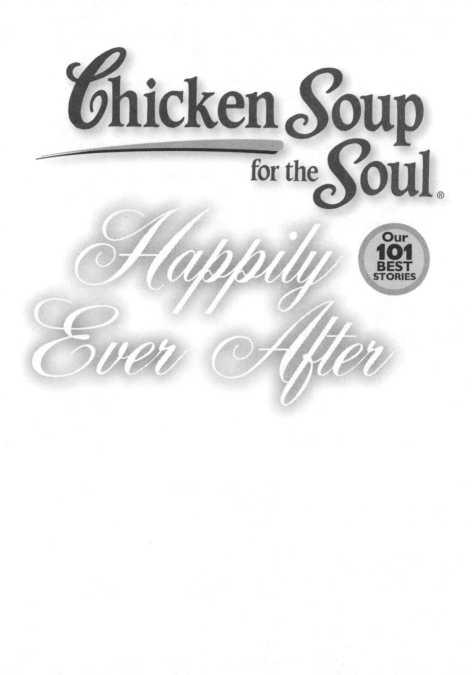

Chicken Soup for the Soul®

Our **101** BEST STORIES

Happily Ever After

Chicken Soup for the Soul® Our 101 Best Stories:
Happily Ever After; Fun and Heartwarming Stories about Finding and Enjoying Your Mate
by Jack Canfield, Mark Victor Hansen & Amy Newmark

Published by Chicken Soup for the Soul Publishing, LLC   www.chickensoup.com

The publisher gratefully acknowledges the many publishers and individuals who granted Chicken Soup for the Soul permission to reprint the cited material.

Cover and interior illustration courtesy of iStockPhoto.com/Simfo

Cover and Interior Design & Layout by Pneuma Books, LLC
For more info on Pneuma Books, visit www.pneumabooks.com

Distributed to the booktrade by Simon & Schuster. SAN: 200-2442

Publisher's Cataloging-in-Publication Data
(Prepared by The Donohue Group)

Chicken soup for the soul. Selections.
    Chicken soup for the soul : happily ever after : fun and heartwarming stories about finding and enjoying your mate / [compiled by] Jack Canfield [and] Mark Victor Hansen ; [edited by] Amy Newmark.

    p. ; cm. — (Our 101 best stories)

ISBN-13: 978-1-935096-10-8
ISBN-10: 1-935096-10-9

1. Marriage--Literary collections. 2. Love--Literary collections. 3. Mate selection--Literary collections. 4. Marriage--Anecdotes. 5. Love--Anecdotes. 6. Mate selection--Anecdotes. I. Canfield, Jack, 1944- II. Hansen, Mark Victor. III. Newmark, Amy. IV. Title.

PN6071.M2 C293 2008
808.8/0354   2008931087

PRINTED IN THE UNITED STATES OF AMERICA
on acid∞free paper
16 15 14 13 12 11 10   04 05 06 07 08

Chicken Soup for the Soul® Happily Ever After

Fun and Heartwarming
Stories about Finding
and Enjoying Your Mate

Jack Canfield
Mark Victor Hansen
Amy Newmark

Chicken Soup for the Soul Publishing, LLC
Cos Cob, CT

Contents

❶
~The Power of Love~

❷
~Worth the Wait~

❸
~Wedding Laughs~

❹
~Meant to Be~

❺
~Making It Work~

⑥
~Wasn't the First Love Story in a Garden?~

⑦
~We Didn't Give Up on Us~

⑧
~Live, Love, Laugh!~

⑨
~Finding the Right Mate~

⑩
~ I'm So Grateful to Have You in My Life~

⑪
~Military Marriages~

⑫
~Holding Memories Close to Your Heart~

A Special Foreword

by Jack and Mark

For us, 101 has always been a magical number. It was the number of stories in the first *Chicken Soup for the Soul* book, and it is the number of stories and poems we have always aimed for in our books. We love the number 101 because it signifies a beginning, not an end. After 100, we start anew with 101.

We hope that when you finish reading one of our books, it is only a beginning for you too—a new outlook on life, a renewed sense of purpose, a strengthened resolve to deal with an issue that has been bothering you. Perhaps you will pick up the phone and share one of the stories with a friend or a loved one. Perhaps you will turn to your keyboard and express yourself by writing a Chicken Soup story of your own, to share with other readers who are just like you.

This volume contains our 101 best stories and poems about dating, romance, love, and marriage. We share this with you at a very special time for us, the fifteenth anniversary of our *Chicken Soup for the Soul* series. When we published our first book in 1993, we never dreamed that we had started what became a publishing phenomenon, one of the best-selling series of books in history.

We did not set out to sell more than one hundred million books, or to publish more than 150 titles. We set out to touch the heart of one person at a time, hoping that person would in turn touch another person, and so on down the line. Fifteen years later, we know that it has worked. Your letters and stories have poured in by the hundreds of thousands, affirming our life's work, and inspiring us to continue to make a difference in your lives.

On our fifteenth anniversary, we have new energy, new resolve, and new dreams. We have recommitted to our goal of 101 stories or poems per book, we have refreshed our cover designs and our interior layout, and we have grown the Chicken Soup for the Soul team, with new friends and partners across the country in New England.

Dating and courtship, love and marriage are always popular subjects and we had a hard time choosing our best 101 stories and poems for you from our rich 15-year history. These heartwarming stories will inspire, amuse you, and maybe even give you some new ideas for your own loving relationship, whether you are just starting to date, or whether you are a veteran of a long marriage.

We hope that you will enjoy reading these stories as much as we enjoyed selecting them for you, and that you will share them with your families and friends. We have identified the 30 *Chicken Soup for the Soul* books in which the stories originally appeared, in case you would like to explore our other titles. We hope you will also enjoy the additional books about men and women, families, pets, and life in general in "Our 101 Best Stories" series.

With our love, our thanks, and our respect,
~*Jack Canfield and Mark Victor Hansen*

Chapter 1

Happily Ever After

The Power of Love

Love is composed of a single soul inhabiting two bodies.
~Aristotle

With These Rings

If you don't like something change it;
if you can't change it, change the way you think about it.
Mary Engelbreit

I was a new pastor's wife when my husband took me to a small town in Oklahoma. We fought until we learned to love each other during the two years we spent there. I was the new girl in town. I knew no one and barely knew my husband, Brad. He was busy with his church, and there I was, stuck. No money, no job and no friends. I was uncomfortable in my new role and resented it when others referred to me as "the preacher's wife." I failed to see what an honor that was.

The parishioners made attempts to befriend me, but I was too busy being lonely and angry, and was bound and determined to let Brad know it. I pouted and packed, whined and packed, and threw things at him and packed. "I'm leaving!" I would scream when he came home. With the fifty cents I had in my pocket and no gas money, I don't know where I thought I was going, but I was adamant.

"Don't do me any favors," he would reply, which only caused me to turn on my heels and shout, "I'm staying, and don't try and stop me!" Who did he think he was? I wasn't about to let him kick me out.

Somewhere between my daily suitcase-packing episodes, I remembered that I had promised to love him for better or for worse. In desperation, I found ways to entertain myself. I spent hours picking from the six pecan trees in the front yard. I quickly realized that even though we had no money, the pecans made great Christmas gifts. I even found a job. Then my husband came home one day and announced that he had an interview at a church in Louisiana. I had just learned to live in Oklahoma!

True to form, I pouted and griped on the way to Louisiana. Then something stopped me in my tracks. We were on our way through Texas when we ran right into what looked like a giant crystal bowl. An ice storm had hit the area a few days earlier, and it was the most beautiful sight I had ever seen. And there I was, gnawing on my husband. Somewhere between Denton and Sulphur, I had taken off my wedding rings and tucked them into the folds of my skirt so that I could apply some hand cream. The ice we were skidding on distracted me just enough that I forgot to put my rings back on.

Three hours later I looked down and realized that I had lost my rings out on the highway when I had stepped out of the car to take a picture of a horse and buggy driving by. But which highway? Everything looks the same in an ice storm, especially when you are in unfamiliar country.

"I'll buy you another ring," my husband said.

I knew he meant well, but the ring was a family heirloom. "That ring can't be replaced," I cried.

"Honey, we don't even know where to begin looking," he said. "No, we're NOT going back," he insisted as he turned the car around and headed back to look for the rings.

It was hours before we found a location that seemed familiar. Occasionally some well-meaning person would pull his car over to the side of the road, roll down his window and yell, "Hey, buddy, what'd ya lose?" At one point, there must have been ten cars stopped on the side of the road, all abandoned by the occupants who had joined in the search. But with the sun going down, it was obvious that our chances of finding the rings were slim. I was crushed.

"Face it, Honey, they're gone," Brad said. "I know you're upset. I promise to try and find a suitable replacement."

I knew he was right. The walk in the cold that day had given me time to think about the day's events. I played the scene over and over in my mind, and what I saw was not a pretty sight. I had ranted and raved, nagged and wailed, and acted like a spoiled brat. I took a good long look at my husband pacing back and forth in the freezing cold. He had driven three hours back to this desolate area in the middle of a treacherous ice storm without one thought for himself, attempting to find something that was important to me.

The rings might be gone, but there could never be a suitable replacement for my husband. Suddenly, the rings seemed so unimportant. I resolved right then and there to stop thinking only of myself.

It was at that very moment that I opened the car door and began to step inside. Something on the floor caught my eye. My rings! I grabbed them and waved them in the air. Brad rushed to my side and put them back on my finger. "This is where these rings belong," he whispered. I looked into his eyes, and knew that I had found what I was looking for. It wasn't my rings that were lost that day — I was the one who had been missing.

Life in the pastorate hasn't changed. The only thing that has changed is me. We still move around more than I like. And I still have to start over again every time we do. But I've learned to appreciate when people call me "the preacher's wife," because etched into my mind is a frozen road in Texas, and a voice that whispers, "This is where these rings belong."

~Sharon M. Palmer
Chicken Soup for the Christian Family Soul

Te Amo, Te Quiero, Cariña

They met in the dawn of their childhood.
As kids they would play man and wife.
And they knew even then, before they were ten,
They'd share the rest of their lives.
They played in her tea-castle garden,
'Neath the shade of an old tamarind tree.
In his poor Key West clothes, he gave her a rose
And whispered these words tenderly:
"Te amo, te quiero, cariña"
He said as he whispered her name.
"I love you, I want you my precious one."
These words set her heart all aflame.
And they danced 'neath the stars to the sound of guitars,
"Te amo, te quiero, cariña."
In the noon of their lives they courted,
No longer young children at play.
And they spoke not a word, only heartbeats were heard,
As they kneeled to worship and pray.
They married in an old Spanish churchyard,
'Neath the shade of an old tamarind tree.
In his best Key West clothes, he gave her a rose
And whispered these words tenderly:
"Te amo, te quiero, cariña"

He said as he whispered her name.
"I love you, I want you my precious one."
These words set her heart all aflame.
And they danced 'neath the stars to the sound of guitars,
"Te amo, te quiero, cariña."
In the twilight of life she goes walking,
To where their song was first sung.
And she sees his sweet face in memory's fond place,
In a time when they were both young.
Now he sleeps in an old Spanish churchyard,
'Neath the shade of an old tamarind tree.
In her old woman's clothes she brings him a rose
And whispers these words tenderly:
"Te amo, te quiero, cariño"
She says as she whispers his name.
"I love you, I want you my precious one."
These words set her heart all aflame.
She can't hold back the tears after all of these years,
"Te amo, te quiero, cariña."

~Patrick Mendoza
Chicken Soup for the Bride's Soul

A Fall from the Sky

Attitudes are contagious. Are yours worth catching?
~Dennis and Wendy Mannering

One day, some years ago, my friend Beverley and I decided that we'd each like to experience the thrill of a tandem skydive—when a novice leaps out of an airplane without a parachute while attached to an experienced jumpmaster who is wearing two, just in case. The jumpmaster keeps everything safe and stable so that even novices—in this case Beverley and I—can experience thirty seconds or more of weightless free fall.

We had heard about Kevin McIlwee's skydiving school—named after his war heroes, the Flying Tigers—and about his excellent reputation. Yes, even on a small island called Jersey, fourteen miles off the north coast of France, one can leap out of airplanes. As it happened, Kevin was presenting an introductory skydiving seminar at a local hotel, and so we eagerly attended. He was most impressive—a professional skydiver for twenty years who had completed over four thousand jumps, and the first British qualified tandem instructor.

During that first meeting, Kevin won our confidence, so Beverley and I signed up for our first tandem skydives. As time passed, Kevin won more than Beverley's confidence; he won her heart.

In the spring of 2001, Kevin and Beverley married. And now Mr. and Mrs. McIlwee prepared for their honeymoon. They packed their suitcases—and of course their skydiving rigs—and they set out on their journey. Kevin piloted their light aircraft from Jersey to the parachute center in Vannes, on the south coast of Brittany in France.

By this time, Kevin and Beverley had completed over fifty tandem skydives together and were looking forward to their long weekend in Vannes. The French parachutists welcomed them and invited Kevin to participate in some big formation skydiving. So the first two days of their honeymoon were spent doing tandem skydives together and making new friends.

On their last day in Vannes—Sunday, June 3—they decided to do one last tandem skydive before flying home to Jersey.

During their free-fall, they marveled once more at the spectacular view across Brittany. Then it was time to pull the ripcord and open the chute at 5,500 feet. Kevin looked up and saw that the parachute hadn't inflated. Kevin had to take immediate action. Built into his parachute rig was an automatic opening device that operated the reserve parachute. If Kevin didn't act quickly, the reserve would be released automatically, and it would almost certainly become entangled with the main chute. The result would be fatal.

Kevin yelled to Beverley to put her arms and legs back into free-fall position while he attempted to jettison the main chute. It wouldn't release despite Kevin's repeated efforts. Meanwhile, the ground was approaching at over 100 miles an hour. Kevin made a life-or-death decision—he deployed the reserve parachute with the main parachute still attached to the rig. It was an extremely dangerous maneuver, but his only chance of slowing their fall.

The chutes didn't entangle, but the reserve parachute started to spin, almost colliding with the main parachute. Kevin worked furiously to keep the two parachutes apart, knowing that they mustn't become entangled or the parachute would go out of control—and that would be the end.

Beverley stayed calm. In that moment, it was the only help she could offer. She trusted her husband to protect her as best he could. Meanwhile, Kevin was extremely busy: The parachutes would almost collide, then separate, then almost collide again, which sent Kevin and Beverley in and out of dives, their speed varying from a float to a plummet. The odds of their survival were not great. He decided to tell Beverley in case she might wish to say a prayer.

"Beverley, I don't think we're going to make it. I love you."

"I love you, Kevin," she replied. "Very much."

Beverley relaxed into her fate, whatever it might be; she felt no sense of panic, although she did say a quick prayer. Kevin prepared for a crash landing. The ground raced up at them, and he was horrified to see that they were coming down among trees, buildings and combine harvesters at work. By sheer luck, or the grace of God, they fell clear of any obstacles, but they hit the ground with massive force.

They woke in a nearby hospital where a team of medical experts set to work. Beverley had broken both legs and her feet as well. Kevin's lower left leg bones had broken and shattered his kneecap. The surgical team in France provided lifesaving initial emergency care, but it was decided that they should be flown home by air ambulance to Jersey since they were going to need extensive long-term treatment. There, the surgeon said that Beverley's feet were so severely broken that she might never walk again. Kevin's kneecap was shattered in so many pieces that it couldn't be saved. The surgeon told Kevin that he would walk, but that he would never be able to run or exercise to any great extent. Thus began a long process of operations and rehabilitation.

One year after the accident, a party of us celebrated Beverley's birthday at a local restaurant. Her ankles aren't so flexible anymore, and she has metal pins in her feet, but she looked stunning. And I saw something that night that will stay with me always and remind me what strength of character really means. When she was walking towards me, her heel pressed down on one of the metal pins and for an instant, I saw her wince in excruciating pain. Then she smiled, straightened her shoulders and said, "Oh, it's nothing. Have you all got enough to eat?"

Kevin has shown his own special brand of courage. Since leaving the hospital, he has worked out every day in the gym, without exception. He goes to spinning classes, and he works on the leg press to increase the flexibility in his left leg and strengthen the muscles around his knee. He cycles to and from work every day. His work has paid off. He passed his physical and got the all clear to pilot planes again.

According to the surgeons in France and Jersey, their injuries indicate they must have hit the ground at around sixty miles per hour. That they survived at all was a miracle—a honeymoon miracle. God must have known that they had more life to live together. And the paramedics who first arrived said that it was "good luck" that Beverley landed on top of Kevin, which prevented him from moving. Any slight movement could have severed the main artery of his leg that was still connected, and he would have likely died.

That day in Vannes, when Beverley and Kevin fell from the sky, lives that might have been lost were changed forever. Beverley's radiant blue eyes still shine as she reflects on how that accident opened her to new insights. "I can't wear high heels anymore, or run the way I used to—and I'll probably never ski again. But I've developed patience, acceptance and a new sense of perspective. The day we married, I would never have believed that we could be even closer, but we are. My brave husband saved my life, and this experience has bonded us forever."

~Joanne Reid Rodrigues
Chicken Soup to Inspire the Body & Soul

Princess Bride

*B*rooke was our little princess. She was spoiled not only by me, but by her father and four older brothers as well. She was beautiful and intelligent, but also compassionate and loving. She never put herself first; she lived to make others happy. She made our souls sing.

Brooke met Dan in her junior year of college. I loved her phone calls even more now. Her laughter and giggles when she talked about Dan made my heart smile.

But when he graduated, Dan took a position two states away with an esteemed accounting firm. Over the next year, Dan and Brooke kept in constant contact. I could tell my daughter was in love, so I prayed nightly their hearts would remain strong and true, and would someday be united as one.

Brooke graduated with honors and applied for several jobs near Dan's home. It didn't take her long to be offered one. Now they were not only close in heart, but also close in proximity as they shared day-to-day life. Two years passed before I got the phone call I dreamed of and prayed for.

My princess was getting married!

They set a date for the following summer. Since it was already January, we had a year and a half to prepare for this joyous occasion. Brooke and I began planning a fairy-tale wedding—the only kind fit for a princess.

But on December 2, the fairy-tale world came crashing down.

A simple yearly exam revealed horrifying news: Brooke had breast cancer and it was already quite advanced. We cried for hours.

Why was this happening? Why Brooke? Why my baby? Why not me? I just didn't understand. I was terrified, confused and angry all at the same time. But I soon brushed all my emotions aside to put Brooke first.

I assured her we would beat this thing and life would go on as planned. She would grow old with Dan and the children they would one day have. I knew my princess would be okay. She had to. She was my baby and I would not say goodbye to her. After all, this wasn't the way things were supposed to happen.

But the doctors were honest from the beginning. They only gave Brooke a 20 percent chance of survival. Because of her cancer's advanced stage, a regimen of drugs and chemotherapy began immediately.

After only a month or so of treatment, the disease spread and my daughter got weaker. We knew Brooke had only a short time left. My heart was broken and beaten.

Throughout, Dan remained strong. He was there for Brooke every step of the way. She had lost all of her hair, dropped so much weight she couldn't even sit without help and could stay awake no longer than ten to twenty minutes at a time. Yet Dan was there to love and support her.

One day, Dan asked for our blessing to marry Brooke before she passed away. He had loved her so long and only wanted one thing in his life: Brooke as his wife. Even if her days left on Earth were uncertain, he wanted them to be spent as a married couple.

We knew she still dreamed of the fairy-tale wedding she would now never have. But we also knew she would not want Dan to marry her when they both knew she was dying. So, we decided the wedding would be a surprise. With help and cooperation from the hospital staff, Dan secretly arranged a lovely ceremony.

When Brooke first realized what was happening, she strongly objected. But Dan explained the most important thing in his life was her. And all he wanted was her as his wife—be it for fifty years or for only a day. Brooke sobbed, but agreed. It was her dream, too.

Dan brought a simple but beautiful white gown, delicate lace scarf and sheer veil to her hospital room. The nurses and I dressed the fragile bride, using the scarf to cover her smooth head and draping the veil gently over it. Even pale and broken, my princess daughter shined. This was her day, the day she had dreamed of and planned for.

There was no elegant church as we'd once imagined. None of her family and friends were in attendance as we'd once hoped. But her beloved Dan was there, they were getting married and that was what mattered most. The two exchanged vows and a touching, sweet wedding kiss. It may not have been the fairy tale, but it was still a dream come true.

Brooke spent sixteen days as the wife of the man she adored and loved. And it wasn't until after she passed away that I found a letter tucked into her hospital nightstand.

In it, Brooke wrote that she had only ever wanted to love, be loved and to matter to others. She expressed her gratitude for wonderful brothers and loving parents. The day Dan married her, she said, all her dreams came true. She had truly lived her life's dream. Brooke felt her life was complete; she was neither afraid nor disappointed. And, compassionate to the end, she wished only that none of us had to suffer her loss.

Today, we often see Dan and we love him as our son and Brooke's husband. After all, he made our daughter a princess when she most deserved to be.

~Veneta Leonard
Chicken Soup for the Bride's Soul

Hot Lips

Anywhere is paradise; it's up to you.
~Author Unknown

"Loose Lips Sink Ships," the poster warned.

After a week of censorship duties, I was sure that the squadron harbored no loose lips. But we sure had plenty of "hot lips," and I was growing sick of playing censor.

Every night, a pile of mail was plunked down in front of me, and my job was to pore over it for any information that might be useful to the enemy or unnerving to the home front. It was a lousy way to spend an evening.

My eyes blurred, and my brain turned numb as I read the contents: Complete recitations of the daily menus. Wild guesses at when the war was going to end. Complaint after complaint about fellow soldiers. What else was there left to write about after years of war?

Love letters, of course. Boy-girl letters that positively sizzled with passion. I had my doubts about a number of those fiery attestations of undying love. I'd seen some of those "faithful" boyfriends in action in the "rest camps."

But the husband-wife letters—they were different. They were real, and playing Peeping Tom to them was hard. I still remember one particular letter as clearly as if I had read it in this morning's mail, though it's been forty-five years now.

The letter was written by a ground crewman I didn't know, and the separation from his wife had become unbearable for him. "I must meet you tonight," the man wrote his wife. "And tomorrow night. And the night after that."

What was he talking about? We were on Corsica, an island thousands of miles away from her in the States. "Nine P.M.," he reminded her. "Meet me by the light of the moon." He even specified where he would meet her—a little building near the squadron operations office. That would be a trick, I thought. Besides, 9 P.M. here was full sun back in the States.

I folded the letter, placed it back in the envelope and finished my pile. It isn't any business of mine anyway, I told myself.

But as 9 P.M. drew near, my curiosity got the best of me, and I strolled by the operations office in the direction of that little building. A full moon was out, and I could see everything clearly. I stopped short when I saw the figure outlined in the moonlight. A lone man. His head was bowed toward his shadow on the ground, his eyes closed in disappointment. Surely he hadn't really expected her to be there?

Yet as I studied the husband's face in the moonlight, his eyes tightly shut, I read not disappointment but intense concentration. That's when I realized what was happening. As far as he was concerned, he wasn't standing by an old operations building in Corsica at all. He had transported himself to be with his wife, just as she had done, and was doing whatever it is married lovers do when they rendezvous unnoticed by the world in a private little corner, after long months of separation.

I quickly turned and walked off into the night, ashamed that I had played voyeur to such an intimate rendezvous. As I walked back to my tent, though, I couldn't help but feel warm inside. I had just seen devotion that defied time and space. It was a love that nothing could censor.

~Philip Weiner
Chicken Soup for the Veteran's Soul

When Snowball Melted

Love is the condition in which the happiness of another
is essential to your own.
~Robert Heinlein

Lovebirds. That's what all our friends called us when we first married.

I guess Don and I deserved it. Money was tight because we were both full-time students, working to pay our way through school. Sometimes, we'd have to save up days just for an ice cream cone. Still, our tiny, drab apartment seemed like paradise. Love does that, you know.

Anyway, the more we heard the term "lovebirds," the more we thought about birds. And one day we started saving up for a couple of lovebirds of our own: the feathery kind. We knew we couldn't afford to buy both birds and a nice cage, so in his spare moments, Don made the cage himself.

We set our cage in front of a shaded window. Then we waited until the crumpled envelope marked "lovebirds" was full of bills and spare change. At last the day came when we were able to walk down to our local pet store to "adopt" some additions to our little family.

We'd had our hearts set on parakeets. But the minute we heard the canaries singing, we changed our minds. Selecting a lively yellow male and a sweet white female, we named the youngsters Sunshine and Snowball.

Because of our exhausting schedules, we didn't get to spend too much time with our new friends, but we loved having them greet us each evening with bursts of song. And they seemed blissfully happy with each other.

Time passed, and when our young lovebirds finally seemed mature enough to start a family of their own, we went ahead and prepared a nest area and lots of nesting material for them.

Sure enough, one day they began to find the idea very appealing. Snowball was a very exacting supervisor in designing and decorating their nest just so, while Sunshine, his face aglow with love, bent over backward to put everything just where she ordered.

Then one day an egg appeared. How they sang! And a few weeks later when a tiny chick hatched, their happiness seemed to know no bounds. I don't know how it happened genetically, but that baby canary was bright orange. So right off we named him Punkinhead.

The sunny days passed. How proud all of us were when our fledgling tottered out of the nest onto a real grown-up perch!

Then one day, Punkinhead suddenly plunged headlong from his perch to the bottom of the cage. The tiny orange bird just lay there. Both parents and I rushed to his rescue.

But he was dead. Just like that. Whether he'd had a heart attack before he fell or broke his neck in the fall, I'll never know. But Punkinhead was gone.

Though both parents grieved, his little mother was inconsolable. She refused to let either Sunshine or me get near that pitiful little body. Instead of the joyful melodies I usually heard from Snowball, now she gave only the most excruciating cries and moans. Her heart, joy and will seemed completely melted by her sorrow.

Poor Sunshine didn't know what to make of it. He kept trying to push Snowball away from her sad station, but she refused to budge. Instead, over and over she kept trying to revive her adored child.

Finally Sunshine seemed to work out a plan. He convinced her to fly up and eat some seeds every so often, while he stood duty in her place. Then each time she left, he'd quietly place one piece of nesting straw over Punkinhead's body. Just one. But in a few days, piece by piece, it was completely covered over.

At first Snowball seemed disoriented when she looked around, but she didn't try to uncover the chick. Instead, she flew up to her normal perch and stayed there. Then I was able to quietly reach in and remove the little body, straw shroud and all.

After that, Sunshine spent all his time consoling Snowball. Eventually she started making normal sounds, and then one day, her sorrow finally melted and she sang again.

I don't know if Snowball ever realized the quiet labor of love and healing Sunshine had done for her. But they remained joyously devoted for as long as they both lived. Love does that, you know.

Especially to lovebirds.

~Bonnie Compton Hanson
Chicken Soup for the Pet Lover's Soul

I Love You Anyway

Make your optimism come true.
~Author Unknown

*I*t was Friday morning, and a young businessman finally decided to ask his boss for a raise. Before leaving for work, he told his wife what he was about to do. All day long he felt nervous and apprehensive. Finally, in the late afternoon, he summoned the courage to approach his employer, and to the businessman's delight, the boss agreed to the raise.

The elated husband arrived home to a beautiful table set with their best china and lighted candles. Smelling the aroma of a festive meal, he figured that someone from the office had called his wife and tipped her off! Finding her in the kitchen, he eagerly shared the details of his good news. They embraced and danced around the room before sitting down to the wonderful meal his wife had prepared. Next to his plate he found an artistically lettered note that read, "Congratulations, darling! I knew you'd get the raise! This dinner is to show you how much I love you."

Later on his way to the kitchen to help his wife serve dessert, he noticed that a second card had fallen from her pocket. Picking it up off the floor, he read, "Don't worry about not getting the raise! You deserve it anyway! This dinner is to show how much I love you."

~Joe Harding
Chicken Soup for the Romantic Soul

Josef and Rebecca

*I*n 1996, I decided to participate in the March of the Living, an international program that brings six thousand Jewish teenagers and a thousand adults from forty-five countries to Poland to retrace the death march from the concentration camp at Auschwitz to nearby Birkenau. The group then tours Poland visiting the Treblinka and Majdanek concentration camps and other sites of Jewish interest. Finally, we travel to Israel for Holocaust Remembrance Day and Independence Day.

Three months before the march, we were all given identification cards and told to take good care of them, that they were important and that someday we would do something with them.

I was given a copy of identification card #07175, issued 22 September 1941, by the Nazis, to Josef Bau, a Jew living in Krakow. It said that Bau was born in Krakow on June 18, 1920, exactly one year and five days after my father was born in Brooklyn. Josef went to Hebrew High School, was in the Boy Scouts and worked as a drafts-man at the hard labor concentration camp in Plaszow.

I learned that Bau was at Plaszow when he fell in love with Rebecca Tannenbaum, also a prisoner. They met one gray morning when he stood outside, holding up a blueprint frame toward the low autumn cloud. His thin body seemed overburdened by the weight. She asked if she could help him.

"No," he said. "I'm just waiting for the sunshine." Then he said, "Why don't you be my magical sunshine?"

They were eventually separated when the Germans constructed an electrified fence between the men's and women's prisons.

Undeterred, Josef found a dead woman's dress in the clothing warehouse, and after roll call in the men's lines, he would go to the latrines, put on the long gown and place an Orthodox bonnet on his hair. Then he would come out and join the women's queues. With thirteen thousand women prisoners, he would pass into the women's compound and spend the night sitting up in Hut 57 keeping Rebecca company.

Josef married Rebecca on a fiercely cold night in February. As there was no rabbi, Josef's mother officiated. Their wedding bands were crafted in the prison workshop out of a silver spoon Mrs. Bau had hidden in the rafters.

Ten minutes after the wedding, Josef was discovered missing from his barracks. Unwilling to compromise the women in the barrack, he kissed his wife and ran from the hut.

In the fence between the men's and women's camps in Plaszow ran nine electrified strands. In spite of this, Josef launched himself high. He landed on the wires and hung there. He thought the coldness of the metal was the first message of the current. But there was no current. He vaulted into the men's camp.

As I traveled through Poland, I found it hard to connect with Josef Bau and his young bride, Rebecca. I couldn't relate to their lives in this horrible place. Instead, all I wondered about was where they had lost their lives, where they had been exterminated. Auschwitz, Birkenau, Majdanek, Treblinka—so many dead, so much unbelievable suffering.

On our first evening in Israel, we were asked to take out our identification cards. We were asked to think about our "Krakow connection" as real people: How old was Josef Bau when the war interrupted his life? What kind of life was he leading at the time? How would it have been similar to my own life? What kind of a life would he have had if he had survived?

Shortly after, we arrived at Atlit, the displaced person camp near Haifa that was run by the British after the war. We were welcomed in a small auditorium and the speaker introduced the guests who had joined us that night. They were the Krakow Jews whose identification cards we had carried all these months.

I stood there in utter disbelief—Josef and his bride Rebecca were standing there, right in front of me. I had not passed them in the ovens of Auschwitz or at the ash heap at Majdanek. Tears rolled down my face.

Slowly, I went over to meet Rebecca and Josef, sitting with their two daughters. Josef had survived Auschwitz and Rebecca had been a "Schindler Jew," on that fortunate list that spared her life. They reunited and made a life together in Israel.

They couldn't speak English, and I do not speak Hebrew, but that didn't matter. For me, nothing needed to be said.

~Mark I. Farber
Chicken Soup for the Traveler's Soul

Hello, Young Lovers

*H*e appeared almost Lilliputian, dwarfed by the big hickory rocking chair he occupied on the porch of the old Riverside Hotel in Gatlinburg, Tennessee. But we could hardly help noticing him on that warm mid-April day: While others lounged about in casual attire, he wore a dark-blue pinstripe suit, a Harvard-crimson necktie and a straw boater. The gold watch chain draped across his tightly buttoned vest glinted in the sunlight as he rocked ever so deliberately.

He watched bemusedly as I stepped from the Jaguar XK-150, my pride and joy, and walked to the opposite side to open the door for Diane, my bride. His eyes followed as we trailed self-consciously behind the luggage-laden bellboy, and he smiled a knowing smile when we neared his rocker.

"Hello, young lovers," he said. Our honeymooner status was unmistakable.

The man we came to know as Mr. B was in the dining room, sitting alone with a cup of tea, when we entered late the next morning. His eyes came to life when he saw us. He rose with some effort and beckoned us toward him.

"You'd make an old man very happy if you joined me," he said with an octogenarian's formality. I wonder even now why we did. Perhaps it was the angelic expression his face assumed. More likely, it was our honeymooner self-consciousness—we'd been found out by an elder and felt compelled to comply with his wishes.

He was a Canadian, an attorney, he said, still practicing in Winnipeg. But he'd been spending Aprils in Gatlinburg for almost fifty years. He and his wife would come with their son and daughter and explore the mountains on horseback, getting to know every scenic vantage point of Mount Le Conte, every turn in the tumbling Little Pigeon River.

After the son had died and the daughter was grown, Mr. B and his wife had kept up their visits. And he still made the annual trek even though his wife had died three years earlier. The mountains and the valley were touchstones for him, sites of pleasant memories that were revived with each visit.

"I've had a love of my own," he said, his eyes misting. He asked detailed questions about our wedding and told us in detail of his own, some sixty years earlier. During brief periods when a conversational lapse threatened, he softly hummed "Hello, Young Lovers," the song from *The King and I*.

That night he sat alone during dinner, careful, he later told us, not to "get in love's way." But he glanced often in our direction, and we knew he was not alone; he was deep in reverie, dining with his own true love. Returning to our room following an after-dinner walk, we found a ribbon-bedecked bottle of champagne. An accompanying card read: "See Mr. B in the A.M. for instructions as to its use."

He was waiting for us in his rocking chair after breakfast, the look of a leprechaun on his face. He handed me a piece of paper on which he had sketched the river, a place where we could leave our car, a footpath and points at which large boulders made it possible to cross the cold mountain stream on foot. His shaky-handed path led eventually to a river pool indicated with an X.

"The champagne is to be chilled in the pool," he said. "You are to spread your picnic lunch on the grassy knoll to the right of it. It's very secluded. A very romantic spot." We could only gape at him, certain he was spoofing.

"Your picnic basket will be delivered to you here on the veranda at precisely noon." He was on his feet then, moving away. He turned and added: "It was our favorite spot, our secret place."

We never saw Mr. B again during our honeymoon. We wondered whether he'd fallen ill. But inquiries to the hotel staff were answered with, "Oh, he's around," or "He often likes to be alone."

Our firstborn was almost three when we next visited Gatlinburg, and Diane was six months pregnant with our second son. We approached the aging hotel not in the Jaguar, but in a practical sedan. Our arrival went unnoticed.

But when we walked into the hotel lobby the next morning, our son toddling ahead, the old man was sitting in an overstuffed lounge chair. Seeing the child, he stretched out his arms, and our son, as if drawn by a magnet, ran into them.

"Mr. B!" we exclaimed in unison.

He smiled that beatific smile.

"Hello, young lovers," he said.

~Philip Harsham
Chicken Soup for the Romantic Soul

Ageless

Love is a symbol of eternity. It wipes out all sense of time,
destroying all memory of a beginning and all fear of an end.
~Author Unknown

It was Sunday morning. My grandmother and I were getting ready for church. Lately, I'd been noticing her paying a little more attention to what she was wearing, examining herself for longer periods of time in front of the mirror.

"Is everything okay, Grams?"

She checked if her earrings were on straight and if her blush perfectly matched the color of her dainty pink dress.

"You have no idea what it's like," she said.

"What what's like?"

"To be old and wrinkled."

I chuckled. "Gram, it doesn't matter what you look... I mean, you're... seventy-five!"

She turned away from me and I immediately realized my insensitivity had hurt her feelings. "I'm sorry. I didn't mean seventy-five in a bad way."

"Oh, it's not you I'm trying to impress."

Without speaking further, we drove the short distance to church. I felt horribly guilty, wondering if I should have told her how I really felt about her attractive appearance.

I trailed into the church behind her while a handsome gentleman usher took her arm. Jim, a seventy-four-year-old widower, often walked my grandmother down to her seat. He was so sweet to her and always made sure he had saved a pew for us near the front so we could clearly see the pastor.

Then, like a lightning bolt, I understood what was really upsetting my grandmother! She wasn't depressed or really mad at me! She was feeling insecure because she had fallen in love in her golden years.

"How are you, Loretta?" Jim inquired.

"Well."

"My brother came for a surprise visit," Jim explained. "I'm sorry I missed you at bingo. I heard you won, though. Congratulations."

I scooted down into our pew, determining that Jim must have been asking about my grandmother's whereabouts on Wednesday as well.

Tenderly gazing down into her dark brown eyes, he escorted her to my side. After a moment of embracing her hand, he shakily pulled a crumpled piece of paper from his pocket and placed it in her fingertips.

I waited until he walked away. "What does it say, Grams?"

She blushed. "It has his phone number and says to call him if I'd like to go to the singles dance on Saturday."

I fought back tears of joy witnessing her brilliant smile wipe away all signs of wrinkles. "See, someone else knows how beautiful you are, too, Grams; you're still as perfect as you ever were."

"He just needs a dancing partner, that's all."

I countered, "Gram, he wants to waltz with someone who cares about him."

Her face lit up. "Maybe you're right."

"I know I am."

Watching my grandmother and Jim dance that night was something that took my breath away. My boyfriend Louis and I were worried about her and decided to drop by. With one glance, all our fears disappeared. They were swinging like teenagers, laughing and holding each other underneath the twinkle of the stars.

Nine months later, at the age of seventy-four, Jim dropped down on one knee and asked for my seventy-five-year-old grandmother's hand in marriage.

"Yes," she immediately replied. "But... there's just one thing."

"What's that?" Jim wiped the tears from her rosy cheeks.

"I don't do windows anymore."

He clapped with excitement. And before a man of God, my family and I came together, filling his house to watch them wed by candlelight.

It's been eight years now, and Jim and Loretta are still just as happy as the night they danced until dawn. Every time I see them together, I'm reminded that love is ageless. It's as priceless at eighty as it is at twenty, perhaps even more.

~Michele Wallace Campanelli
Chicken Soup for the Grandparent's Soul

11

A Hero for the Books

is grin and twinkling eyes were the first thing I
noticed.

I was a regular at the public library and had
seen librarians come and go like Heinz goes through tomatoes, but
this guy was different. He talked to patrons like they were special and
the most important people ever to grace the earth. It didn't take many
visits to feel like we were old friends, and trips to the library became
social events.

Sharing New York humor made for some belly grabbing laughs;
Mark's deadpan quips made tears roll down my face. I never tired of
leaning against the front desk to hear his latest spin on some inane
happening, which only he could make into a comedy routine. My
book returns were notoriously overdue, but it was so much fun to
visit with Mark that promptness became my habit.

Over time, though, Mark seemed tired. He would rub his eyes
while in the middle of a story, and his quips weren't as frequent. Yet,
he never lost his smile and always made a point of asking about my
family. We still discussed books and motorcycles and religion, but I
could tell something was wrong in his life. I couldn't just blurt out,
"What's wrong?" based solely on a gut feeling. Or, could I?

It was during one of our chitchats that Mark let slip that he had
taken his wife to the doctor. Not wanting to lose the opportunity, I
pursued the subject. What did he mean by sick?

"ALS, Lou Gehrig's disease," he replied. His answer shoved me into the proverbial brick wall. As a nurse, I had seen the destruction wrought by the disease and knew there was no cure. For once in my life, I was speechless.

Heartbroken for his situation, I gently pressed him for more details. He was willing to talk, and talk he did. His words gushed like water from a crack in a dam, flowing until there was nothing left. He had kept his secret well hidden behind the jokes, the stories, the exchange of wit, but he couldn't mask the pain any longer. The lump in my throat prevented any reply. The tears in my eyes reflected his.

The debilitating disease was diagnosed shortly after their second child was born. Mark and his wife were sucked into the quicksand of illness in the prime of their lives.

They were fast-forwarded through the marriage experiences, living out their vows "in sickness and in health." While other young mothers taught their babies to speak, their little boy translated his mother's increasingly slurred speech. She was now at the point where one blink of the eye meant "yes," two blinks, "no."

After working all day, Mark rushed home to oversee homework, prepare dinner and drive the children to their activities. He survived his first shopping trip with his preteen daughter, and, when their son was old enough to play ball, he purchased a van so his wife's wheelchair could be rolled into it. As long as she had breath in her body, she was determined to see every game. She loved being a mother.

When Mark exhausted his monologue, he poignantly added, "Did you know we both love the beach? One of our favorite things to do together was to sit on the sand at sunset. We'll never be able to do that again." Now, their dates were trips to the hospital during bouts of pneumonia or wild-goose chases to doctors, hoping for a new solution.

On subsequent visits, I learned how draining the responsibilities of caring for a spouse with ALS are. After carrying her into the bathroom and preparing her for bed, Mark then wakes up at least once every hour to turn his wife so she doesn't choke. The muscle activity in her body has diminished, and she has to be physically lifted, rolled over, suctioned and repositioned. He gently rubs her legs to ease the pain, and he whispers in her ear as he wedges pillows around her. A little smile peeks up at him in gratitude, and they drift off for a few minutes sleep, until the routine is repeated. He is up at dawn to send the children off to school, greet the aide and leave for work at the library.

It's been a gift to become a part of his life, to witness the incredible bond of a man's love for a woman. His commitment to her shines like a beacon in a dark world where marriage is devalued. He is a testimony to what men and women are called to do in their lives—to love unconditionally, selflessly and without end.

A lesson that's long overdue.

~Irene Budzynski
Chicken Soup for the Caregiver's Soul

Happily Ever After

Worth the Wait

*I never thought it was worth it, you know waiting for your love,
and then I felt your kiss, I could wait forever for this
~Author Unknown*

12

The Wallet

To love and be loved is to feel the sun from both sides.
~David Viscott, M.D.

As I walked home one freezing day, I stumbled on a wallet someone had lost in the street. I picked it up and looked inside to find some identification so I could call the owner. But the wallet contained only three dollars and a crumpled letter that looked as if it had been in there for years.

The envelope was worn and the only thing that was legible on it was the return address. I started to open the letter, hoping to find some clue. Then I saw the dateline—1924. The letter had been written almost sixty years earlier.

It was written in a beautiful feminine handwriting, on powder-blue stationery with a little flower in the left-hand corner. It was a "Dear John" letter that told the recipient, whose name appeared to be Michael, that the writer could not see him any more because her mother forbade it. Even so, she wrote that she would always love him. It was signed Hannah.

It was a beautiful letter, but there was no way, except for the name Michael, to identify the owner. Maybe if I called information, the operator could find a phone listing for the address on the envelope.

"Operator," I began, "this is an unusual request. I'm trying to find the owner of a wallet that I found. Is there any way you can tell me if there is a phone number for an address that was on an envelope in the wallet?"

She suggested I speak with her supervisor, who hesitated for a moment, then said, "Well, there is a phone listing at that address, but I can't give you the number." She said as a courtesy, she would call that number, explain my story and ask whoever answered if the person wanted her to connect me. I waited a few minutes and then the supervisor was back on the line. "I have a party who will speak with you."

I asked the woman on the other end of the line if she knew anyone by the name of Hannah. She gasped. "Oh! We bought this house from a family who had a daughter named Hannah. But that was thirty years ago!"

"Would you know where that family could be located now?" I asked.

"I remember that Hannah had to place her mother in a nursing home some years ago," the woman said. "Maybe if you got in touch with them, they might be able to track down the daughter."

She gave me the name of the nursing home, and I called the number. The woman on the phone told me the old lady had passed away some years ago, but the nursing home did have a phone number for where the daughter might be living.

I thanked the person at the nursing home and phoned the number she gave me. The woman who answered explained that Hannah herself was now living in a nursing home.

This whole thing is stupid, I thought to myself. Why am I making such a big deal over finding the owner of a wallet that has only three dollars and a letter that is almost sixty years old?

Nevertheless, I called the nursing home in which Hannah was supposed to be living, and the man who answered the phone told me, "Yes, Hannah is staying with us."

Even though it was already 10 P.M., I asked if I could come by to see her. "Well," he said hesitatingly, "if you want to take a chance, she might be in the day room watching television."

I thanked him and drove over to the nursing home. The night nurse and a guard greeted me at the door. We went up to the third floor of the large building. In the day room, the nurse introduced me to Hannah. She was a sweet, silver-haired old-timer with a warm smile and a twinkle in her eye.

I told her about finding the wallet and showed her the letter. The second she saw the powder-blue envelope with that little flower on the left, she took a deep breath and said, "Young man, this letter was the last contact I ever had with Michael."

She looked away for a moment, deep in thought, and then said softly, "I loved him very much. But I was only sixteen at the time and my mother felt I was too young. Oh, he was so handsome. He looked like Sean Connery, the actor.

"Yes," she continued, "Michael Goldstein was a wonderful person. If you should find him, tell him I think of him often. And," she hesitated for a moment, almost biting her lip, "tell him I still love him. You know," she said, smiling as tears welled up in her eyes, "I never did marry. I guess no one ever matched up to Michael."

I thanked Hannah and said goodbye. I took the elevator to the first floor and as I stood by the door, the guard there asked, "Was the old lady able to help you?"

I told him she had given me a lead. "At least I have a last name. But I think I'll let it go for a while. I spent almost the whole day trying to find the owner of this wallet."

I had taken out the wallet, which was a simple brown leather case with red lacing on the side. When the guard saw it, he said, "Hey, wait a minute! That's Mr. Goldstein's wallet. I'd know it anywhere with that bright red lacing. He's always losing that wallet. I must have found it in the halls at least three times."

"Who's Mr. Goldstein?" I asked, as my hand began to shake.

"He's one of the old-timers on the eighth floor. That's Mike Goldstein's wallet for sure. He must have lost it on one of his walks."

I thanked the guard and quickly ran back to the nurse's office. I told her what the guard had said. We went back to the elevator and got on. I prayed that Mr. Goldstein would be up.

On the eighth floor, the floor nurse said, "I think he's still in the day room. He likes to read at night. He's a darling old man."

We went to the only room that had any lights on, and there was a man reading a book. The nurse went over to him and asked if he had lost his wallet. Mr. Goldstein looked up with surprise, put his hand in his back pocket and said, "Oh, it is missing!"

"This kind gentleman found a wallet and we wondered if it could be yours."

I handed Mr. Goldstein the wallet, and the second he saw it, he smiled with relief and said, "Yes, that's it! It must have dropped out of my pocket this afternoon. I want to give you a reward."

"No, thank you," I said. "But I have to tell you something. I read the letter in the hope of finding out who owned the wallet."

The smile on his face suddenly disappeared. "You read that letter?"

"Not only did I read it, I think I know where Hannah is."

He suddenly grew pale. "Hannah? You know where she is? How is she? Is she still as pretty as she was? Please, please tell me," he begged.

"She's fine... just as pretty as when you knew her," I said softly.

The old man smiled with anticipation and asked, "Could you tell me where she is? I want to call her tomorrow." He grabbed my hand and said, "You know something, mister? I was so in love with that girl that when that letter came, my life literally ended. I never married. I guess I've always loved her."

"Michael," I said, "come with me."

We took the elevator down to the third floor. The hallways were darkened and only one or two little night lights lit our way to the day room, where Hannah was sitting alone, watching the television.

The nurse walked over to her.

"Hannah," she said softly, pointing to Michael, who was waiting with me in the doorway. "Do you know this man?"

She adjusted her glasses, looked for a moment, but didn't say a word.

Michael said softly, almost in a whisper, "Hannah, it's Michael. Do you remember me?"

She gasped. "Michael! I don't believe it! Michael! It's you! My Michael!"

He walked slowly toward her, and they embraced. The nurse and I left with tears streaming down our faces.

"See," I said. "See how the good Lord works! If it's meant to be, it will be."

About three weeks later, I got a call at my office from the nursing home. "Can you break away on Sunday to attend a wedding? Michael and Hannah are going to tie the knot!"

It was a beautiful wedding, with all the people at the nursing home dressed up to join in the celebration.

Hannah wore a light beige dress and looked beautiful. Michael wore a dark blue suit and stood tall. They made me their best man.

The hospital gave them their own room, and if you ever wanted to see a seventy-six-year-old bride and a seventy-nine-year-old groom acting like two teenagers, you had to see this couple.

A perfect ending for a love affair that had lasted nearly sixty years.

~Arnold Fine
A Second Chicken Soup for the Woman's Soul

13

The Ageless Dance of Love

Age does not protect you from love,
but love to some extent protects you from age.
~Jeanne Moreau

he hot line rang loudly, awakening me from a sound sleep. I picked up the old-style black phone and heard the voice of an alert dispatcher: "We have an elderly male who is not breathing at Angler Courts, Cabin Four. It's the second cabin on the left from the Fulton Road entrance." I hung up the phone, jumped into my paramedic uniform, and stopped in the bathroom to check my eyes for mascara rings and finger through my big Texas hair. A possible cardiac arrest; the adrenaline streaked through my veins. Our south Texas resort area had mainly trauma in summer and cardiac in winter because of the northern retirees who spent the colder months here.

As I pulled onto the highway in the early dawn, I hit the switch that causes eye-popping lights of red, blue and white to bounce reflections from surrounding buildings. That tends to wake me up. I held off on the siren, since no real need existed at that hour.

I pulled into the given address and parked near a sheriff deputy's car. Volunteer EMTs were already on the scene. As I walked up the steps to the little clapboard cabin, a deputy spoke quietly to me. "It looks like he's been down a while, Wendy."

I saw a small woman standing by the bed, clutching the front of her blue quilted robe. Her short white hair fluffed into curls around her face and reminded me of a Tiny Tears doll I had as a child. As I placed the jump kit on the floor and the Life-Pak heart monitor on the bed, I asked the burly EMTs what they had assessed to this point.

"We found him breathless and pulseless. We didn't start anything, but if you want us to...." I picked up the old man's hand; they were right. Lying on his back, pillow under his head, he looked peaceful. The thought passed through my mind that he had no problem greeting death tonight. I placed the paddles on his chest to monitor his heart rhythm and found none. An absolute flatline. I asked for his age. "He would have been eighty-six next February," his wife said softly. I asked the deputy to notify the funeral home in the next town. We all knew it would take at least an hour. We would wait with her.

Another paramedic stood with me as I took the miniature-looking hand of the new widow. "Ma'am, I am sorry, but your husband's heart has stopped, and it has been too long for us to attempt any sort of resuscitation. It appears that he may have died quietly sometime in the night." She acknowledged by gently nodding her head.

"When did you notice that he wasn't breathing?"

"Well, sweetie," she said, "we went to bed around midnight. We just lay there and talked, like we do every night. We aren't like most folks our age; we stay up late and sleep late. Our friends just hate that about us. Anyway, we talked until about 1 A.M., then we began to make love."

There was a sharp intake of breath from the paramedic next to me and he suddenly began to fidget with the gear on his belt.

"I'm sorry, ma'am, you did what at about 1 A.M.?"

"We were having sex, making love." She graciously deadpanned her delivery. "We finished about an hour later, and I got up to go to the bathroom. When I came back, he was lying just like that, like you see him now. I told him goodnight, but now that I think about it, I'm not sure he answered."

Every person in the room had discovered some obscure duty that demanded their immediate attention. No one would look in our direction. Backs were shaking slightly from held-in laughter. Law enforcement officers suddenly needed to go outside, medics were packing up equipment, and no one, absolutely no one, would make any eye contact. This precious little woman never shied away from her description of the evening, had no embarrassment of it, and seemed to believe their behavior standard—for octogenarians to engage in sex for one hour.

"When I woke up to visit the bathroom at 6 A.M.," she said, "I couldn't arouse him." Poor choice of words with this audience. We were instantly alone in the room. The guys nearly knocked down the door getting out. I envisioned the chuckle-stifling crew hidden on the other side of the ambulance.

"I just cannot imagine it, though. We have sex most every night and it never killed him before." But instead of laughter, I felt immediate respect and admiration for this couple who had remained close emotionally and physically until their ultimate separation.

"You must have had such a grand love for one another." I moved her to a chair and had her sit down. "May I make some coffee while we wait for the funeral home folks? Do you want to talk for a while?"

"That would be nice. You've all been nice and so prompt. Yes, coffee… I suppose. I have a lot of things to do now. I should call my daughter in Illinois. I should…" She looked at her husband as her eyes welled up with tears. "I will miss him, I already do…. You know, I remember the day we met."

"Please tell me about it. We can make the calls later, after they have come for him. How did you meet?"

I sipped hot coffee and held the hand of a lovely farm girl from Kansas. As she spoke, I saw in her eyes a twenty-year-old seeing her first love, her only love, her constant love. Through the hardships of farming, raising children, losing two children and growing old, they had remained true to each other.

A habit had formed early. Each night they talked in bed for about an hour and then made love to one another. Emotional and physical communication had kept their relationship fresh for sixty years. They never viewed each other as old, never saw wrinkles, never noticed the changes that naturally happen to a body with age. At night, they were ageless—connecting, moving and swaying to a dance of their own creation. No "if onlys" will exist in her mind, only dear sweet memories of a man and a marriage made in heaven.

~Wendy J. Natkong
Chicken Soup for the Romantic Soul

14

Chain of Love

Whatever our souls are made of, his and mine are the same.
~Emily Brontë

on's eyes brightened when I walked into the restaurant. Always attentive, he took my coat and pulled out my chair. I avoided his eyes and wondered how to start.

We had dated for two years before getting engaged a week earlier. During that time we had decided to avoid physical intimacy. We wanted to remain objective about the relationship and thought this would help. And we were true to our agreement even though it became increasingly difficult as we fell more deeply in love. Now that we were engaged, it seemed silly to continue our abstinence.

Yet I wanted to do just that.

How would Ron react when I told him? Would he think I was hiding something? Would he think I was afraid of intimacy? Worst of all, would he think I didn't love him?

Setting down my glass of water, I reached for his hand across the table.

"Ron, you know how much I love you," I began. "And I think our 'agreement' has both tested and strengthened our relationship."

I faltered. Ron sat, silent. Waiting. My eyes focused on our clasped hands, then rose to meet his.

"I... I want to continue this way." I took a deep breath. "I want to wait until our wedding night."

Ron was grave as he pondered my request. I shredded the corners of my paper napkin—and waited. After a long pause, he looked up and met my anxious gaze.

"Agreed."

"Really?" I gasped.

"Really."

My heart filled with new respect and appreciation for the man I was going to marry. Yet, as we left the restaurant, Ron seemed distracted. In the parking lot, I suggested dessert at the local ice cream parlor.

"I have something important I need to see to," he declined. He had already started driving away when I realized he had forgotten his coat. I tried to flag him down but he didn't even see me.

Why was my attentive fiancé suddenly so absent-minded? I returned home uncertain where we stood, not sure I had really gotten what I wanted.

Later that night, the phone rang.

"I need to see you. I need to come over." There was urgency in his voice.

"Why? What's wrong? Ron?" He had already hung up.

Fifteen minutes later, Ron arrived carrying a large cardboard box. My heart sank. Was he returning all the gifts I had given him? I twisted the week-old diamond ring on my finger. I started to slide it off.

Ron held out the box. "Open it."

I swallowed hard and lifted the lid. Inside the box was a paper chain.

I pulled out length after length after length. On each link was a date, beginning with the current day and numbering into the future.

I knew my face mirrored the questions churning inside me. I looked at Ron.

He smiled at my puzzlement but quickly grew serious.

"I thought about your decision," he said. "And I plan to honor it—although it will be a great sacrifice." He nodded at the chain draping from my hands. "The chain represents that sacrifice."

Ron asked me to hang it in my bedroom and tear off a link every night. As our wedding neared, the chain would shrink and so would the sacrifice.

"With each torn link, pray for me to have the strength to be true to this commitment." Ron gazed into my eyes. "Will you do this for me?"

Tearfully, I accepted the chain and the commitment. All the love I felt poured forth when I kissed him like never before. Ron pulled away.

"If you want me to keep my promise, you had better stop giving such wonderful kisses," he teased. I laughed... and blushed... and showed him to the door. With my heart still racing, I suddenly recognized this would be a sacrifice for me too.

The chain circled my bedroom three times. I delighted in the evening ritual as I tore a link, thought about Ron's—our—sacrifice, and said a prayer just as he'd asked.

Soon only seven links remained. Then three. And, finally, the day before our wedding, only one. I didn't tear the last circle; I packed it in my suitcase.

On our wedding night, I showed Ron the final link of the chain. Smiling, we each took one side... and pulled. Then, together, we offered a prayer that our love—rooted in mutual sacrifice—would blossom and flourish.

~Kathleen Happ
Chicken Soup for the Bride's Soul

15

Bowled Over

"I know it's the last minute," Carl said timidly when I answered the phone, "but I, um, need a date for tonight." A date? Carl had never once mentioned the "D" word to me before, and it left me speechless. "I hope you're available," he added.

I glanced at the clock. It was after four. How many other numbers had he dialed first? He probably thought, maybe I'll try ol' reliable Jan. She's usually home on a Saturday night.

"It's my company party—a bowling party," he said. He needs a date for bowling? "Okay, sure," I replied.

When I hung up the phone my thoughts drifted back to two years ago when Carl first joined our church singles group. He wasn't what you'd call a hunk and didn't have a sparkling personality, but there was an instant tug at my heart. It wasn't his steel blue eyes, the premature gray hair or warm smile that attracted me, but an obvious strength of character. I wanted to know this man.

After the singles meetings, a few of us would meander over to the coffee shop. I'd linger, making sure I found myself alone with Carl. One night we talked until the late hours, conferring about everything from childhoods to politics to the Bible.

"You have firm opinions, and you're not afraid to state them," he told me. "I like that." Feeling as flimsy as a soggy piece of toast, I gazed longingly at him, but I received only congenial smiles in return.

Every week my heart fluttered at his warm "Hello." I knew he must be attracted to me, too, but this guy guarded his heart like a sentry over the crown jewels.

A few months later at our group's annual country hoedown, Carl and I square-danced together most of the night, twirling, tripping and laughing like teenagers.

He offered to drive me home after we cleaned up. "I have a view of the valley from my deck," I said, nudging Carl through the front door to the backyard. "Come and see." As we stood close together, watching the city lights flicker, I thought my anxious heart was about to explode like a pan of sizzling popcorn. This is the perfect moment to sweep me into his arms. Then, abruptly, he said, "I've really got to go now."

"He's driving me crazy," I later told my best friend, Jeanne.

"Could you be misinterpreting his attentions, just a bit, Jan? He's still healing from a recent divorce. He's got to test the single waters and see which way to steer his boat."

"But, but..." I was about to counter with "He likes to be with me, and we have so much in common, and doesn't he realize I'm perfect for him?" What was the matter with me? I'd been single again for ten years. A mature, professional woman, a singles group leader, not a schoolgirl dizzy with her first crush.

Jeanne piped in. "Earth to Jan—remember that seminar on dating and healthy relationships? The tricky little 'I' word?"

Infatuation, the chemistry that turns the sensible into silly. Yes, and it's the mystery, the uncertainty that keeps the fires of infatuation going.

"I must be imagining things that just aren't there."

"You're in love with the idea of falling in love."

I suppressed some tears. "I feel like a fool."

"Let it go, Jan. The timing is wrong," Jeanne urged.

Yes, and if Carl were the right man for me, it would happen in God's time with no plotting on my part. I asked myself, do I care about Carl enough to want the best for him, even if it is never me? I wrestled with it all night. How is it possible to have a platonic relationship while a medley of feelings dances on my heart?

"Give it to God," Jeanne said. She was right, but why do fantasies feel so comfortable, like a soft, cuddly lamb's-wool rug in front of a warm fire? It was hard to let go, but even harder to spark a romance with only one flame.

Carl was a popular guy in our group, friendly with everybody, and in the next year he had his share of women chasing him. He did have some dates, but none with me. He was like a cat with a dish of cream, lapping up strokes to his self-esteem. He was in his single heyday. Finally content to be his pal and cheerleader, life went back to normal.

But then came the telephone call, and that "D" word. I raked over my closet trying to find the perfect bowling outfit. Oh, here I go again, feeling all giddy. After all this time? Get a grip, girl.

We met for dinner at Garcia's, a Mexican restaurant near the bowling lanes, and before the fajitas stopped sizzling, the atmosphere shifted. This was not our usual "Let's grab a bite to eat." This was a lingering-over-the-meal, his-eyes-riveted-on-me, soaking-in-my-every-word-as-if-I-hadn't-existed-before kind of thing. This was a real date! And to cinch it, he paid for my dinner! While I didn't make any strikes later at the bowling alley, there was a telltale twinkle in his eyes that showed me I'd made a big strike with him. Bowled over, my emotional alarm clock started to go off.

Jeanne was half asleep when she picked up the phone at midnight. "What are you so afraid of?"

"That old floating-on-a-cloud feeling. I don't want to go back there."

"I like you better sane, myself."

Three weeks went by and no telephone call from Carl. It figures. He's probably back at Garcia's sampling the chili rellenos with somebody else. That's fine. At least I got a nice dinner out of it.

It was time for our singles Saturday social: a trip to San Francisco, a bike ride in Golden Gate Park and an optional dinner cruise on the bay. We rendezvoused at the grocery store parking lot.

"Lover Boy just showed up," Jeanne announced as Carl began to unload his bike from the back of his car. I bolstered myself. Be mildly sociable, but aloof. Let him come to you. After biking along the beachfront, ten of us changed into dinner clothes and boarded a blue-and-gold double-decker boat. As it headed out in the choppy waters, we all stood on the lower deck, watching the blazing sun slip under the Golden Gate Bridge, coloring the sky like a dream. I was spellbound by the lights emerging from the bridge. I barely noticed the music starting to signal dinner being served. I saw Jeanne and the group go below, and suddenly the deck was empty. Except for me and Carl.

As the boat began to circle, a cold blast of sea breeze made me shiver. Carl slid his long arms around my shoulders. This was no benign hug. Suddenly, I froze like a petrified tree.

Gently, he lifted my chin and looked down at me. He's going to kiss me. In the most romantic place in the world he's going to kiss me. Wait a minute. I have a few questions.... But I closed my eyes, slipped my arms around his neck and just let it happen.

"I knew you wanted me to do that long ago," he finally said, "But I couldn't. I was nowhere near ready for a committed relationship, and it wouldn't have been fair. I needed time—to become the right man for a woman like you."

Eleven months later we were married. During our wedding vows, Carl said, "Thank you for waiting for me, Jan." When it was my turn, I shared something I'd tucked away in my heart. It was from one of those dating seminars: "Love is a friendship that has caught fire."

~Jan Coleman
Chicken Soup for the Single's Soul

16

Mom, Can You Pull Some Strings?

"Mom, you can't die. I'm a late bloomer," I pleaded at my mother's bedside, as she lay dying of pancreatic/liver cancer. This couldn't be happening! My beautiful, vibrant, effervescent, fifty-nine-year-old mother couldn't be sick! It was all so unreal. Just two months ago she was fine, and yet now here she was, days from death.

"Mom, you have to meet my future husband and kids. You're not done."

"Oh, Carol, I would have loved that," she said wanly.

"Okay, Mom. If you're not going to meet him, you have to send him to me! Will you pull some strings for me up there?" I asked, trying to make her feel better.

"Yeah, Mom, you're on loser patrol. Carol needs help," my older sister, Linda, chimed in. We'd both moved home to nurse Mom and were with her night and day. Linda was right. I did need help. I'd dated a string of unavailable men. I'd been broken-hearted several times.

"Oh, my God. I don't want that job! I'm supposed to be resting up there," Mom exclaimed, knowing all too well how difficult the subject of "Mr. Right" was for me.

"Well, in that case, Mom, while you're at it, do you think you could get me a book deal?" asked Linda only half-joking. She'd been working on a book for three years and had a handful of rejection slips from numerous publishers.

"Gee, you two! I'll see what I can do," she said, smiling weakly.

A few days later, Mom passed away peacefully, the two of us praying by her side, our weeping father at the foot of the bed.

At her memorial service, Linda and I recounted for the over 300 attendees what a giving, selfless, loving mother she was.

I told the story of the first time she met the most significant boyfriend in my turbulent past, Bill. Bill was a professional harmonica player. On this first meeting, we went to brunch with my parents for Easter. Bill was my first real boyfriend after high school—the first relationship I'd had in six years. My parents were understandably excited to be meeting him. I was very nervous and hopeful that all would go well.

Much to my horror, my father barraged Bill with a series of annoying questions before we'd even ordered. "When was the harmonica invented? What keys do they come in? How many can you play?" And on and on. I wanted to melt underneath my chair! I looked desperately to my mother for help. Noticing my frantic eyes, she chimed in, "So, Bill, how long have you two been seeing each other?"

This was helping?!

"Uh, about six months," Bill replied.

"Gee," said Mom, leaning forward and grinning widely, "Any thoughts of this getting serious?" I wanted to die.

"Not until this very moment," Bill responded dryly.

In spite of it all, Bill and I went on to date for three years. He treated me like a queen and I grew to love him more every day. He felt ready to get married. I did not. We consequently broke up. I felt certain a world of wonderful men was waiting for me with open arms. I was wrong. With every new failed relationship, I'd weep to Linda, "Bill was so much better for me." He, on the other hand, was in a committed relationship almost immediately after we broke up. I was devastated!

Bill and his new love moved 1,000 miles away to New Mexico after a year. I hoped this would make things easier. As fate would have it, Linda called one day to inform me that she and her family had discovered an incredible land opportunity through Bill and were moving to New Mexico as well, with Bill and his girlfriend right next door. They would never be out of my life.

For Christmas, three months after Mom's death, my father and I went to see Linda and her family. I was very depressed without Mom.

We went to a big Christmas dinner. Bill was there. His girlfriend was away working for a few months. For the first time in the four years since we'd broken up, I felt very comfortable — as if he were an old friend. I was finally over it.

Two nights later, I was still really missing Mom. I decided to talk to her — something I had not yet done since she had died. I was staying by myself in a trailer a few minutes from Linda's. I lit a candle and said, "Mom, I miss you. Come be with me." The whole trailer immediately filled with brilliant white light. It was like nothing I had ever seen before. I could see it just as brightly with my eyes closed. "Mom, is that you?" I asked. The light flickered in response. She had come! Very at peace, I went to sleep, the light of my mother's essence encircling me.

Later that week, I had dinner with Bill. He confessed that he was still in love with me and that he couldn't get me out of his mind.

"How long have you been feeling this way?" I asked, incredulous.

"It's been especially intense since I saw you after your mother died. One look, and I knew we'd be together," he explained. I was completely in shock. "I've been talking to your mother about this," he said sweetly. "And you remember that first dinner I had with your mother when she asked if we were getting serious?" he said with a twinkle. "I think that meant she approves."

We were married nine months later.

Linda sold her book to a very reputable, successful publishing company the month before our nuptials.

I sure hope Mom can get that rest now.

~Carol Allen
A Second Chicken Soup for the Woman's Soul

17

One True Love

Have courage for the great sorrows of life and patience for the small ones;
and when you have laboriously accomplished your daily task,
go to sleep in peace.
~Victor Hugo

When Henri Bissette of Sherbrooke, Québec, went off to fight in World War I in 1917, he left behind his love of four years, Émilie Chevrier. The two wrote to each other faithfully. Letters could not always cross the battle lines, however, and eventually their writing became less frequent.

Émilie missed Henri terribly and constantly prayed for his safe return. One day in April 1918, Henri's family received a letter informing them that their son was "missing in action."

When Émilie heard the report she was devastated and refused to believe that Henri was gone. Six months later, when no further information had been received, Émilie finally realized that she would never see her beloved again.

Five months after the armistice was signed, ending the Great War, Émilie received a letter that Henri had written almost one year earlier. In it, he wrote about his feelings of desperation and his longing to leave the horrific war. His only desire was to return home to Canada so that he and Émilie could be married. The letter reassured Émilie that Henri's love was a true one, and although she kept all his letters, she treasured this one the most.

Émilie felt deep in her heart that she could never love another man as much as she loved Henri. He was her one true love, and she promised herself that she would never marry. In 1921, however, she met a kind, caring man named Joseph who she married shortly thereafter. They moved to Ottawa, where they raised a family of four children and lived happily until Joseph passed away in 1959.

Émilie was sixty years old when Joseph died, and her full-grown children were living lives of their own. Finding herself alone, she decided to return to her hometown of Sherbrooke, Québec, to enjoy her retirement years.

One day while out shopping, Émilie met an old school friend and the two reminisced about their past. During their conversation her friend mentioned Henri—she hadn't known about his war experience or his being "missing in action." When Henri's name came up, Émilie told her friend about everything that had occurred over forty years ago.

When she heard the story, her friend replied, "How odd! I'm sure I remember hearing that Henri bought a farm up north in the 1930s."

Émilie assured her friend that she must have been misinformed. After the two parted company, however, Émilie couldn't help wondering about the woman's story. Could it be true? she wondered. Surely, if Henri were alive, the two of them would be together now. Émilie needed to know the truth, but Henri's family had long since passed away. She began to investigate on her own and soon discovered that there was a Henri Bissette—he owned a farm just west of Trois-Rivières, Québec. Émilie decided to visit Trois-Rivières and make a trip out to the farm. She did not hold out much hope that she would really find her Henri. It was over forty years since she had received word of his death. In all likelihood, when the farmhouse door opened, she would simply find some farmer standing there—one who might be amused by her story.

When Émilie arrived at the farm and knocked on the door, however, she received the shock of her life. As the door opened, a farmer indeed stood there, but it was her own beloved Henri! He was greatly aged, of course, but still as handsome as she remembered. Henri gasped, recognising her instantly, and whispered, "Émilie!"

The two fell into each other's arms, so overcome with emotion that for several minutes all they could do was hug each other, crying and trembling. A lifetime had passed since they had last seen each other, but now it felt as if no time had passed at all.

When they calmed down, they both started to talk at once about what had happened over the years. Henri explained that after being wounded, he had spent over a year and a half recuperating in a hospital in Europe. When he finally did return to Sherbrooke, his family told him that the heartbroken Émilie, believing he was dead, had married and moved to Ottawa. They had no other information about her whereabouts. Henri was greatly saddened, but didn't want to disrupt Émilie's happiness in her life. He bought his farm shortly after, and had lived alone there all these years. He had never married because he knew that Émilie was his one true love.

With tears running down her face, Émilie pulled Henri's wartime letters from her purse.

"I never forgot you either, Henri," she said. "These letters have meant more to me over the years than you can ever know. I would always read them over and over when I began to feel sad, and it made me so happy to remember that you were the most special part of my life."

All at once the forty years of separation melted away. Finding each other had made them happier than they had ever been. Shortly after their reunion, they were married, and spent the rest of their days together on Henri's farm.

~Crystal Wood
Chicken Soup for the Canadian Soul

18

Treasure Hunt

It was so much fun, we proposed to each other all day long.
~Melissa Errico

Andrea slammed the phone into its cradle and shrieked, "I can't believe him!"

Her mom entered the room. "Jeff?"

"Yeah. He just did everything he could to pick a fight!" Shaking her head, she added, "I haven't seen him in three days and it doesn't even bother him. He says he's busy at work and can't break away. I don't know how much longer I can take this."

"Don't get impatient," Emma smiled slightly and patted her frustrated daughter's shoulder. "The best things in life are worth waiting for. Trust me."

"I don't know, Ma. Maybe he's the one that should be doing the waiting." She stormed out of the room.

Emma's smile widened.

Not an hour later, the doorbell rang. Andrea rushed to answer it. It just has to be Jeff, she thought. He'd never hang up angry.

Emma stood back, wiped her hands on a flowered apron and reclaimed her mischievous smile.

Andrea tipped the young messenger and rushed the package into the house. Under the watchful eye of her curious mother, she tore through the brown wrapping. It was the most beautiful dress she'd ever laid eyes on. As she lifted the white lace into the air, a piece of stationery floated to the floor. It read:

Baby Cakes,

Sometimes I say things I don't mean. Sometimes I'm stubborn and defensive. Sometimes I want to go to you, but fear rejection. Andrea, I love you, and because I love you I'll try harder to be understanding and have more patience. Forgive me. I saw this dress and thought how beautiful you'd look in it. Please wear it tonight and meet me at Capriccio's at 6:00. Can't wait to see you!

Love,
Jeff

As she wiped her eyes, Andrea caught her mother's grin. "I'll be there, "she smirked. "But this time he's gonna wait!"

Her mother just laughed.

It was almost 6:30 when Andrea screeched into Capriccio's lot. She intended to be a few minutes late, allowing extra time to get ready. She wanted his wait to be worth it when he saw her. The valet attendant took one look and swallowed hard. She noticed and smiled. The extra time had paid off.

Greeted by the maitre d', she expected him to escort her to Jeff's table. Instead, the older gentleman smiled and handed her a dozen long-stemmed roses.

"Mr. Stanton called and said he was running late. He said that the card would explain."

Blowing a wisp of hair from her eyes, Andrea reached into the baby's breath and retrieved the card.

Babe,

I would say I'm sorry, but those would just be words that you have heard many times before. This time, I'll say I love you, a truth that lives within my heart.

Meet me at the Eagle for drinks at 7:00.
Jeff

Andrea looked at the maitre d' who continued to grin. "Did he say anything else on the phone?"

"Not exactly," the kind man muttered. "Just that he can't wait to see you."

"It certainly doesn't seem that way," she lamented.

As she reached the parking lot, she was surprised to find that her car hadn't been moved. The valet attendant opened the door, smiled sweetly and said, "Best of luck!"

"Same to you," she replied, confused by his curious comment.

Within ten minutes she was at the Eagle waiting in the lounge. She would give him ten minutes to show; otherwise she'd go home to contemplate their future.

The bartender sauntered over. "What'll you have, Miss?"

"Margarita, no salt and a cup of ice on the side."

"Cup of ice on the side?" the man questioned with a silly grin dancing across his face.

"Yeah," she confirmed, her irritated tone approaching anger. If she didn't know any better, she'd swear she was the butt of some cruel joke. She checked her watch again. He had seven more minutes. Looking down at the beautiful white dress she wore, she shook her head. What a waste, she thought, fighting back the tears.

Within seconds, the bartender returned with a bottle of champagne and the same smile he'd left with.

"I ordered a margarita," she roared, then realizing her rude outburst, quietly added, "I'm sorry; it's just that my boyfriend was supposed to..."

"Meet you here at 7:00? I know. He called and asked that I pour you a glass of champagne and give you this card." With a wink, the bartender was gone. Andrea reluctantly opened it.

Sweetie,

Please bear with me! There are going to be times when other things might seem more important than you, but you have to trust that they're not.

The rest is up to faith. I'll be at the Dockside at 7:30. I'm hoping more than anything that you meet me. Please be there with the champagne.

Jeff

Andrea stood and noticed that every patron in the bar was gawking. She was right; it was a conspiracy. Her first thought was to go home and put an end to Jeff's foolish game.

Then it hit her. There was no way Jeff would have had the time to drop off both cards. Realizing it was all a carefully planned scheme; she smiled back at the crowd. Her excitement grew and, within minutes, she was in her car speeding to the Dockside.

As expected, Jeff was nowhere to be found. Instead, a white stretch limousine idled in front of a dilapidated shack. The chauffeur held a sign that read Andrea Evans.

With her dozen red roses, bottle of champagne and tears in her eyes, she climbed into the car. The driver offered a familiar smile and handed her a tiny card.

I knew you wouldn't give up on me. Enjoy the ride. I'm waiting! I love you!

Jeff

Andrea enjoyed the ride and when the car stopped, she stole a peek out the window. She was at the beach and Jeff was waiting somewhere in the dunes.

The driver parked the car, opened the door and assisted her out. "Have a beautiful time," he said. "I'll be here when you get done!"

Andrea felt like hugging him for his smile — the same one she had seen on the faces of strangers all day. Something big was up and the quest was not yet complete. Not forgetting her roses and champagne, she kicked off her shoes, grabbed them and started for the ocean.

A path of small seashells glimmered under a full moon. It was obvious each shell had been carefully placed, looping through the shifting dunes until they reached several large conch shells. Arranged in the shape of an arrow, they were the last clue on Jeff's peculiar map. She took a deep breath before stepping over the last dune.

The sight nearly brought her to her knees. Jeff was seated at a small round table in the middle of the beach. Dressed in a black tux, he stood when he saw her. She hurried toward him.

On the table, a hurricane lamp illuminated two place settings, an empty vase and empty ice bucket waited to be filled, and soft music drifted through the breeze.

As she reached him, she expected Jeff to embrace her, but he didn't. Instead, he dropped to his knees, grabbed her hand and blurted, "Be my wife, Andrea. Spend the rest of your life with me."

Instinctively, Andrea dropped to meet him in the sand. "Yes!" she answered through her sniffles. "I thought you'd never ask!"

Jeff laughed and pulled her to him. "I love you," he whispered.

"And I love you," she countered. Gesturing toward the table, she added, "I love all of this! But why?"

"Because I needed to know that you wouldn't give up on me when you thought I may have given up on you. I needed to know you love me as much as I love you."

"Do you know now?"

"I do," he whispered.

"Good," she giggled. "Because this is the last time I chase you!"

~Steve Manchester
Chicken Soup for the Bride's Soul

19

Five Dates, Eleven Hundred Letters and Fifty-Five Years Later

The U.S. Army arranged their brief meeting in September 1944. Nathan Hoffman, a soldier from Texas, was waiting at Camp Shanks in New York to ship out for the war in Europe. He decided to use his first leave pass to visit the Big Apple only thirty-five miles away. Little did Nathan know that what awaited him that night would change his life forever.

One of his fellow soldiers—whose parents lived in the city—wanted to drop in and surprise his parents with a hello. No one was at home, so Donald rang the doorbell at a neighbor's house where his parents often went to visit. Evelyn, the neighbors' twenty-one-year-old daughter, answered the door.

"Where's my mom?" Donald asked.

"She's in Brooklyn with my folks."

Donald nonchalantly said, "Say, I'm on a pass with two of my friends from Camp Shanks. Care to join us downtown?"

Evelyn and one of her friends agreed to go. The soldiers and the young ladies took off for a night on the town, escorting the Texan on his first tour of New York City. The evening ended with dancing at the Bal Tabarin in Times Square.

Before the evening was over, Nathan asked Evelyn, "Would you see me on every pass?" The vivacious young woman replied, "Sure! I'd love to!" Nathan used each pass to see Evelyn, for a total of five romantic dates.

On date number two, the handsome, serious soldier and the attractive, quick-witted young woman again laughed and danced at the Bal Tabarin. The band played "I'll Be Seeing You." Dates three, four and five passed all too quickly, with Nathan visiting Evelyn at her parents' home each night. They hoped for more dates, but the army intervened again.

Nathan's division was restricted to camp. At the camp P-X, Nathan ordered Evelyn an orchid corsage, and wrote on the card in his neat script, "I'll Be Seeing You." The corsage arrived for Evelyn while Nathan was on the ship to Europe, and she wore it proudly to the high holy day services at her synagogue, thinking, "How nice if he were here with me."

Before their fifth and last date, Nathan and Evelyn had vowed to write daily. And they kept that vow. For the next sixteen months, the soldier from Texas and the girl from the Bronx sent each other eleven hundred letters.

From the beginning, they were much more than just pen pals. Letters to him were addressed, "Nat dear," while she was "Evelyn dearest." He wrote candidly in his October 26, 1944 letter:

Baby, I am not asking you to make any promise with regard to the future... who knows how long it will be before the other end of our round-trip ticket to the States. I do know, though, that I want you to feel about me as you do now for a long, long time because it is mutual and maybe both of our prayers together will help our wishes materialize.

The sweethearts identified their favorite passages in books they were both reading and then compared opinions. While Nathan was still in England, Evelyn described the record albums of classical music she bought. She asked him, "What do you think of fine music?" He replied by sending her a program from a concert he attended in an

English cathedral. He wrote that he especially enjoyed *Symphony No. 5 in C Minor* by Beethoven.

The Texas soldier turned out to be very special to Evelyn. They enjoyed the same music, books, art and entertainment, had the same religion and philosophy of life.

Despite the German surrender in May, Nathan remained in Germany during the summer of 1945, wondering whether he would be sent to the Pacific if Japan refused to surrender. In June, he wrote Evelyn, telling her he would understand if she chose not to wait for him. It would probably be another fifteen months before he could return.

The courtship continued, and their letters gave life to their transatlantic romance.

Their letters dated August 8 through 15, 1945, record their mutual celebration, a celebration tinged with a somber recognition that the world was forever changed:

August 8, 1945 — Nathan [in Germany]

Evelyn, from this day on the world as it has been up to now is through. The A-bomb and its successors could become a Frankenstein eventually destroying its creators and the whole planet.

August 11 — Evelyn [in New York]

Now the end is in sight, a matter of days. Shredded paper comes from the office windows at every new announcement. People are touchy and suspenseful. This time they say there will be no unofficial V-J Day. We're all waiting for President Truman's peace declaration.

August 11 — Nathan [in Germany]

I've just heard the good news about the war. Honey, I'm so happy I could holler, shout, raise hell, cry and do anything. If someone tells me it's a false alarm, I will keel over and drop

dead. Hopefully, now the whole damned war is "kaput" and this
wholesale slaughter can be brought to an end.

August 15 — Evelyn [in New York]

The sirens are wailing. The noise and celebration in the streets are
deafening. I can hardly steady my hand. I have a deep peaceful
feeling and a million prayers of thanksgiving. I can't remember
what peace was like. Most of all, it means our husbands, fathers,
brothers, boyfriends and relatives are coming home. We can
start our lives again. Pray there will be no more wars.

After the peace declaration, Nathan had to wait his turn, while the
soldiers who had fought in Europe the longest went home first.
September, October and then November dragged on. The sweethearts grew impatient with their matchmaker, the army. In all their
letters, an electric undercurrent of anticipation for their sixth date
grew stronger.

Everywhere his unit was sent, Nathan carried with him in his
one duffel bag the hundreds of letters Evelyn had sent. Before he
finally received orders to go home, he needed to lighten his duffel bag
for the trip. He sent the letters home by mail in a twenty-three-pound
package.

Nathan's final correspondence of the war, penned on the last day
of 1945, reads like this:

This should be the last letter that I shall write to you from here.
When you next hear from me it will be by phone or in person....
S'long, honey, pucker up, 'cause here I come... with love.

When Nathan returned home in January 1946, Evelyn was there at
the Discharge Center to meet him. A month later, on February 24,
1946, they were married in Nathan's family's synagogue.

• • •

Fifty years later, as they renewed their vows in the same synagogue where they were married, Nathan shared: "After fifty golden years, I can say that our years together seem to me but a few days because of the love I have for her. And I would wait for her all over again."

"World War II brought us together," said Evelyn. "In Hebrew, we have a word beshert—divinely appointed, meant to be. That is what Nathan and I are, beshert—we are each other's perfect soul mate."

The twenty-three-pound package of letters Nathan had sent home from the war, along with the letters Evelyn had lovingly saved, are now preserved within two large, bound volumes. The Hoffmans compiled these letters in book form as a labor of love to pass along as a special legacy for their children, grandchildren and friends.

On September 9, 1944, among eight million people in New York, Nathan and Evelyn fatefully crossed paths.

Five wonderful, whirlwind dates, eleven hundred letters and fifty-five years later, their love that endured a war is still going strong.

~Amy Seeger
Chicken Soup for the Golden Soul

20

Tattooed Dreams

Ididn't like going to the beach, but I had no choice. My boys were at that age where it was best to keep an eye on them. It wasn't that I didn't like to sit in the sun and feel ocean breezes tease through my hair, but at forty-five, I felt fat and out of shape. Middle age was not a good time.

Sounds of the old beach stirred up emotions. I sat in the sand chair wrapped like a mummy in a long beach cover-up. Ageless aromas breezed from concession stands carrying memories of my teenage years, especially the good times with Jimmy. We had spent summers on the beach jumping through waves, kissing under bubbling foam, holding hands as we walked under starry summer skies.

Mother never liked Jimmy. Her comments were always laced with negative remarks. "He's irresponsible. He'll never amount to anything."

For me, it was love at first sight. Jimmy was cool. He drove a souped-up Plymouth sedan. He wore chino pants and white T-shirts. His dark, shiny hair dipped across his forehead in an enviable wave. It didn't take long to learn his tough veneer covered a sensitive, loving person. He treated me like the best thing that had ever happened to him.

Sitting on the old beach, listening to the rhythmic sounds of rolling waves, the toasty sun lulled me back to the past. Sleepily, I eased from my beach chair to stretch out on the striped towel, and then discreetly slipped off my cover-up.

Daydreams wandered off to the time when Jimmy and the guys had gotten tattoos. A flowery heart surrounded my initials, CLG. At first, I was annoyed. I didn't like my middle name and never used the initial, but when Jimmy rolled up his sleeve, I was proud of the statement his tattoo made: I was his girl.

We made plans to marry right after high school. Then Jimmy broke my heart. He and a couple of friends quit school. "We joined the army." Mother was thrilled over his enlistment. It was as if her prayers were answered.

He shipped out to the Far East. I spent my senior year alone. During the following summer, Mother found me a promising husband. She promoted my relationship with Chet, an engineer with an engaging personality. At Mother's urging, our marriage took place, quickly. Chet and I moved across the country to California and began our new life.

Through the years, I had no contact with Jimmy. Every once in a while, thoughts about him slipped through daydreams. When I asked Mother if she'd heard how he was, she'd always cut the conversation short. "Heard Jimmy married one of those overseas girls," or "Heard Jimmy was MIA."

I tried to be an attentive wife, but I felt empty inside. Every once in a while, I escaped the confusion of marriage with thoughts of my first love. When I did, it seemed as if Chet could read my mind. He'd become nasty and lectured blatantly about the responsibilities of marriage. He didn't seem to care how I felt or that past times needed closure. I quietly submitted to his demands and covered up my feelings.

Chet's controlling directives forced me into a Stepford wife existence to promote his advancements at work. Unexpectedly, my life took a dramatic turn. While away on business, Chet had a heart attack. He died in the Chicago airport.

For the first time, I took control of my life. Somehow, I managed to keep all the balls in the air, except for money issues. Moving back East with Mother had helped financially, but had stirred up the past.

Lately I had been thinking that if I could drop a few pounds and tone up this mess, I could settle down, again. But this time, do it right.

"Ma! Ma!" A panicked call broke beach daydreams. My son screamed as he struggled through the waves trying to rescue his brother, who'd been caught in a riptide. I bolted to the water's edge. The lifeguard's chair was empty.

Suddenly, a man dashed past and dove into the water. He swam, hard and strong, out to my son, who wrapped his arms around the man's neck and almost drowned them both. The man managed to make headway when the lifeguards showed up and pulled them to safety.

My son was fine. The middle-aged man gasped breathlessly. "How can I ever thank you?" I said.

"Don't worry," he replied. "Saving your son is thanks enough. I only wish the same had been done for me." His eyes teared.

"Why?" I hesitated, and then asked, "What happened?"

"Several years ago, we capsized off the 'Nam coast. Soldiers pulled me in, my wife and son drowned." He brushed tears away. The kids and I were devastated. I didn't know what to say. My boys gathered around and sat quietly with our heroic stranger. His friendly manner eased us into conversation. As I looked into his eyes an old, comfortable feeling washed through my thoughts. I forgot about my middle-aged appearance. I forgot I wasn't hiding under my cover-up.

As we talked, one of my sons asked, "What's that picture on your arm?" My son's directness embarrassed me.

Our rescuer chuckled, "It's a tattoo."

"Like Popeye?"

"That's right. And it had my girlfriend's initials right there," he said pointing to the flowery heart. "Under that blue line. I covered them up because I married someone else."

"That's kinda like my first boyfriend, Jimmy," I blurted. "He had my initials tattooed on his arm." My boys' eyes widened. "Wonder what he did?"

The kids gasped, then giggled. Our new friend chuckled. For the first time, I took a hard look at our rescuer. His bald head was fringed with gray, and his belly overlapped his bathing trunks. I wondered, Could he be...? I glanced at his eyes.

He grinned. Then his upbeat voice distracted me. "Guess he did what I did," he laughed.

Something seemed familiar about his tone. I don't know why I said, "You're kinda like him." Our hero filled my nagging emptiness. Maybe daydreams tricked me. I liked not having to cover up my feelings or my middle age. Then, I remembered, through all our conversation, we hadn't introduced ourselves. I smiled and extended my hand. "I'm sorry. I should have introduced myself. I'm Carol...."

"Yes, I know," he interrupted gently. "You're Carol Lee Gebhardt. And yes, I'm Jimmy. And you haven't changed a bit."

As impossible as it seemed, it was true—we had found each other again. Our magical reunion turned into a marriage that has been solid for eighteen years. His wonderful, caring personality won the boys over, and they think of him as a father figure.

When people see the blanked-out area inside the tattooed heart on Jimmy's arm they think somebody else's initials are under there. I laugh and say, "I'm really under there!"

~Carol MacAllister
Chicken Soup for the Romantic Soul

Chapter
3

*Happily
Ever After*

Wedding Laughs

I dreamed of a wedding of elaborate elegance, a church filled with family and friends. I asked him what kind of a wedding he wished for, he said one that would make me his wife.
~Author Unknown

21

What's So Funny?

*A little girl at a wedding afterwards asked her mother why the bride changed
her mind. What do you mean? responded her mother. Well, she went down
the aisle with one man, and came back with another."*
~Author Unknown

t was a beautiful wedding. The dresses, the candles, the
flowers—especially the flowers. They were wonderful.
The candle glow and smell of roses heightened the inten-
sity of the ceremony.

"And do you, Peggy, take this man..." the pastor began.

Yes of course I do. He's sweet and gorgeous and...

"I do," I said.

"And do you, Dickey, take this woman, Peggy..."

Yes, of course he does.

"Please kneel. Father, we ask your special blessing on this husband and this wife," the pastor continued.

Wait, is someone giggling?

"Bless their union..."

Who is giggling?

It's his mother! Why is she laughing? What does she know that
I don't?

"And all of us gathered here promise to offer support..."

Now his mother's laughing out loud. And so is everyone else.
Wait! May I ask a question before we continue?

"I now introduce Mr. and Mrs..." the pastor concluded, although he seemed a little confused, too.

They're still laughing.

But the music swelled and this man I was no longer sure of whisked me out of the church.

"Wow!" I said with a catch in my throat. "They all seemed to enjoy the service." I turned to Dickey, fishing for an explanation.

Dickey had a look of suspicion on his face as he leaned against the wall. He lifted one shoe and then the other.

"My little sister! I'm going to get her!" he groaned, shaking his head. Then he showed me the bottom of his shoes.

Written in big red letters were the words "HELP ME!"

~Peggy Purser Freeman
Chicken Soup for the Bride's Soul

22

The Missing Candelabra

Small deeds done are better than great deeds planned.
~Peter Marshall

It was one of the largest weddings ever held at Wilshire. Fifteen minutes before the service was scheduled to begin, the church parking lots were overflowing with cars, and scores of people were crowding into the foyer, waiting to be properly seated. It was the kind of occasion that warms the heart of a pastor.

But that was fifteen minutes before the service.

At exactly seven o'clock the mothers were seated, and the organist sounded the triumphant notes of the processional. That was my cue to enter the sanctuary through the side door at the front and begin presiding over the happy occasion. As I reached for the door a voice called from down the hall, "Not yet, Pastor. Don't open the door. I've got a message for you."

I turned and through the subdued lighting I saw the assistant florist hurrying as fast as she could toward me. Her speed didn't set any records, because she was about eight months pregnant and waddled down the hall with obvious difficulty. She was nearly out of breath when she reached me. "Pastor," she panted, "we can't find the candelabra that you are supposed to use at the close of the ceremony. We've looked everywhere, and it just can't be found. What on earth can we do?"

I sensed immediately that we had a big problem on our hands. The couple to be married had specifically requested that the unity candle be a part of the wedding service. We had gone over it carefully at the rehearsal—step by step. The candelabra, designed to hold three candles, was to be placed near the altar. The mothers of the bride and groom would be ushered down the aisle, each carrying a lighted candle. Upon reaching the front of the sanctuary, they were to move to the candelabra and place their candles in the appropriate receptacles. Throughout the ceremony the mothers' candles were to burn slowly while the larger middle one remained unlighted. After the vows had been spoken, the bride and groom would light the center candle. This was designed to symbolize family unity as well as the light of God's love in the new relationship.

I felt good about all this at the rehearsal. I had a special verse of scripture that I planned to read as the couple lighted the middle candle. We had it down to perfection.

We thought.

The notes from the organ pealed louder and louder as I was stalled in the hallway. I knew that the organist by now was glancing over her left shoulder wondering where in the world the minister was.

"Okay," I said to the perplexed florist, "We'll just have to wing it. I'll cut that part out of the ceremony and improvise at the close."

With those words I opened the door and entered the sanctuary, muttering behind my frozen smile, "What on earth are we going to do?"

The groom and his attendants followed me in. The bride and her attendants came down the left aisle of the sanctuary. When the first bridesmaid arrived at the front, she whispered something in my direction.

The puzzled look on my face was a signal to her that I did not understand.

She whispered the message again, opening her mouth wider and emphasizing every syllable. By straining to hear above the organ and through lip-reading, I made out what she was saying: "Go ahead with the unity candle part of the ceremony."

"But... how?" I whispered through my teeth with a plastic smile. "Just go ahead," she signaled back.

We made it through the first part of the ceremony without any difficulty.

Everyone was beaming in delight because of the happy occasion—everyone except the first bridesmaid who had brought me the message. When I looked in her direction for some additional word about the candelabra, she had a stoic look on her face and her mouth was tightly clamped shut. Obviously, she was out of messages for me.

We continued with the ceremony. I read a passage from Corinthians 1:13 and emphasized the importance of love and patience in building a marriage relationship. I asked the bride and groom to join hands, and I began to talk about the vows they would make. There wasn't a hitch. I was beginning to feel better, but I still had to figure out some way to conclude the service. Just now, however, we needed to get through the vows and rings.

"John, in taking the woman whom you hold by your hand to be your wife, do you promise to love her?"

"That's the funniest thing I've ever seen," the bride interrupted with a loud whisper. I turned from the bewildered groom to look at her and noticed that she was staring toward her right, to the organ side of the front of the sanctuary. Not only was she looking in that direction, so were all the attendants, and so was the audience! One thousand eyes focused on a moving target to my left. I knew it was moving, for heads and eyes followed it, turning ever so slightly in slow-motion style.

The moving target was none other than the assistant florist. She had slipped through the door by the organ and was moving on hands and knees behind the choir rail toward the center of the platform where I stood. The dear lady, "great with child," thought she was out of sight, beneath the rail. But in fact, her posterior bobbled in plain view six inches above the choir rail. As she crawled along she carried in each hand a burning candle. To make matters worse, she didn't realize that she was silhouetted—a large, moving, "pregnant" shadow—on the wall behind the choir loft.

The wedding party experienced the agony of smothered, stifled laughter. Their only release was the flow of hysterical tears while they fought to keep their composure. Two or three of the bride's attendants shook so hard that petals of the flowers in their bouquets fell to the floor.

It was a welcomed moment for me when the vows were completed and I could say with what little piety remained, "Now, let us bow our heads and close our eyes for a special prayer." This was a signal for the soloist to sing "The Lord's Prayer." It also gave me a chance to peep during the singing and figure out what in the world was happening.

"Pssst. Pssst!"

I did a half turn, looked down and saw a lighted candle being pushed through the greenery behind me.

"Take this candle," the persistent florist said.

The soloist continued to sing, "Give us this day our daily bread...."

"Pssst. Now take this one," the voice behind me said as a second candle was poked through the greenery.

"...as we forgive those who trespass against us..."

I was beginning to catch on. So I was to be the human candelabra. Here I stood, with a candle in each hand and my Bible and notes tucked under my arm.

"Where's the third candle?" I whispered above the sounds of "...but deliver us from evil..."

"Between my knees," the florist answered. "Just a minute and I'll pass it through to you."

That's when the bride lost it. So did several of the attendants. The last notes of "The Lord's Prayer" were drowned out by the snickers all around me.

I couldn't afford such luxury. Somebody had to carry this thing on to conclusion and try to rescue something from it, candelabra or no candelabra. I determined to do just that as I now tried to juggle three candles, a Bible and wedding notes. My problem was complicated by the fact that two of the candles were burning, and the third one soon would be.

The dilemma was challenging, a situation that called for creative action—in a hurry. Nothing in the *Pastors' Manual* addressed this predicament. Nor had it ever been mentioned in a seminary class on pastoral responsibilities. I was on my own.

I handed one candle to the nearly hysterical bride, who was laughing so hard that tears were trickling down her cheeks. I handed the other to the groom, who was beginning to question all the reassurances I had passed out freely at the rehearsal. My statements about "no problems," and "we'll breeze through the service without a hitch," and "just relax and trust me," were beginning to sound hollow.

I held the last candle in my hands. They were to light it together from the ones they were each holding. Miraculously, we made it through that part in spite of jerking hands and tears of smothered laughter. Now we had three burning candles.

In a very soft, reassuring voice, I whispered, "That's fine. Now each of you blow out your candle."

Golly, I said to myself, we're going to get through this thing yet.

That thought skipped through my mind just before the bride, still out of control, pulled her candle toward her mouth to blow it out, forgetting that she was wearing a nylon veil over her face.

Poooff!

The veil went up in smoke and disintegrated.

Fortunately, except for singed eyebrows, the bride was not injured.

Through the hole in the charred remains of her veil she gave me a bewildered look. I had no more reassurances for her, the groom or anybody. Enough was enough.

Disregarding my notes concerning the conclusion of the ceremony, I took all the candles and blew them out myself. Then, peering through the smoke of three extinguished candles, I signaled the organist to begin the recessional... now! Just get us out of here! Quickly!

Everything else is a blur.

But I still turn pale when prospective brides tell me about "this wonderful idea of using a unity candle" in the ceremony.

~Bruce McIver
Chicken Soup for the Romantic Soul

23

Keeping the Tradition

he year was 1972. Noel and I had just gotten married in Southern California and were traveling — by car — to our new life together in Pennsylvania. My in-laws offered to pack the top layer of the wedding cake in dry ice and mail it after we got settled in our attic apartment.

Sure enough, a few weeks later the package arrived. We eagerly unpacked it and placed it in our "freezer," a small metal box mounted inside the back of the refrigerator. The cake filled the entire compartment. Now we had a serious choice to make.

After some thought, a little deliberation, and a lot of conversation, we decided to forfeit ice cube trays and ice cream for the next twelve months — in honor of tradition. It was a big price to pay, but eating the cake top on our first anniversary would make it worthwhile.

One year later our anniversary arrived. I gently removed the package from the freezer and was relieved to see that our perfectly preserved top layer looked as fresh as it had on our wedding day. I made a nice dinner while it defrosted and Noel prepared for our celebration. When the meal was over, I ceremoniously handed the cake knife to Noel and asked him to do the honors and cut the first slice.

Noel pressed down on the knife.

"Something doesn't feel right," he said, pressing harder. We heard a strange noise, a squeaky crunch.

"Something doesn't sound right."

What was wrong with the cake? Noel slid the small piece onto a dessert plate. We stared in disbelief, caught each other's eyes, and burst out laughing.

Styrofoam! Our "cake" top was iced Styrofoam!

And, to think, for an entire year we had sacrificed cold drinks and frozen desserts in anticipation of this traditional event. After we finally quit chuckling, we raced straight to the store. Now we would really celebrate... by stocking the freezer with ice cube trays and our favorite ice cream.

~Dr. Denise Enete
Chicken Soup for the Bride's Soul

24

The Ideal Invitation

A friend lost her mate several years ago and recently developed a friendship with a man who had also lost his spouse. They seemed a perfect match, and all their children agreed they should get married. While they were excited about the upcoming nuptials, they didn't need more crystal vases, blenders, toasters, etc. So this was their invitation:

Phil, Richard, Karen and Allison
and
John, Matt and Steve
request the honor of your presence
at the marriage of their
Mother and Father.
Because they are combining two households,
they already have at least two of everything.
So please, no presents!
Reception and garage sale immediately following the ceremony.

~Del Chesser
Chicken Soup for the Golden Soul

Popping the Question

When you realize you want to spend the rest of your life with somebody,
you want the rest of your life to start as soon as possible.
~Nora Ephron, When Harry Met Sally

It was a typical Tucson winter day, cool and sunny. I met my boyfriend for lunch at a sandwich shop near the college I was attending. We had limited time so we ate quickly. Jeff had to get back to work; his afternoon would be busy. Before parting, Jeff asked if I wanted to go to Happy Hour that evening. I agreed and we kissed goodbye.

That afternoon biology class was dismissed early. I jumped into my car to drive home, change clothes, and freshen up before our date. As I headed up the ramp to the freeway, my cell phone rang.

"I'm off early. Had to go to the post office and bank," Jeff explained. He was in his car only minutes ahead of me.

"Isn't this great? We have plans and we both got out early!"

"Where are you?" Jeff asked.

"Still a couple of miles behind you." I gave him my cross streets.

Jeff suddenly interjected, "I'm sorry I haven't been very romantic lately."

"No, I guess you haven't," I agreed. "But we've been busy, it's okay."

"Valentine's Day is coming up. I promise to do something romantic, at least get you a card."

"That's a start."

"Where are you now?" he asked, more impatiently. I looked at the street signs and read them off to him. "Well, hurry up. I want to get to Happy Hour."

We had plenty of time. Why the hurry? He was acting so strange.

"I can meet you at the restaurant if you prefer," I suggested. "Or, if we meet at the house we can ride together and catch up on our day." He agreed, and we hung up again.

My cell phone rang again.

"Beth, I just got home. What happened to the garage door? Did you break it this morning?" The garage door was our main entry to the house.

"It was fine when I left. Maybe your automatic opener isn't working?" Minutes later I pulled beside Jeff's car in our driveway. I repeatedly pressed the button on my garage opener. Nothing. With a shrug, I walked up to the front door and turned the knob.

As I stepped into the living room, my jaw dropped and my eyes grew big. A camera flashed.

I was swimming in a sea of balloons. Balloons on the floor. Balloons on the ceiling. Dozens and dozens... hundreds of colorful balloons. Jazz music played in the background.

After my eyes adjusted, I saw Jeff sitting on the couch, camera in hand. He said, "You agreed I wasn't very romantic, so I decided to whip something up."

Still in shock, I trudged through the balloons to hug him. I felt like I was in slow motion.

Jeff nodded toward the coffee table. "You have something to open." There sat a bucket with a champagne bottle on ice, two crystal champagne flutes, two candles and a blue ribbon... tied around a little blue box.

I picked up the box and slowly pulled the ribbon. Inside was a ring box. I lifted the lid and found... a gold stickpin? I looked at Jeff with raised eyebrows.

He folded his arms across his chest, settled back and grinned. "It looks like you have some popping to do."

"What?" I looked around the room. "Oh!"

Not wasting a moment, I grabbed the pin and began sticking balloons. Laughing all the while, I searched for "the" balloon. But there were so many, I finally started shaking them and throwing them to the side.

"Don't forget there are balloons on the ceiling," Jeff reminded me. I looked up.

After an eternity, I shook a red balloon. Something rattled! When I poked it with my gold stickpin, shiny heart-shaped confetti cascaded around me. A blue ring bag fell to the carpet.

Trembling, I tipped it open until a ring fell into my hand. Jeff gently took it and urged me to sit on the couch.

"You know me. I have to do this the traditional way." As he lowered himself to one knee, his brown eyes gazed into mine. He asked me to be his wife and slipped the princess-cut diamond on my finger.

After my eager "Yes!" and many kisses later, Jeff said, "Oh... and... by the way... we are not going to Happy Hour."

~Elizabeth L. Blair
Chicken Soup for the Bride's Soul

26

Our Honeymoon Flight

Charming people live up to the very edge of their charm,
and behave as outrageously as the world lets them.
~Logan Pearsall Smith

Dennis and I almost missed our honeymoon flight and were unable to get seats together. When we were airborne, I wrote my new spouse a flirtatious note: "To the man sitting in 16C. I find you very attractive. Would you care to join me for an unforgettable evening? The lady in 4C." A flight attendant delivered it.

A few minutes later she returned with a cocktail. The man in 16C was flattered, she told me, but said he must decline my offer since he was on his honeymoon. I was still laughing when we landed. "Thank you for the drink," I said to my groom.

"But I didn't send you one," he replied.

He had been sitting in 14C.

~Cindy J. Braun
Chicken Soup for the Romantic Soul

Chapter
4

Happily Ever After

Meant to Be

I married the first man I ever kissed.
When I tell my children that, they just about throw up.
~Barbara Bush

27

A Thousand Ways

Challenges make you discover things about yourself
that you never really knew.
~Cicely Tyson

Heavy snow fell outside the home of Dick Osborn's parents in Boise, Idaho. Dick sat quietly in his room brooding about a dating relationship that had ended. Reaching for his Bible, he read Proverbs 16:33: "The lot is cast into the lap, but its every decision is from the Lord."

Normally Dick wasn't the type to give God an ultimatum, but this particular evening, he felt lonely and depressed thinking about his ex-girlfriend, Sandy. He reached in his pocket for a quarter and flipped it up in the air, saying, "Lord, if it lands heads up, I will get back with Sandy and marry her someday. If it doesn't, I know that isn't your will." The coin landed tails up.

"No, Lord," Dick said, "that's not the right answer. Let's go two out of three." He tossed the coin into the air once more, and it landed tails up again. After the fourth time, Dick groaned, "Well, this is just a bunch of hokey anyway."

Glancing around the room, Dick's gaze fell on a magazine lying upside down on the rug. On the back was an advertisement for the book *Parables for Young Teens*. He pleaded, "Lord, who am I going to marry, then?" Staring at the book's picture, he read the author's name and said, "Susan F. Titus?" Again, he flipped his coin up in the air, but this time it landed heads up.

"Well, that just proves that this really is a bunch of hokey. I don't even know anyone named Susan F. Titus, let alone what state she's in. How could I possibly marry her?" He soon forgot the incident and tried to move on in his life.

Months later, Dick sat laughing and talking with his church group.

"The thing I miss most from my previous marriage is the baseball tickets to the California Angels," one young woman said.

"It happens that I've got season tickets to a box seat. Maybe we can go sometime," Dick said.

She whispered discretely, "I'd like to, but I'm dating someone."

Dick smiled and responded glibly, "Let me know if you ever change your mind."

Several months later, Dick was disappointed to learn that his old girlfriend, Sandy, was engaged to someone else. The following Sunday he walked with his baseball-fan friend from the church sanctuary to the parking lot. She stopped and said, "Dick, remember what you said about my telling you if I ever changed my mind about going out with you?"

"Yeah."

"Well, I'd like to."

A smile lit his face. "Okay."

They had lunch the following Wednesday, and soon their romance blossomed. Before long, they were engaged. One day, while Dick was carrying some of her son's things upstairs, he noticed a framed poster hanging on the hallway wall, which read: Parables for Young Teens by Susan F. Titus.

He stared openmouthed, then turned to his fiancée. "Sue, did you write that book?"

"Yes," she answered. "Why else would I have it hanging on my wall?"

He didn't respond, but just stared incredulously.

Later on their honeymoon, one evening Dick squeezed Susan's hand and said, "I have a story to tell you, and you're going to find it hard to believe. " Before he started the story, however, Dick took a coin from his pocket and flipped it. "Heads. I won," he said, and then he began.

~Susan Titus Osborn
Chicken Soup for the Christian Woman's Soul

28

How David and Lily Got Together

When the world says, "Give up,"
Hope whispers, "Try it one more time."
~Author Unknown

This is the story of how David and Lily got together, or at least, what they always told us. We didn't learn the truth till many years later.

Some years ago, a good family moved into the third-floor apartment of the tenement where we lived in the Bronx. David was the son, and he was going to medical school. He was also an avid reader, so he spent most of his free time in the library.

The librarian there was a pretty, soft-spoken young woman named Lily. We kids all loved her. If we couldn't find a book, she would stop whatever she was doing, smile at us warmly and launch a search to find it for us. She was a hard worker.

She also secretly admired our new neighbor, David. Whenever he entered the small neighborhood library, Lily's eyes lit up and observed his wandering path through the stacks of books. She never struck up a conversation with him, though. She was much too shy, and in those days, a woman didn't talk to a stranger without a formal introduction.

One evening, as Lily was closing up the library, her assistant bent down near the desk to retrieve an unopened envelope from the floor. She showed it to Lily, and they noted that it was sent from a major city hospital.

"It looks so important," the assistant said. "Some poor person is probably looking for it frantically. It must have fallen out of his pocket or book."

Lily glanced at the address of the recipient and was surprised to see it was for the building right next to hers. She took the letter so she could drop it by the man's apartment on her way home.

She turned out the lights, locked up the library and hurried home, where she quickly set down her bags. Clutching the envelope, she ran across the way, entered the front lobby next door and scanned the mailboxes. She found a "Gordon," the same last name listed on the envelope, and rang the bell for that apartment.

"Who's there?" called out a woman's voice over the scratchy intercom.

"I'm the librarian," Lily answered. "We found a letter on the library floor addressed to a David Gordon. Does that name mean anything to you? The letter looks important."

After a pause, the voice replied: "Yes. Could you bring it up for me, Apartment B3? I fell a few weeks ago and can't walk the stairs."

Lily walked up the three flights of stairs and was greeted at the door by a sweet, older woman who was leaning on a crutch.

"Oh, thank you so much," she said. "As you see, I really can't walk the stairs."

Lily smiled. "I understand. Well, here's the letter. Is David Gordon your husband?"

"Oh, no," she answered. "That's my son. We were wondering where that letter went." She looked Lily up and down. "You say you found the letter at the library?"

"Yes," said Lily. "I'm the librarian there, but I live in the building next to you, so it was no trouble to bring you the letter."

"Well, look at us standing here like strangers," the woman said, smiling brightly. "Come and sit for a moment and have some tea. Please."

As she motioned Lily to a chair, the lady talked about the letter.

"When I get mail for my son, I always put it on the kitchen table so he can find it when he comes home. This letter was important, so I stuck it in his book. You see, he is going to medical school to be a specialist," she said proudly.

Just then, the door opened, and in walked her son, David. Upon seeing that he was the young man she had admired so long, Lily felt her heart beat faster. His mother excitedly explained to him what had happened to the letter.

David looked at Lily in astonishment. "Gosh! You're from the library. Thank you! I was looking high and low for that letter." He turned to his mother. "You see, I was accepted to the hospital's medical program."

Then he turned back to Lily and smiled shyly. "Thanks again, Miss, errrr, I didn't get your name."

"Lily," she said, smiling her warmest smile. Her heart was still pounding, and she felt sure her cheeks were flushed.

Meanwhile, Mrs. Gordon was hobbling around, setting the table for tea and cookies. "Sit! Sit!" she urged the young couple.

"Have you decided which branch of medicine you want to specialize in?" Lily asked David.

"Cardiology," David answered, still smiling. "And this is the letter that will start me on my career. I was really worried when I hadn't heard from the hospital. I was considering going out west someplace, but I'd much rather stay at this hospital, here in the city."

And then, out of the blue, David blurted: "Would you care to go to a movie with me Saturday night?"

Before Lily could catch her breath, Mrs. Gordon grabbed her hand and said, "Oh, yes, Lily! Please say yes!"

Lily laughed. "I'd love to!"

And so began Lily and David's life together.

But now for the whole story. After they'd been married twenty-five years, he told us the truth about the letter. David was a cardiovascular specialist by then, and his dear Lily, the mother of their three children, was sitting by his side as he told us.

You see, David wasn't that avid a reader, as it turns out. He just wanted to see that pretty young librarian. He told his mother about the girl at his local library, but he was shy and didn't know how to approach her. His mother devised a scheme. Every time David went to the library, he was to drop an envelope addressed to himself on the floor. David's mother hoped Lily would retrieve it for him, call him over to the desk and give him a chance to strike up a conversation. So David dutifully dropped a letter each time he visited the library, but each time, someone would see the envelope fluttering to the floor and rush to reclaim it for him. "Oh, sir!" he'd hear someone cry out, but when he turned, it was never Lily.

On the day he finally met Lily, David waited till no one was left in the building but Lily and her assistant. Once again, he dropped his letter by the desk. The next day, he hoped, he could come back and ask Lily if she had found an envelope with his name on it. The plan worked far better than he imagined when Lily showed up in person to deliver the letter.

While David was telling this story, his beautiful wife Lily began laughing hysterically.

"David," she said, when she caught her breath. "You didn't seal that envelope very well. We opened it at the library. I saw that there was nothing but a blank piece of paper inside. I was dying to figure out what you were up to, so I played along. David, you were a terrible actor!" She turned her twinkling eyes to her husband's.

"But, oh, David! I loved you so!"

And that is how David and Lily really got together.

~Arnold Fine
Chicken Soup for the Single's Soul

29

A Novel Experience

*We must be willing to get rid of the life we've planned,
so as to have the life that is waiting for us.*
~Joseph Campbell

After I boarded the plane in Atlanta for the flight to Spokane, I eagerly opened a highly recommended novel. I anticipated seven relaxing hours of good reading. Just as the attendants were closing the doors for takeoff, a late passenger rushed on, breathlessly looking for her seat. Before I finished thinking, *I hope it's not the empty seat next to me,* the tiny bundle of energy plopped down right beside me and exclaimed, "Gracious, I thought I could never make this flight!" I closed my book and didn't open it again for the rest of the flight.

Her name was Thelma. She was from New York and was dressed stylishly. Her enthusiastic explanation of her life's work at a children's center in upstate New York captivated me. I could feel Thelma's dedication as she shared one story after another about the children. Her delightful sense of humor shone through as she described her all-out efforts to fill the role of surrogate grandmother to the many hurting children.

Thelma also told me of her daughter's recent tragic death from breast cancer and that she was flying to Spokane for a reunion with her son-in-law and his family. She was eager to meet and hold a new great-grandson and to see the lovely new home of her son-in-law on Lake Pend'Oreille, Idaho.

Thelma was obviously coming to terms with her daughter's death. She emphasized that her daughter had not wanted her to mourn but to continue her worthwhile work of helping children without parents. I silently prayed, "If I am ever faced with losing a child, let me handle it with her kind of courage, grace and dignity."

I confided in Thelma that my trip to Spokane was one of compassion. Our youngest daughter, Debbie, had just divorced after twenty-two years of marriage and needed a "Mom fix." Debbie and I had talked endlessly by telephone, and mother's intuition told me she needed loving arms to hold her, along with words of encouragement.

As the plane landed, Thelma and I were astounded that the flight had passed so quickly. We exchanged addresses, promising to write. At the gate we each walked into the arms of waiting loved ones and turned to wave goodbye to each other.

My daughter and I had a wonderful visit. We shopped for items Debbie needed in her new apartment. We talked long into the nights, discussing her plans for the future. Debbie had decided to continue her photography business but needed my reassurance. I agreed that she had made a sound decision. Debbie's two children were in college, and it seemed for the first time in many years my daughter had the complete freedom to think and plan for herself. She held fast to the hope for renewed happiness. Winging my way back to Atlanta, I was confident that Debbie would be just fine in her new life. I knew that a loving man who would appreciate her qualities was somewhere in her future.

Months later a ringing telephone hurried me into the kitchen, and a breathless voice said, "Hi, Mom! I have some exciting news for you. I've been dating a man who is great fun and loves to dance. His name is Don. And he's asked me to marry him. He's a widower with four grown children, a darling little grandson, and he has a beautiful new home on Lake Pend'Oreille, Idaho."

Flashing lights went off in my memory! I asked Debbie, "Would it be possible to call Don and ask him if he has a mother-in-law named Thelma, from New York?" I knew the answer before her return call.

Thelma's son-in-law Don and my daughter Debbie were married at the lovely home on Lake Pend'Oreille on March 7, 1993. Thelma carried on with her life after her daughter's death, and by her example she encouraged Don to go on living as well. The results? Debbie has a wonderful husband—every mother's dream for her daughter.

As for the bestselling novel I planned to read on that milestone flight from Atlanta to Spokane? Well, I eventually read it, and it was okay. But that opportune meeting with Thelma was just the beginning of a beautiful, unfolding story of life, love and family—much better than a book!

~Phyllis S. Heinel
Chicken Soup for the Golden Soul

30

A Friend, Indeed!

"Mom... it's over!" I wailed into the telephone. After being wined and dined for two years, I'd been dropped like a hot potato. My first heartbreak.

In the following days, tears gave way to a blank sadness and the bitter taste of betrayal. By Wednesday evening, I was lying on the living room floor curled in a ball, trying to ease an inner pain that would not cease. Then I heard a voice in the distance.

"Julia... come on... get up! Get dressed! We're going out."

I looked up with glazed eyes, dazedly recognizing my old friend Alex, whom (guiltily, I realized) I had not made much time for during the past couple of years.

"No," I muttered with self-pity. "I'm not going anywhere."

I felt myself elevated by strong, sturdy arms and gently placed on my feet. "Get dressed, Jules," he repeated. "I'll wait right here until you're ready."

Thus began the healing process. Through Alex, I reunited with friends I had somehow drifted away from through the years. He appeared at my doorstep each evening with a new agenda for the night, gently prying me from my misery as our mutual respect and quiet love for each other grew in friendship.

After a particularly difficult day, he took me to a lively café. Drowning my sorrows in a frothy latte, I blurted, "Alex, will I ever meet the right guy?"

His deep brown eyes danced with laughter. "Jules, one thing I can promise you—someday, I'll be dancing at your wedding."

I gazed at my trusty, dependable friend. Taking in his broad stance, olive complexion and endearingly familiar smile, I tried to picture Alex waltzing with his date at my wedding. But I couldn't. Something didn't seem quite right. I resolved that this could only mean one thing—I might be destined to never get married. With a sigh, I turned my attention back to the latte.

As the years passed, I decided to concentrate on my career as an artist rather than on my downfalls with men. Alex was there to share my disappointments and successes, no matter how large or small. He helped me recover from the likes of Brad, Lou and John—although failed relationships no longer shocked my system.

I occasionally shot him an earful of advice on the ladies and suffered only mild pangs of jealousy toward the women in his life. But it wasn't until Dan that I truly opened my eyes.

Dan. He was thrilling, exciting, handsome—and famous, too. What more could a girl want? Our dates consisted of exclusive shows and private parties, a fantasy come to life. So why did I find myself comparing him to Alex?

In fact, I realized most of the men I'd dated couldn't hold a candle to Alex's kindness. None had his sense of humor or rich, hearty laugh. None had his overwhelming compassion and genuine optimism. None had the qualities I had taken so for granted in Alex.

So, when Dan left me behind to go on tour, I didn't feel disposed of like the crumpled, used tissue I thought I'd be. I had Alex and that was what mattered.

One summer night, to celebrate our "thirteen years of friendship," Alex invited me to dinner at a quiet Italian restaurant in the city. Afterwards, we cruised around town with the car's top down. I laughed happily at the sheer joy of the evening, loving the freedom of wind tumbling my hair and the comfort of Alex beside me.

On a whim, he parked the car near the harbor.

"I know it's getting late," he said. "But it's too beautiful for the night to end."

"It is gorgeous out tonight," I agreed, taking his hand as I climbed from the car. We strolled along serenely, oblivious to the world, until Alex stopped suddenly.

"What is it?"

"Look," he pointed. "We're right beneath the CN Tower."

The massive grand structure—landmarking Toronto's skyline—was directly in front of us. I had lived with the majestic view of this building all my life, but I had never seen its towering frame silhouetted against a blazing moon. Judging by the look on Alex's glowing face, he hadn't either.

Then, all at once, I realized it wasn't the tower but me he was looking at.

"Alex," I began shyly, not knowing how to respond to this new feeling. "Do you find it... odd... that I didn't notice the tallest freestanding structure in the world? Especially since we're standing right beneath it?"

"No, actually... not odd at all," he drew me closer. "Because when I'm with you, the world seems to disappear."

The moment his lips touched mine, breathless yearning and passion laced the deepest love I could ever imagine and poured from his heart to mine. It only took one kiss to change my life. One kiss to see what had been right before my eyes, right beside me all along.

"Julia," he whispered. "I am so in love with you!"

"I love you, too, Alex. So much. And I think maybe I always have."

"Well," he smiled. "I need to clarify one thing, though."

"What's that?"

"Remember the promise I made a few years ago... to dance at your wedding?"

"Uh-huh."

"I lied." He broke into a big grin. "I should have told you I plan to dance at our wedding."

~Sylvia Suriano
Chicken Soup for the Bride's Soul

31

How I Stopped Looking for Mr. Right

It's so easy to fall in love but hard to find someone who will catch you.
~Author Unknown

I'll never forget that Christmas season of 1986. It was the year I went into a full-fledged panic. It happened after hearing a panel of experts on the subject of single women declare on a TV talk show: "Any woman not married by the age of forty has a better chance of being shot by a terrorist than she has of finding her 'Mr. Right.'"

I was forty-four years old and hadn't married. Obviously, the experts were talking about me. Their words hit me like a lightning bolt, jolting me into the reality of my bleak future. A silent scream choked in my throat.

My imagination soared. Who and what was waiting for me in my future... spinsterhood... the man of my dreams... or a terrorist? That night, I found it impossible to sleep. Visions of terrorists and lonely spinsterhood invaded my thoughts. The next morning, I reluctantly but bravely walked to work, looking over my shoulder every step of the way.

At the office, my coworker Mable noticed my depressed state of mind and quickly attributed it to my advanced age. She suggested that I was probably going through "the change," and advised me to drink a glass of vinegar and water spiked with a clove of garlic to set me right.

Change? I bristled to myself. What sort of change was Mable talking about? Was I suddenly going to sprout fangs and furry knuckles and commence baying at the full moon? Nothing less would induce me to indulge in a diet of garlic and vinegar.

Mable went on to compare my plight with that of her aged Aunt Agatha who, at my age, had begun taking daily doses of the concoction. The potent mixture had sustained the old woman well into her nineties.

Mable's story made me feel worse. The following day, I launched a frantic campaign to find my Mr. Right. I begged for advice from all the married women I knew. Mable was quick to tell me I was too old to be particular. She said I should hang around singles bars, where she found her Benji.

My friend Jane told me her aunt had actually found her husband several years ago by reading books on "how to find a man." There was a long list of these books available, some that guaranteed the reader a husband in one month's time: where to go, how to look, walk and talk—all the important nuances for finding a husband. I was so desperate to find a Mr. Right before Christmas, I scoured the bookstores and immediately went on a reading binge.

I feverishly read each paragraph and page. One book suggested I hang around the frozen-food sections of my local supermarkets. The book assured me that single men were sure to be there buying their dinners. But after two weeks of buying frozen dinners, all I had to show for it was a freezer full of frozen foods, and the only people I had met were young housewives and old married couples. I also spent long, frantic hours loitering in sporting-goods shops where, the books promised, I'd find a treasure trove of rich, handsome bachelors buying sporting equipment. But the only shoppers I found turned out to be young athletic women, soccer moms and little boys in the peewee league. After weeks of lingering and loitering at these shops, the only thing I got was some strange looks from the store security.

In desperation, I followed the books' advice and took night

classes in carpentry and automotive repair; these classes were supposed to be full of men. The books were several years old and so were their statistics. The classes were filled with women. Even the teacher was a woman.

I tried beauty treatments and a whole new wardrobe, but still no luck. After months of following every instruction to the letter, the only bachelors I met were boys barely old enough to shave and men my grandpa's age.

Finally, I surrendered to defeat. I couldn't fight the Fates any longer. If I was going to end up an old maid, or worse, then so be it. I conceded that the experts were right and with a sense of freedom and relief, I chucked every one of books in the office Dumpster.

That night was Christmas Eve. Every year after work, the staff gave an office party for the workers. I decided to stay after work and have a cup of eggnog with the girls. The lights of the office were dimmed for atmosphere; the glow of flickering candles cast dark shadows in every corner of the room. About twenty minutes into the party, I was bored and decided to leave.

As I started down the long, darkened office corridor to the exit elevators, I was aware of someone in the shadows—a tall silhouette of a man in a dim corner of the hallway. The sinewy figure sprang toward me from the darkness. A glimmer of light reflected off a black shiny object he held at his side.

Was it the barrel of a gun? Was this the deadly terrorist the experts had warned me about? Was I about to meet my fate? I wasn't going to wait around to find out. In sheer panic, I bolted for the exits, running as fast as my shaky legs could carry me. Down the dark corridor I ran. The tall figure followed me in quick pursuit, catching up with me at the elevator.

"Hey, wait up," his voice shot through the darkness.

I spun around, my back pinned against the elevator door. With nowhere else to go, I faced him straight on: "Take one more step closer, and I'll scream!" I heard my voice cry out.

A complete look of bewilderment crossed over my handsome

pursuer's face. "What did you say?" He asked quizzically, while holding in his right hand a large black umbrella.

Just then the elevator doors pulled open, putting some light on the subject. I soon realized that my overactive imagination had gotten the best of me. This very attractive man was no more a terrorist than I was. Trying to cover up my stupidity, I quickly introduced myself. "Hello, my name is Rosalie. What's yours?" I asked, trying to change the subject.

"I'm Dan," he answered. "I've been trying to meet you all month, but you always have your head buried in a book!"

That was me, all right, so preoccupied with my frantic search for Mr. Right, I'd overlooked what was right in front of me all along.

I wasted no time that night digging up some information on this handsome hunk. I couldn't believe my ears when the girls in the office told me his name was actually Dan Wright—Mr. Wright! All the time I'd had my head buried in those books, he was working just across the hall from me. And he was single. I would have learned all these facts if I hadn't stopped taking coffee breaks with the office girls to read those darn books.

It never dawned on me, all the while I was looking so hard for Mr. Right, that Mr. Wright was trying equally hard to find me.

We were married the following year and marked the occasion with a grand wedding celebration. Finding Mr. Wright, and marrying for the very first time at age forty-five, was a small miracle in itself. But more than that, it proved that even experts on finding true love can be wrong. And we should hang on to our hopes and dreams no matter the odds against them. And a little advice, just from me to you: If you're looking for something, or someone, don't look so hard for it that you don't see what's been right there in front of you all along.

~Rosalie Wright
Chicken Soup to Inspire a Woman's Soul

32

A Happy-Ever-After

"Is this Jenna?" the voice on the phone asked.

Jenna clutched the receiver with a trembling hand. That voice was exactly as she had dreamed it would sound. Just exactly like his father's.

Jenna had known for thirty years that this day would come. Adopted children seem to want to know all about their natural families. Feelings of dread, but a sort of elation, filled Jenna while she carried on a conversation with the young man on the phone.

In 1967, Jenna was in love with David. But David's family was from the poorer section of town. Jenna's father was controlling and abusive, and he would not allow her to date David. With the help of friends, they sneaked around to see each other.

When Jenna discovered that she was pregnant, her father became enraged. He forced the teen to go away to live with an aunt until the baby was born. Heartbroken, David joined the army and went to fight in Vietnam. He wrote some letters to Jenna, but her father threw them away. David even tried writing letters to one of Jenna's friends, hoping to get some word to the girl he dearly loved. Jenna never received any of the letters, and she didn't know how to contact David.

Jenna came home after the baby was born. She dreamed constantly of the tiny infant she had held for only a second. She wondered what his adoptive parents were like, where they lived, and what the baby was growing to look like. She also dreamed of the day she would be old enough to leave home and get away from her controlling father. After graduation, Jenna went to college, then got a good job in a large city. She never returned to her hometown, still angry that her father had not allowed her to keep her child and marry David.

Memories of a lost love and a son she had to give away caused Jenna to never marry. She kept busy with her job as a school teacher. Organizations for battered women and unwed mothers became her passion. Jenna worked very hard to help others all her adult life.

But in the back of her mind, she always knew that this day would come. Her son would find her and want to know why she hadn't loved him enough to keep him.

"Can we meet sometime soon?" the young man asked. His name was Bradley. Jenna agreed to allow him to fly to her city and meet her. He was thirty years old and married. He had two children.

After she hung up, Jenna wished she had asked if Bradley had been able to find David. She let the thought die and began to prepare for the visit from her son in two weeks.

The days dragged. Jenna's emotions flew. She went from excitement at seeing her son at last, to dread that he wouldn't like her or wouldn't understand.

Finally, the day arrived. Jenna drove to the airport two hours early because she was too nervous to stay home alone. She paced and bit her nails.

Bradley's flight was announced. Jenna got as close to the gate as she was allowed, craning her neck to watch for the family she was about to claim. A lifetime of nightmares and regrets filled her mind.

Suddenly, there he was, right in front of her. A hug so tight that he picked her up was the first touch from her son in thirty years. They hugged and cried for several minutes. Then a little boy tugged at Bradley's shirt.

"Daddy, I'm thirsty." Jenna hugged her grandson, then his older sister. She hugged her daughter-in-law, and then hugged Bradley some more. The little boy began to shout and run toward another man. "Grandpa!" he yelled.

Jenna stopped and stared. It can't be. But how? Is it really him?

Bradley dropped a soft kiss on Jenna's cheek. "Yes, it's really him. I found him last week, and he has been to the house to visit us. He was very excited to know that I was meeting you today. He's never married, either, you know."

David picked up the little boy, then his eyes met Jenna's. He gently put the boy down. In an instant, he reached Jenna. She was in his arms a long time before they pulled apart to look at each other.

The weekend ended much too soon. Bradley and his wife made Jenna promise to come visit in a few weeks. When they went to the airport, David helped Bradley's family get situated.

"Where are you flying out from?" Jenna asked.

"I'm not," he answered. "I've extended my vacation. We have a lot of years to make up for."

Bradley was able to witness his parents' marriage at Christmastime that year.

Yes, there really are some happily-ever-afters.

~Mary J. Davis
A Second Chicken Soup for the Woman's Soul

Storybook Proposal

True love stories never have endings.
~Richard Bach

Emily and I met in our first semester of college and dated for almost six years. Regardless of how crafty and intuitive my ideas, I was never able to surprise her with anything. Emily was investigative and I was naive—not a good combination for a surprise. Leave it to me to accidentally leave behind a receipt or just happen to be checking voicemail on a speakerphone when the restaurant or florist would call to confirm.

Time after time, I tried to surprise her. Time after time, I failed.

When I began to think about a long-overdue proposal, I wanted nothing more than to surprise her. So I embarked upon a personal journey to find a unique and special way to pop the question.

After much thought—and some interesting suggestions from friends and coworkers—I decided to incorporate two of Emily's loves: reading (her graduate-school pursuit) and pigs (her favorite animal since childhood) into a storybook proposal. My dream was to create and publish a children's book in which two little pigs, Emmy and Matty, would parallel the story of Emily and me.

I was working in public relations for a school district. I asked an art teacher if she knew any students skilled in cartoon illustration. Without hesitation she put me in touch with Jeremy, a tenth grader who excitedly showed me his portfolio. I hired him on the spot. Page by page, I sent the manuscript to Jeremy for custom drawings. And I began to write.

I wrote about two little pigs who meet in a college computer lab, just like Emily and me. My story detailed Emmy and Matty's journey through the years. On page eight, the two little pigs find themselves in front of a sunset.

"One fall evening, Matty had an important question for Emmy," the page read. The proposal page followed.

Upon completion of the illustrations, text and layout of the story, my creation was ready to be printed. It came back in the form of a real book, hardbound. I had done it. I successfully produced the entire book in complete secrecy. After all these years, I would surprise Emily.

On a random Thursday, I told Emily I had found a couple of cute children's books on sale for her collection. Naturally she wanted to take a look, so the first one I gave her was *The Story of the Two Little Pigs*.

As she read the first couple of pages, she started to catch on that I had written a book for her, but had no I idea it would change both of our lives forever.

As she approached the proposal page, I asked her to stand up. I bent down on one knee as I watched her eyes follow the words on the paper that simply said, "Emily Suzanne ...Will You Marry Me?" She was speechless as she looked up and saw me with a ring in my hand.

Stunned, she closed the book and gave me a big hug. "Yes, yes and yes! Of course. I love you!"

We hugged for a couple of minutes and I wiped the tears from her eyes. I urged her to turn to the last page of her storybook proposal—an illustration of pigs dressed in wedding gown and tuxedo.

It read, in appropriate storybook fashion: "Emmy and Matty lived happily ever after."

~Matthew Cummings
Chicken Soup for the Bride's Soul

Two Coins in a Fountain

Even as a kid, my cousin Andrea always had big dreams! When we talked about being teachers or secretaries, Andrea talked of being a movie star. When we dreamed of going to the Mediterranean on holiday, Andrea dreamed of the Caribbean! (A long way from Scotland!)

As we grew up, she was not the prettiest of us, yet she had the most boyfriends. She was a little overweight and not that tall. But Andrea sparkled, both physically and mentally, and young men seemed to find that attractive.

Once on a double date, I marveled at her because she never had one moment of self-doubt or of feeling self-conscious. Because of this, she had the ability to say exactly what she was feeling; she made it seem like you were sharing something very personal with her.

It wasn't a surprise when she came in and announced, "Well, I am off to Rome to work as a nanny!" We all knew that Andrea had long ago decided she was in love with Rome and always said that is where she wanted to live.

She openly told us, "I am convinced I will meet this gorgeous Italian prince and we will fall madly in love!"

We laughed at that, but were all sad to see her go. She kind of spread light around her and it was all much duller when she left.

Andrea arrived in Rome and settled in with the family for whom she was to be the nanny. They gave her a little apartment, and she already spoke Italian having always known she would need to use it!

Andrea took her young charge out a fair bit, to the Coliseum, the Spanish Steps, but mostly they went to the Trevi Fountain. "To anyone who has never seen it," she wrote to us, "you think of a little fountain in a square. It is huge, like a giant monument with water; it is breathtaking and beautiful."

She told us that you throw one coin in the fountain to return to Rome, two coins to find true love. "I have spent a fortune. I throw two coins in every time I pass, but it is an investment. I know it will work!" We laughed at that letter; same old Andrea, still the same big dreams!

One beautiful, sunny Roman morning, Andrea took Pier Luigi out early, and they came to the Trevi Fountain. Andrea could not pass it by without throwing in her two coins, so they went down the steps and she threw in her coins.

She glanced up and two very handsome young men were watching her. The taller of the two asked her, "You weesh to return very much, eef you throw in two coins no?"

Andrea looked at this gorgeous young man, his hair a light gold brown, but his face somehow very Italian. "One is to return to Rome, two is for love!"

They both smiled and walked over to her, and the one who had spoken introduced himself. Marcello continued to study her smiling as he asked, "So you want to find true love, here on your vacation?"

"I live in Rome. I love Rome and I have always dreamed of falling in love with someone here. I am sure it will happen," she beamed at him. He kept smiling at her and asked where she came from, and the four of them ended up having coffee together in a little café.

Whatever she said at that first meeting, he seemed to be really taken with her and asked if she would go out with him.

Andrea met Marcello the next evening and asked him what he did for a living. It turned out that he played for Roma FC, the football team. Not only did he play for them, he was one of their star players. Andrea's Marcello was a very famous and much admired young man throughout Italy because he played for the national side as well.

When she wrote and told us about him and sent photographs,

we agreed with how gorgeous he was. My younger sister Bertha said that she had read about him and that he was usually with some tall, long-legged blond model or something. It would have made the rest of us wonder what he could see in someone ordinary like us. Andrea never gave that a second thought; she was already nuts about him and fully expected him to be nuts about her!

The thing was, amazingly, he was nuts about her. She wrote and told us that she saw him nearly every day, she had met his family. Then that he wanted her to give up her work and live with him in his beautiful villa high up in the hills that surround Rome. Finally we flew over to visit her, and lying at the side of his huge swimming pool, surrounded by hills and the distant tops of the buildings of Rome, she beamed at us. I asked her, "So is Marcello the Italian prince you always dreamed of?"

"Oh yes, Joyce, and more, he has asked me to marry him!"

When we met him, it took us all of five minutes to realize he was not just in love with Andrea, but he adored her. He smiled every time his eyes rested on her. "There is no one like her," he told us. "She is so full of effervescence; she is like a bottle of champagne and I could not go back to drinking wine. She drifts off on flights of fancy, and I am running behind trying to find wings to fly with her. I love her very much."

They have been married for fifteen years and have three kids. She has seen a fair bit of the world, as she somehow always knew she would. Mainly though, she lives in her beautiful house with her gorgeous Italian.

I said to her one day about all her dreams coming true and she laughed. "You have to be determined to achieve your dreams, like throwing two coins in the fountain every time you pass, to make sure they come true!"

~Joyce Stark
Chicken Soup for the Romantic Soul

35

Coming Full Circle

Forgiveness does not change the past, but it does enlarge the future.
~Paul Boese

*I*met Sara during preschool. I was three years old and she was four. We were kindred spirits, alike in so many ways—inseparable sisters who became family through our own self-created love.

But one thing that differentiated the two of us was the fact that my parents were still married, while her parents were divorced.

Jim and Teresa's divorce had shocked everyone who knew them. They were high school sweethearts who married right after graduation. Then two years later, shortly after Teresa gave birth to Sara, Jim divorced her and moved to another state.

"Why did your father leave?" I'd asked Sara.

"I don't know." She shrugged her shoulders and flipped her ponytail like she didn't care. But deep down I knew she did.

Although Sara did not see her father often, he called regularly, encouraged and rewarded her good grades, kept abreast of her activities, and provided the family with more than enough money. So in spite of the separation, she always felt he cared about her.

Teresa never discussed why she and Jim divorced. Family and friends reminisced about their once-passionate relationship. But Teresa's bitterness was apparent.

During her freshman year of high school, Sara met Brad, a sweet, smart and handsome young man who eventually won over all of us.

All except her mother—who objected when Brad proposed four years later.

Teresa repeatedly explained how painful marriage could be, especially at such a young age. She did not want to see her daughter go through the same hurt she'd experienced. Sara insisted she loved Brad, and their situation wasn't the same as her mother's. Defeated, Teresa accepted Sara's decision to marry.

The day of Sara and Brad's engagement party, the couple's families and friends enjoyed meeting one another and celebrating the upcoming nuptials. Brad tried hard to entertain and talk to Sara's mother in spite of her persistent coldness.

Toward the end of the evening, Sara's dad startled everyone when he walked through the door. I watched Sara run across the room and throw herself into his arms. Surprisingly, even Teresa looked pleased.

After meeting Brad and congratulating the couple, Jim spotted his ex-wife and immediately went to her table. He kissed her cheek, gave her a lingering hug and sat beside her. The two talked away the evening.

The day of Sara and Brad's wedding was magical. As maid of honor, it was my responsibility to tend to my best friend. As I straightened her veil, there was a slight knock at the dressing room door.

Teresa walked in and quietly gave Sara her blessing, apologizing for being so doubtful in the beginning. Then she admitted to Sara that she'd been in regular contact with Jim since the engagement party. They had done lots of talking and, for the first time, Jim explained why he'd left, apologized for his immaturity, his panic as a young parent and his wrongdoings. More importantly, he begged for forgiveness.

Teresa explained how this conversation helped her deal with the resentment she'd felt and the lonely void caused by his absence. After all these years, she discovered she still loved him. Thrilled with the reconciliation, mother and daughter embraced.

Sara's father escorted her to the altar where she joined hands with Brad. Then Jim sat next to Teresa; they joined hands, too.

During the reception, everyone danced, ate and toasted the evening away. And Sara's parents did not leave each other's side. When a slow song began to play, Jim asked Teresa to dance. Suddenly he got down on one knee and took his ex-wife's hand in his. A clamorous crowd circled the pair.

"I love you," Sara's father began, "and I need for everyone to know how sorry I am for what I did to you and our daughter."

Sara's mother couldn't utter a word, because her other hand was covering her mouth in shock.

"And I want you to be my wife. Again. Will you marry me, Teresa?"

She pulled Jim into her arms.

In Sara's eyes, that moment made her wedding day perfect. Not only did she marry the man she loved but, after eighteen years of hope, tears and prayers, her mother and father reunited. Like the wedding band her husband slipped on her finger, Sara felt like her life had come full circle.

~Denise N. Wheatley
Chicken Soup for the Bride's Soul

36

Ben and Virginia

The greatest discovery of my generation is that a human being can
alter his life by altering his attitude.
~William James

In 1904, a railroad camp of civil engineers was set up near Knoxville, Tennessee. The L&N campsite had tents for the men, a warm campfire, a good cook and the most modern surveying equipment available. In fact, working as a young civil engineer for the railroad at the turn of the century presented only one real drawback: a severe shortage of eligible young women.

Benjamin Murrell was one such engineer. A tall, reticent man with a quiet sense of humor and a great sensitivity for people, Ben enjoyed the nomadic railroad life. His mother had died when he was only thirteen, and this early loss caused him to become a loner.

Like all the other men, Ben sometimes longed for the companionship of a young woman, but he kept his thoughts between himself and God. On one particularly memorable spring day, a marvelous piece of information was passed around the camp: The boss's sister-in-law was coming to visit! The men knew only three things about her: She was nineteen years old, she was single and she was pretty. By mid-afternoon the men could talk of little else. Her parents were sending her to escape the yellow fever that was invading the Deep South and she'd be there in only three days. Someone found a tintype of her, and the photograph was passed around with great seriousness and grunts of approval.

Ben watched the preoccupation of his friends with a smirk. He teased them for their silliness over a girl they'd never even met. "Just look at her, Ben. Take one look and then tell us you're not interested," one of the men retorted. But Ben only shook his head and walked away chuckling.

The next two days found it difficult for the men of the L&N engineering camp to concentrate. The train would be there early Saturday morning and they discussed their plan in great detail. Freshly bathed, twenty heads of hair carefully greased and slicked back, they would all be there to meet that train and give the young woman a railroad welcome she wouldn't soon forget. She'd scan the crowd, choose the most handsome of the lot and have an instant beau. Let the best man win, they decided. And each was determined to be that man.

On Friday evening, as the other men tried to shake the wrinkles out of their Sunday best and draw a bath, Ben sat down on a log next to the campfire. Something glinted orange in the firelight. Idly, he reached down and picked it up. His friends had been so busy and full of themselves, they'd left the girl's picture lying on the ground.

The men were too preoccupied to see Ben's face as he beheld the picture of Virginia Grace for the first time. They didn't notice the way he cradled the photograph in his big hands like a lost treasure, or that he gazed at it for a long, long time. They missed the expression on his face as he looked first at the features of the delicate beauty, then at the camp full of men he suddenly perceived to be his rivals. And they didn't see Ben go into his tent, pick up a backpack and leave camp as the sun glowed red and sank beyond a distant mountain.

Early the next morning, the men of the L&N railroad camp gathered at the train station. Virginia's family, who had come to pick her up, rolled their eyes and tried unsuccessfully not to laugh. Faces were raw from unaccustomed shaves, and the combination of men's cheap colognes was almost noxious. Several of the men had even stopped to pick bouquets of wildflowers along the way.

At long last the whistle was heard and the eagerly awaited train pulled into the station. When the petite, vivacious little darling of the L&N camp stepped onto the platform, a collective sigh escaped her would-be suitors. She was even prettier than the tintype depicted. Then every man's heart sank in collective despair. For there, holding her arm in a proprietary manner and grinning from ear to ear, was Benjamin Murrell. And from the way she tilted her little head to smile up into his face, they knew their efforts were in vain.

"How," his friends demanded of Ben later, "did you do that?"

"Well," he said, "I knew I didn't have a chance with all you scoundrels around. I'd have to get to her first if I wanted her attention, so I walked down to the previous station and met the train. I introduced myself as a member of the welcoming committee from her new home."

"But the nearest station is seventeen miles away!" someone blurted incredulously. "You walked seventeen miles to meet her train? That would take all night!"

"That it did," he affirmed.

Benjamin Murrell courted Virginia Grace, and in due time they married. They raised five children and buried one, a twelve-year-old son. I don't think they tried to build the eternal romance that some women's magazines claim is so important. Nor did they have a standing Friday night date. In fact, Ben was so far out in the sticks while working on one engineering job that one of their children was a full month old before he saw his new daughter. Ben didn't take Virginia to expensive restaurants, and the most romantic gift he ever brought her was an occasional jar of olives. If Virginia ever bought a fetching nightgown and chased him around the icebox, that secret remains buried with her to this day.

What I do know is that they worked on their relationship by being faithful to one another, treating each other with consideration and respect, having a sense of humor, bringing up their children in the knowledge and love of the Lord, and loving one another through some very difficult circumstances.

I am one of Benjamin and Virginia's great-grandchildren. He died when I was a baby, unfortunately, so I have no memory of him. NaNa (Virginia) died when I was twelve and she was eighty-five. When I knew her, she was a shriveled old woman who needed assistance to get around with a walker and whose back was hunched over from osteoporosis. Her aching joints were swollen with arthritis and her eyesight was hindered by the onset of glaucoma. At times, though, those clouded eyes would sparkle and dance with the vivaciousness of the girl my great-grandfather knew. They danced especially when she told her favorite story. It was the story of how she was so pretty that once, on the basis of a tintype, an entire camp turned out to meet the train and vie for her attention. It was the story of how one man walked seventeen miles, all night long, for a chance to meet the woman of his dreams and claim her for his wife.

~Gwyn Williams
A 5th Portion of Chicken Soup for the Soul

37

Mom's Last Laugh

Next to a good soul-stirring prayer, is a good laugh.
~Samuel Mutchmore

onsumed by my loss, I didn't notice the hardness of the pew where I sat. I was at the funeral of my dearest friend — my mother. She finally had lost her long battle with cancer. The hurt was so intense; I found it hard to breathe at times.

Always supportive, Mother clapped loudest at my school plays, held a box of tissues while listening to my first heartbreak, comforted me when my father died, encouraged me in college, and prayed for me my entire life.

When Mother's illness was diagnosed, my sister had a new baby and my brother had recently married his childhood sweetheart, so it fell to me, the twenty-seven-year-old middle child without entanglements, to take care of her. I counted it as an honor.

"What now, Lord?" I asked, sitting in the church. My life stretched out before me as an empty abyss.

My brother sat stoically with his face toward the cross while clutching his wife's hand. My sister sat slumped against her husband's shoulder, his arms around her as she cradled their child. All so deeply grieving, they didn't seem to notice that I sat alone.

My place had been with our mother, preparing her meals, helping her walk, taking her to the doctor, seeing to her medication, reading the Bible together. Now she was with the Lord. My work was finished, and I was alone.

I heard a door open and slam shut at the back of the church. Quick footsteps hurried along the carpeted floor. An exasperated young man looked around briefly and then sat next to me. He folded his hands and placed them on his lap. His eyes were brimming with tears. He began to sniffle.

"I'm sorry I'm late," he explained, though no explanation was necessary.

After several eulogies, he leaned over and commented, "Why do they keep calling Mary by the name of 'Margaret'?"

"Because Margaret was her name. Never Mary. No one called her 'Mary,'" I whispered. I wondered why this person couldn't have sat on the other side of the church. He kept interrupting my grieving with his tears and fidgeting. Who was this stranger anyway?

"No, that isn't correct," he insisted, as several people glanced over at us whispering. "Her name is Mary, Mary Peters."

"That isn't whose funeral this is."

"Isn't this the Lutheran church?"

"No, the Lutheran church is across the street."

"Oh."

"I believe you're at the wrong funeral, sir."

The solemn nature of the occasion mixed with the realization of the man's mistake bubbled up inside me and erupted as laughter. I cupped my hands over my face, hoping the noise would be interpreted as sobs.

The creaking pew gave me away. Sharp looks from other mourners only made the situation seem more hilarious. I peeked at the bewildered, misguided man seated beside me. He was laughing, too, as he glanced around; deciding it was too late for an uneventful exit. I imagined Mother laughing.

At the final "Amen," we darted out a door and into the parking lot.

"I do believe we'll be the talk of the town," he smiled. He said his name was Rick and since he had missed his aunt's funeral, he asked me to join him for a cup of coffee.

That afternoon began a lifelong journey for me with this man, who attended the wrong funeral, but was in the right place. A year after our meeting, we were married at a country church where he was the assistant pastor. This time we both arrived at the same church, right on time.

In my time of sorrow, God gave me laughter. In place of loneliness, God gave me love. This past June we celebrated our twenty-second wedding anniversary.

Whenever anyone asks us how we met, Rick tells them, "Her mother and my Aunt Mary introduced us, and it's truly a match made in heaven."

~Robin Lee Shope
Chicken Soup for the Christian Family Soul

Happily Ever After

Making It Work

For two people in a marriage to live together day after day is unquestionably the one miracle the Vatican has overlooked.
~Bill Cosby

38

Discretion Is the Better Part of Marriage

Soul-mates are people who bring out the best in you. They are not perfect but are always perfect for you.

~Author Unknown

Seventeen years ago on a cold and blustery Saturday, I stood in the arch of a sanctuary with baby's breath in my hair and a foolish grin on my face, too big of a ninny to realize that I ought to be scared to death.

As a swell of Mozart filled air that was thick with my great aunt's Chantilly, my nervous, tuxedo-clad father bent down to whisper what I thought would be words of paternal wisdom. "It's not too late," he hissed, waving a wad of bills. "If you want to weasel out of this, I'll give you five hundred bucks and a Greyhound ticket any place you want to go."

I didn't tell my soon-to-be husband, Jeff, this story for several years. It wasn't that Dad didn't like "that tall kid"—he did—but the combination of watching my sister's impulsive first marriage unravel and knowing that Jeff and I had met less than five months before was making him a little gun shy.

That problem was soon remedied. As some wit said, marriage remains the most efficient way to get acquainted. We met over Labor Day, got engaged at Thanksgiving and married in the windiest January on record. Between immediately moving out east where neither of us knew a soul and then having a child before our second anniversary, we got to know each other (as my southern Missouri relatives would say) right soon.

Though seventeen years hardly qualify us for one of those fatuous anniversary greetings from Willard Scott, we've been married long enough to know a thing or two. Before the honeymoon was over, we were certain that the bozo who wrote "Love means never having to say you're sorry" had obviously never been married. While having the last word might be intellectually satisfying, it's mighty chilly on your own side of the bed. We've also been married long enough to know how much fun it is to have private jokes that drive our children crazy. It would take us a very long time to explain to them why the terms "garlic milk shakes" and "bluebird watching society" set us off, and besides, you had to be there.

We were relieved to discover that we don't have to enjoy the same things to enjoy each other. We both like long road trips on blue highways, old houses and junk shops. After that, we part company. I like Victor Borge; he likes Jimi Hendrix. I love exotic travel; he has never had a passport. He loves musicals where the ruddy villagers burst inexplicably into song; I like Ingmar Bergman dramas in which pale, suicidal sisters communicate in cryptic whispers. He likes to dance; I have two left feet.

Over the years, we've discovered that discretion is the better part of matrimony. He has not once pointed out that I am routinely responsible for 75 percent of the long distance calls on the phone bill. When I see the telltale yellow of a parking ticket on his chest of drawers, I permit myself no more than a raised eyebrow. He doesn't comment when I stay up until 2 A.M. reading a mystery even though I've been whining about how much I have to do the next day; I pretend I don't know he blows half an hour and a few bucks at the video arcade each time he takes the boys to the mall. I nod in agreement when, with ambition born of a Saturday morning, he says he's going to patch, sand and paint the bedroom after going into the office in the morning and before running errands in the afternoon (even though

I know he'll be "resting his eyes" in his favorite chair before the first dribble of paint hits the dropcloth).

And perhaps most astonishingly, of all the innumerable times over the last seventeen years I have put something on and asked if it makes me look fat, he has always feigned astonished denial. Not once has he said, "What do you mean? You are fat."

We have learned that, "How can I help?" works better than "I told you so," and that "I love you" works better than "What's your problem?"

Still, if I had it to do over, I'd take the bus ticket and the money my dad offered instead of the dyed-to-match shoes, the sterling flatware and the obligatory feeding-each-other-cake shot in the deluxe portrait package. But wherever I went, I'd take Jeff with me.

~Rebecca Christian
A 6th Bowl of Chicken Soup for the Soul

39

The Parable of the Coffee Filter

See everything; overlook a great deal; correct a little.
~Pope John XXIII

My brother Dan said, "I'm going home! Your bickering is making me crazy. You two fight constantly—and it wears me out."

I defended our behavior, "Hey, it's not like we disagree about everything. Ron and I agree on all the major issues. We hardly ever fight about 'big stuff' like where to go to church, how to raise Nick or who's a better driver (me); we just disagree about the 'little stuff.'"

He sighed and said, "Well, I'm sick of hearing you go to war over where to put the towel rack, which TV shows to watch or who did—or didn't—use a coaster. It's all dumb stuff. None of it will matter a year from now. I can tell that Ron is really mad by the way he stomped up the stairs. Why did you have to criticize the way he mowed the lawn? I know it wasn't perfect, but couldn't you just let it go?"

"No," I replied. "We are having company tomorrow, and I want the yard to be perfect. So I told him to fix it, big deal! Anyway, I won, because he removed it."

Dan shook his head, "If you keep this up, you may win the arguments, but lose your husband."

I slugged his arm. "Oh, stop being so melodramatic!"

The next evening, Ron and I went out to dinner with some friends we hadn't seen in several years. We remembered Carl as being funny and outgoing, but he seemed rather quiet and looked exhausted. His wife, Beth, did most of the talking. She told us about her fabulous accomplishments and then endlessly bragged about her brilliant, Mensa-bound children. She only mentioned Carl to criticize him.

After we ordered our dinner, she said, "Carl, I saw you flirting with that waitress!" (He wasn't.)

"Caarrrrlll," she whined, "can't you do anything right? You are holding your fork like a little kid!" (He was.)

When he mispronounced an item on the dessert menu, she said, "No wonder you flunked out of college, you can't read!" She laughed so hard that she snorted, but she was the only one laughing.

Carl didn't even respond. He just looked over at us with an empty face and a blank stare. Then he shrugged his sad shoulders. The rest of the evening was oppressive as she continued to harangue and harass him about almost everything he said or did. I thought, I wonder if this is how my brother feels when I criticize Ron.

We said goodbye to Beth and Carl and left the restaurant in silence. When we got in the car, I spoke first. "Do I sound like her?"

"You're not that bad."

"How bad am I?"

"Pretty bad," he half-whispered.

The next morning, as I poured water into the coffee pot, I looked over at my "Devotions for Wives" calendar.

"The wise woman builds her house, but the foolish tears it down with her own hands." Or with her own mouth, I thought.

"A nagging wife annoys like a constant dripping." How can I stop this horrible pattern?

"Put a guard over my mouth that I may not sin with it." Oh Lord, show me how!

I carefully spooned the vanilla nut decaf into the pot as I remembered the day I forgot the filter. The coffee was bitter and full of undrinkable grounds. I had to throw it away.

I thought, the coffee, without filtering, is like my coarse and bitter speech.

I prayed, "Oh, please Lord, install a filter between my brain and my mouth. Help me to choose my words carefully and speak with smooth and mellow tones. Thank you for teaching me the 'Parable of the Coffee Filter.' I won't forget it."

An hour later, Ron timidly asked, "What do you think about moving the couch over by the window? We'll be able to see the TV better."

My first thought was to tell him why that was a dumb idea. The couch will fade if you put it in the sunlight, and besides, you already watch too much TV. But instead of my usual hasty reply, I let the coarse thoughts drip through my newly installed filter and calmly said, "That might be a good idea. Let's try it for a few days and see if we like it. I'll help you move it."

He lifted his end of the sofa in stunned silence. Once we had it in place, he asked with concern, "Are you okay? Do you have a headache?"

I chuckled, "I'm great honey, never better. Can I get you a cup of coffee?"

Ron and I recently celebrated our twenty-fifth wedding anniversary, and I am happy to report that my "filter" is still in place (though it occasionally springs a leak). I've also expanded the filter principle beyond my marriage and found that it's especially useful when speaking to telemarketers, traffic cops and teenagers.

~Nancy C. Anderson
Chicken Soup for the Christian Soul 2

40

A Mistake I Will Not Repeat

To get to a woman's heart, a man must first use his own.
~Mike Dobbertin, age thirteen

Ah! Valentine's Day... a day for lovers, romance and flowers. A day for hearts, candy and jewelry, but apparently not a day for appliances.

I give up. I will never be able to figure out the unspoken language between men and women. And to think I got married two months ago secure in the knowledge that I had finally figured out how to play the game. I was wrong.

You see, I proudly presented to my new wife, on our very first Valentine's Day as young newlyweds, a food processor for her St. Valentine's Day gift. She gazed upon this appliance—one she had mentioned week after week that she desperately needed—and said, "Oh. A food processor."

I have always heard that when someone says what the gift is upon receiving it, it's not a good gift (i.e., "Oh. A Chia pet"). Did I mention that my wife has repeatedly said how much she wanted a food processor?

See, I am of the school of thought that says when I ask, "What's wrong?" and my wife answers, "Nothing," I assume nothing is wrong. And when my wife tells me she wants something, I want to get it for her. She wanted a food processor. She got it. So why did I have to sleep on the couch Wednesday night?

My coworkers laughed at me when I pleaded my case to them. I guess they all attended Gift-Giving 101. I must have missed that class. My boss asked me, and I quote, "Are you an idiot?" I suppose I am.

To make matters worse, my wife's coworkers scoffed at my gift, wondering why she would even consider marrying a heathen like me. How dare I? A food processor, indeed!

I'm not a complete idiot. It's not like I gave her a lawn mower or a subscription to *Sports Illustrated*. I didn't even get her that certificate for a free oil change I was tempted to buy. I gave her what she wanted. And she didn't want it.

I was informed by a female friend of mine that the proper action to take was to buy my wife the food processor on Arbor Day or Flag Day or some random Monday. Never on Valentine's Day.

Another friend said gifts like mine conjure images of housework and stuff that has absolutely nothing to do with romance. What happened to "It's the thought that counts?"

I had no idea there were guidelines for which days to give what. The food processor, I am told, was not personal enough for Valentine's Day. How personal do I need to get? I'm not buying underwear, or anything else she would have to wear, for that matter. If you knew anything of my fashion acumen, you'd agree with me.

I was probably the only person in the world who knew she wanted a food processor. Everyone else got flowers and candy. She got a major appliance. That's pretty personalized, don't you think?

I think my gift blunder has less to do with outright stupidity on my part and more to do with a general communication breakdown between the sexes. I have recently discovered that "Watch whatever you want" does not include *SportsCenter*. I just learned that "Whatever you want to do" does not mean that I can play golf with my friends on Saturday afternoons. I used to think that females found the stereotypical male behaviors cute, even charming. You know, hanging my ties on the doorknob, never making my bed, cold pizza for breakfast, memorizing *Caddyshack*, cleaning out my refrigerator maybe once every time Neptune orbits the sun.

It's all so guy-ish and adorable.

I was wrong on all counts. And I obviously didn't know that "I really wish I had a food processor" meant "Don't you dare give me anything with a cord and a plug for Valentine's Day!" I know now. And I promise to spread the word to all males who are considering shopping at Sears or Home Depot for Valentine's gifts.

For now, I guess I'd better start thinking of a way to make this up to my wife. I should probably start by returning the sewing machine I was going to give her for her birthday next week.

~Michael Seale
Chicken Soup for the Romantic Soul

Love That Lasts

I have a friend who is falling in love. She honestly claims that the sky is bluer; she's noticed the delicate fragrance of the lilacs beside her garage, though she previously walked past them without stopping; and Mozart moves her to tears. In short, life has never been so exciting.

"I'm young again!" she shouts exuberantly. I have to admit, the guy must be better than Weight Watchers. She has lost fifteen pounds and looks like a cover girl. She's taken a new interest in the shape of her thighs.

As my friend raves on about her new love, I've taken a good look at my old one. My hubby, Scott, hasn't yet had his mid-life crisis, but he's entitled to one. His hairline is receding. He's gained fifteen pounds. Once a marathon runner, all muscles and sinew, he now only runs down hospital halls. His body shows the signs of long work hours and too many candy bars. Yet, he can still give me a certain look across a restaurant table, and I want to ask for the check immediately and head for home.

My natural glow has dimmed a bit after twenty-five years. I can look pretty good when I have to, but I don't think twice about hanging around the house in my baggy sweat pants, old softball jersey and my husband's gray wool socks.

My friend asked me, "What will make this love last?" I told her the truth: "I don't know." Then she asked, "Why does your love last?" I told her I'd think about it.

I've run through all the obvious reasons: commitment, shared interests, unselfishness, physical attraction, the ability to communicate. Yet, there's more.

We still have fun. Spontaneous good times. Yesterday, after slipping the rubber band off the rolled-up newspaper, he flipped it playfully at me: this led to all-out war. Last Saturday, while at the grocery store, we split the list and then raced each other to see who could gather the required items and make it to the checkout stand first. We've made an art form out of our prepared gourmet dinners. Even washing dishes together can be a blast. We enjoy simply being together.

And there are surprises: surprises in daily living. One time I came home from work to find a note on the front door. This note led me to another note, then to another, until — many notes later — I was directed to the walk-in closet. I opened the door to find Scott holding a "pot of gold" (my cooking kettle) and the "treasure" of a gift package. He had been jumping back in the closet for an hour, every time he heard footsteps on the stairs. Ever since then, I often leave him notes on the mirror or slip little presents under his pillow.

There is understanding. I understand why he must play basketball with the guys regularly. And he understands why, about once a year, I must get away from the house, the phone, the kids — and even him — to meet my sisters somewhere for a few days of nonstop talking and laughing.

There is a lot of sharing. Not only do we share the bills, the household worries, the parental burdens and the cooking, we also share ideas. Scott came home from a medical convention last month and presented me with a copy of a thick historical novel. Then he touched my heart by telling me he had read the book on the plane. This confession comes from a man who loves science fiction and Tom Clancy thrillers. He read it because he wanted to be able to share ideas about the book after I'd read it.

There is comfort. It's the comfort in knowing that I can tell the waitress waiting for our dessert order, "Just bring me a fork. I'll have a bit of his." I know that one bit is allowed. If Scott really wants every single bit of his dessert to himself, I know he will say, "Sorry, order your own!" And if he's not up to sharing, I'm not offended.

There is blessed forgiveness. When I'm too loud and crazy at parties and have embarrassed us both by not knowing when to shut up, Scott forgives me. He knows I can't resist a good one-liner. I forgave him when he came home and confessed he'd lost some of our investment savings in the stock market. I gave him a hug and bravely said, "It's okay. It's only money."

There is "synergism." That is, we can produce something that is greater than the two of us. (Take, for instance, our kids.) When we put our heads together to identify a problem and all the possible solutions, sometimes we're absolutely, as a team, nothing short of brilliant.

There is sensitivity. I know not to jump all over him for being late when he comes home from the hospital with a certain look in his eyes; I can see that it's been a tough day. Last week, he walked through the door with that look. After he'd spent some time with the kids and had eaten his warmed-up dinner, I asked, "What happened?" He told me about a sixty-year-old woman who had a stroke.

He'd worked with her for hours, but she was still in a coma. When he'd returned to her hospital room to check on her, he had been moved to tears by the sight of the woman's husband standing beside her bed, stroking her hand. Scott wept again as he told me he didn't think the woman would survive. And how was he going to tell this husband of forty years that his wife would probably never recover?

I shed a few tears myself. Because of the medical crisis. Because there are still people who have been married for forty years. Because my husband is still moved and concerned, even after twenty-five years of hospital rooms and dying patients.

There is faith. We both know that God loves us; and that, though life is difficult, He will strengthen and help us. Last week, Scott was on call and already overloaded by the necessary extra hours he spent at the hospital. On Tuesday night, a good friend from church came over and tearfully confessed her fears that her husband, who has cancer, is losing his courageous battle. We did our best to comfort and advise her.

On Wednesday, I went to lunch with a friend who is struggling to reshape her life after her husband left her. Together, we talked, laughed, got angry and figured out the blessings she could still count. On Thursday, a neighbor called who needed to talk about the frightening effects of Alzheimer's disease, because it was changing her father-in-law's personality.

On Friday, my dearest childhood friend called long distance to break the sad news that her father had died. After a minute, I hung up the phone and thought, "This is too much pain and heartache for one week." After saying a prayer, I descended the stairs to run some necessary errands. Through my tears, I noticed the boisterous orange blossoms of the gladiolus outside my window; I heard the delighted laughter of my son and his friend as they created Lego spaceships in our basement.

After backing my van out of my driveway, I caught sight of three brilliantly colored hot air balloons floating in the distant turquoise sky. Moments later, I looked left just in time to see a wedding party emerge from a neighbor's house. The bride, dressed in satin and lace, tossed her bouquet to her cheering friends.

That night, as I told my husband about these events, we acknowledged the cycles of life and the joys that counter the sorrows. We also recognized the satisfaction we felt when we assisted people with the weight of their burdens. It was enough to keep us going.

Finally, there is knowing. I know Scott will throw his laundry just shy of the hamper every night; he'll be perennially late to most appointments; he'll leave the newspaper scattered across the floor three out of five times; and he'll eat the last chocolate in the box. He knows I sleep with a pillow over my head; I'll lock us out of the house or the car on a regular basis; I'll have a pre-trip fit before we leave on vacation; and I will also eat the last chocolate in the box.

I guess our love lasts because it's comfortable. No, the sky is not bluer—it's just a familiar hue. We're not noticing many new things about life nor each other, but we like what we've noticed and benefit from relearning. Music is still meaningful because we know the harmonies. We don't feel particularly young. We've experienced too much that's contributed to growth and wisdom, taken its toll on our bodies, and created our mixed bag of treasured memories.

I hope we've got what it takes to make our love last. As a naive bride, I had Scott's wedding band engraved with this Robert Browning line: "Grow old along with me!" We're following those instructions.

~Annette Paxman Bowen
A 5th Portion of Chicken Soup for the Soul

Overlook It

Attitude is a little thing that makes a big difference.
~Winston Churchill

Sheila and I just celebrated our thirtieth wedding anniversary. Somebody asked her, what was our secret? She answered, "On my wedding day, I decided to make a list of ten of Tim's faults which, for the sake of our marriage, I would always overlook. I figured I could live with at least ten!"

When she was asked which faults she had listed, Sheila replied, "I never did get around to listing them. Instead, every time he does something that makes me mad, I simply say to myself, 'Lucky for him, it's one of the ten!'"

~Tim Hudson
Chicken Soup for the Romantic Soul

Everyday Heroes

I don't remember having a hero as a child, although there have been individuals throughout my life who I greatly respected. I found my hero much later in life, and he wasn't at all like I imagined a hero should be. He wasn't rich and famous. He wasn't a star athlete or a movie star. He was just a guy I'd taken for granted all of my life. This is a story about my hero, who also happens to be my big brother.

My brother, Tony, met his wife, Sheila, while he was in medical school. I remember attending his graduation and meeting her for the first time. Sheila was from England, and she was full of life. She had a smile that brightened any room and she loved to laugh. Sheila was a nurse, and at that time, nurses were in high demand. She had been recruited by U.S. hospitals, was given a work visa and settled in the Dallas area. Sheila met my brother at Parkland Hospital, where she was employed as a nurse and he was a medical student.

Tony had always been too consumed with his schoolwork to become involved with anyone on a regular basis. Somehow, though, I knew that this was more than a casual romance. I caught a glimpse of them sitting quietly in the auditorium, holding hands, deep in conversation.

After graduation, Tony accepted a residency in Louisville, Kentucky. Sheila moved with him. While living in Kentucky, Sheila went on "holiday" to Canada. When she attempted to return to Kentucky, she was refused entry into the United States because her work visa had expired. She was deported to England, and it took a month or so to clear up the mess. Tony, meanwhile, was going nuts without her. The minute Sheila returned to Louisville, they were married. The following year, they flew to England, where along with our parents, relatives and a few friends, they were remarried in a traditional ceremony, top hats and all. So their life together began.

The first few years of their life together went fairly smoothly, other than a few moves — Kentucky to New Mexico, New Mexico to Texas and then back to New Mexico. During that time, their two boys, Cameron and Sheldon, were born, three years apart. My brother had accepted a position with the School of Medicine at the University of New Mexico, and Sheila was working as a nurse in the intensive care unit of the same hospital. In 1989, they bought a beautiful new home in Corrales, New Mexico, complete with a corral and pasture, and with a beautiful view of the mountains. Sheila had always had a passion for horses, and their new home offered her the opportunity to pursue her hobby on a daily basis.

New Mexico can be a really nice place in the spring. One beautiful April spring day, a great day to spend outdoors, Tony decided to take the boys on a fishing expedition. Sheila had a new horse to train. No one knows for certain what happened on that day, but from what information could be pieced together, Sheila was riding in the pasture when her horse fell. Sheila fell forward, facedown into the grass and mud, and the horse landed on top of her, pressing her face into the mud and cutting off her air supply. Across the pasture, their neighbor, who was also a physician, was outside working, when he saw Sheila lying in the pasture. When he reached her, she was unconscious and not breathing. The neighbor began emergency treatment and called the air rescue unit.

Sheila was transported to the hospital where she and my brother both worked. Tony saw the air rescue helicopter from their fishing spot, not suspecting it could be Sheila. Tony and the boys returned late in the day to the news of the accident.

I was preparing to go on a picnic when my mom called and told me. All of my family headed to Albuquerque to be with my brother.

Sheila had a fractured skull, was breathing with the help of a respirator and was comatose. We did not know how long she would remain unconscious or, for that matter, if she would ever wake up. We did not know how much damage had been done to her brain as a result of the trauma.

I remember not knowing what to say to my brother as I watched him by her side, holding her hand and talking softly to her. I watched as the nurses Sheila had worked with the day before cared for her in her unconscious state. I thought about how quickly things can change in life and how different my brother's life might be if she did not recover. Months after the accident, Tony told me that one night he prayed and asked God to take her quickly if she wouldn't be able to live without the artificial support she was receiving. He said he felt a strange calmness after that, and that he just knew everything was going to be okay. Sheila's eyes opened two weeks after the accident. Once again, they began a life together.

The damage from the accident was evident. Sheila had no memory. She could not walk, talk, bathe or feed herself. She needed help with every basic function. The doctors believed that Sheila would eventually regain some of her motor skills, and perhaps some of her memory, but it was going to be a long and difficult journey.

Tony began a daily ritual of reviewing pictures and names with her, working a full day and then returning after work for a couple of hours. Once home with his boys, he fixed meals, read stories and tucked them into bed at night. Although he was exhausted, he never complained.

This ritual continued even after Sheila was transferred to a rehabilitation hospital, where she remained for several months. When Sheila was finally able to come home, she could not walk, her speech was barely audible, she could not write and she had no memory. She did not remember their meeting or courtship, nor did she remember their wedding or the birth of their children. For the longest time, she thought that Tony was an auto mechanic. Still, Tony bathed her, styled her hair, lavished her with gifts and attention. Progress was very slow. As time went on, we began to relish even the smallest accomplishment — new memory, remembering family names, cutting her own food, brushing her own hair, walking a few steps with a harness.

Even though Sheila was making progress toward self-sufficiency, most of her daily care was left up to Tony. This dependency must have been hard on Sheila, and she seemed very depressed. I worried that their marriage would not survive. The love, laughter and life they once shared no longer existed. Every day was a struggle.

Then it happened. The moment that my brother became my hero. I was visiting for the weekend. Sheila sat in her wheelchair. Tony was running around like a madman, cleaning and cooking; the kids were watching television; the stereo was playing — typical Saturday morning chaos.

All of a sudden, Tony turned up the music really loud. He began to snap his fingers and dance all by himself. All of us were looking at him, when the kids giggled and began to dance along. The kids and Tony were laughing and dancing and having a grand time. Tony looked over at Sheila and noticed tears streaming down her face. Sheila loved to dance, and it was as though at that moment, she remembered their life before. Without saying a word, Tony walked over to her and picked her up from her wheelchair. Holding her tightly, he rested her feet on his shoes and began to dance with her around the room.

Time seemed to stand still, and everyone was silent as we watched them dance about. Then, the kids began to smile and giggle, and as everyone joined in enthusiastically, Sheila smiled and started to laugh. It had been a long time since we had seen her smile; it seemed like forever since we had heard her laugh. I looked at my brother as he stared at his wife, and not only could I see the love for her in his eyes, I swear I could feel it from across the room. At that moment, I found my hero.

It has been almost ten years since that awful day in April. Tony, Sheila and their boys still live in their home in Corrales. Tony continues to practice medicine. The boys are now thirteen and eleven, and active in sports and school. Sheila has continued to make progress and is now self-sufficient. Sheila walks with the help of a cane, drives, takes care of their home and once again passed her board exams for nursing. Although she has never regained all of the memories of her past, she is now able to remember much more than ever before. They continue to struggle with the challenges that face those individuals in recovery from a serious accident, but their commitment to one another remains intact. As I have watched them struggle with each of their challenges, I have often been reminded of that simple moment that had such an impact on my life.

I now realize that simple moments and actions are what can make a difference in someone's life. Eleven years ago, I didn't have a hero, but I found one in an ordinary guy that I am also proud to call my brother.

~Shawn Blessing
A 6th Bowl of Chicken Soup for the Soul

44

A Miracle for My Heart

The first duty of love is to listen.
~Paul Tillich

Imagine a boulder jarred loose from its solid rock foundation after a series of earthquakes. Can you see it perched precariously on a crumbling, rocky overhang midway down a steep mountainside, one aftershock away from violent descent and disintegration into millions of tiny fragments? If you have a mental picture of that, then you can visualize my marriage from 1991 to 1996.

After nine sometimes challenging but mostly wonderful years, my standard response to any cheerful, "Hi, how are you?" was a flat, "Hey, just trying to stay married." And I wasn't trying to be funny. I was just keeping it real. When had reality evolved to this? I had to dig deep to resurrect our first reality, the happy one, the beginning....

Our first official date at a restaurant ended with us hanging out at his mother's house with his sister and her boyfriend. Lots of talking and laughing, meaningful glances, teasing, testing. But more than anything, I remember feeling incredibly comfortable and connected. Somewhere near the end of the evening, this funny, spiritual, musical, ambitious, solid-rock-steady, bold, beautiful black man became the brand-new owner of my heart.

Gradually, the tart aftertaste from my previous relationship was invaded by the fresh sweetness of our three-year romance. We laughed and played, kissed and cuddled, shared and dreamed. I didn't have to wonder what heaven was like. Being with this man was the closest I'd ever come to being on hallowed ground.

Now, don't get me wrong. Naturally, I'd always understood God as holy and Creator, but I'd never experienced Him as friend and companion. I realize now that if there had been a simpler, less painful way for me to learn that my God—not my fiancé—was to be the number-one man in my life, events would have unfolded differently.

So what was all the talk about "Marriage is work"? Marriage was marvelous! I didn't know who all the other women in the world had married, but I had a prince! That's why I was careful not to rock the boat, not to say or be anything that might jeopardize this miracle on Earth. I was determined that nothing would separate us—not careers, or children, or "growing apart," or "irreconcilable differences."

I wanted it to be a perfect marriage, but I didn't understand that perfection grows from the seeds of humanness, watered by divine grace. How could I possibly know that the turbulent waterfall we were headed for eventually surfaced in pristine pools of calm, clear, deeply peaceful waters? I had read that God's strength was made perfect in our weakness, but I had to live it to learn it.

It was the mid-1990s. I was oblivious to politics, the economy, world events, whatever. I only knew that I had forgotten what it meant to be a vibrant, versatile participant in a meaningful life. Everything that could possibly go wrong in our marriage gradually did. I suddenly found that my duties as a wife, mother, homemaker, RN, and church deaconess were performed with robotic obligation, completely devoid of joy or purpose. God seemed to be on extended vacation, and I sure hoped He was having fun, because I definitely wasn't.

In fact, if this was to be my life, I was no longer interested. How had my failing marriage come to represent my self-esteem, my accomplishments, my entire world? And when exactly had my emotional whirlwind of anger, resentment, irritability and depression settled into a mindless state of numb indifference? It would take a miracle for my heart to live and breathe and thrive again. And that is exactly what God had in mind.

By the time my husband invited me to hear him play with a jazz band one evening at a local function, I didn't care enough anymore to have any man in my life, divine or otherwise. God, however, was a sweet and faithful song, looking beyond my faults to see my need. Even as I refused my husband's invitation, ignored the flicker of hope that faded from his eyes as I claimed to be without a babysitter, angels must have been hastily dispatched to do the Master's bidding. While I returned to my magazine, he finished loading up his instruments and paused at the door.

"If we can't support each other anymore, there's no reason to stay together. If you really don't want to go tonight, it's okay. But I already packed a bag, and I won't be back after the concert."

He couldn't possibly feel the chill that instantly descended on my heart and stilled the flow of blood in my veins. He could only see my brief upward glance, and the casual shrug of my shoulders. He only heard a flippant "Okay, whatever," before turning slowly and walking out.

I remember the crushing silence that followed the closing of the door. Finally, it could all be over. Why wasn't I relieved? What was that strange stirring in my heart that in some mystical way made me struggle to catch my breath and order my thoughts? Fear? Indecision? Desperation? Or was it simply the unmistakable fluttering of angels on assignment? I tried to refocus on my ridiculous magazine, but the words blurred into a haze of gray and it fell from my hands.

A silent prayer exploded in my mind, God, you said you'd handle this and you didn't! I talked to you over and over again about this and trusted you to work it out, but it's falling apart. What about my children? My family? I did my part but you didn't do yours!

I slid off the couch and collapsed face down on the carpet, knees drawn up under my belly, arms outstretched in abject surrender.

"God, please..." For the first time in my life I felt truly connected to the Savior as my lifeline. "God, please..."

My humanness was swallowed up in His divinity, His peace was mine.

An intense restlessness suddenly dispelled my calm and compelled me to my feet, willed me to the phone. Three attempts. Three failures. No babysitter. A jumble of disconnected thoughts: Maybe my marriage wasn't meant to work? Why can't I just read my magazine? I don't want him to leave! But it's too hard; I already tried. It's too soon to give up; it could work. Swallow your pride. You know you still love him, and you saw his eyes, he loves you back. But I'm so tired.

The shrill ringing of the phone vaporized my thoughts.

"Hello?"

It was a close family friend. "Is there something you'd like to do tonight? I can babysit for you if you want."

"What?" How was this possible? (Obviously my faith was quite a bit smaller than a mustard seed.) "I thought you were at a program tonight," I whispered.

"Well, for some reason I think it's more important that I babysit for you. Do you want me to come?"

A surge of excitement. Crazy hope. "Yes!"

He didn't see me slip silently into an empty seat in an unlit corner, but his eyes periodically swept the room, purposeful, persistent—things I'd always loved about him. When he found me his face lit up like the sun. He grabbed the mike and announced to 150 people that "a very special person has just arrived, and I'd like to ask my beautiful wife to please stand."

Even as my tears threaten to spill over at this moment, I would be lying if I said it was easy after that night. We would return to the brink of collapse more than once. But that night we both knew that God had engineered a miracle to keep us together. And today, two weeks from our twentieth anniversary, I am still amazed at the shift in my chest when I see him across a crowded room, at the ache in my gut when I miss him and hear his voice on the telephone across the miles, at the way I bask contentedly in the warmth of his eyes and the sweetness of his kiss.

And I never cease to wonder that my own personal God loves me enough to send angels on a mission to transform hurt into healing, and grant me a miracle for my heart.

~Karlene McCowan
Chicken Soup for the African American Soul

"Michigan, You Walk a Long Way"

*I*was into my first week of training for the Avon Breast Cancer Three-Day Los Angeles event to raise money to benefit underserved women with breast cancer. The walk is sixty miles long—twenty miles each day.

I nearly skipped my walk that day, thinking that I really should get to work an hour early so I could complete a new business proposal I had started the day before. But I decided to walk first, so that it would help clear my head.

According to the training schedule the walk organizers gave me, I was to walk three miles that day. Each week I would progressively walk farther and farther until I worked up to two, twelve-mile back-to-back sessions in one weekend prior to the big event. To prepare for these, I had spent an afternoon mapping out various locations, to determine how far each one was.

I gathered my things, among them my headphones and a book on tape—*Chicken Soup for the Soul*, tape one, volume one. Because my regular gray sweatshirt was in the wash, I dug out and pulled on a very old sweatshirt, one I hadn't worn in nearly ten years. It was a gift from one of my ex-husband's friends, and it had the Michigan logo across the front of it. Off I went, happily listening to my tape, getting weepy now and again at an especially poignant story, and oh so glad I had decided to walk after all.

About three-quarters of the way into it, I spotted a man about a half-mile ahead of me on the same side of the street. I didn't think much of it. He was going in the same direction, but was way ahead. I didn't think I'd catch up with or pass him before I reached the park and turned around. I continued at my pace, while the words, Stay alert, stay alive, went through my head—instructions I had received at a walk orientation meeting a month or two earlier.

I soon realized I was gaining on the man, and briefly considered crossing the street. Then I saw a female jogger approach and pass him as she came up the street toward me. He hadn't even glanced at her, so I decided he was just out exercising like the rest of us, and I needn't be concerned. I kept walking, listening to my tape, getting closer to him.

I could now see he was an older Asian man, on the stairs about halfway up to the park from the street. He was looking at me. I could tell he wanted to say something, so I stopped, looked up at him, took off my headphones and smiled. He said, "Michigan [referring to the blue and gold logo on my white sweatshirt], you walk a long way. I watch you."

I said, "Yes, sir, I have," and kept smiling and waiting. I felt comfortable talking to him.

He said, "When I was thirty-five years old, I was sick. My doctor told me to start walking every day. Doctor said it make me healthier, stronger."

"Good," I said.

The man held up his arms in a strongman pose: "See: strong and healthy now! From that day I have walked one hour every day, and today I am sixty-five!"

I smiled, enjoying his story. He went on: "Every day I walk, then go home to my wife and tell her I love her. That keeps me healthy, too." He added that he tells her he walks for her, because he loves her. Then he said something that made me catch my breath. He simply said, with force and a pointed finger, "You will live a long time if you do the same—walk an hour every day and tell your husband you do it because you love him."

"...you walk a long way." That statement could be a metaphor for the last two years of my life, and for the lives of those around me. I am a thirty-six-year-old breast-cancer survivor.

I thought I was doing the Avon Three-Day walk because I had received so much help from so many people and organizations, and because my sister had a passion to do it. That nice man made me realize that I am also walking for the same reason that I endured two mastectomies, chemotherapy, radiation therapy and the removal of my ovaries—because I love my husband, children, family and friends so much that I want to be around for a lot more years.

I will walk every day, and I will go home and tell my husband I walk because I love him.

~Donna St. Jean Conti
Chicken Soup to Inspire the Body & Soul

Wasn't the First Love Story in a Garden?

They are not long, the days of wine and roses:
Out of a misty dream
Our path emerges for a while, then closes
Within a dream.
~Ernest Dowson

46

Accidental Blessings

We plant seeds that will flower as results in our lives,
so best to remove the weeds of anger, avarice, envy and doubt...
~Dorothy Day

I was in the hospital mending from a bad car accident when I met Joe. We hit it off right away. It was a cold March in Georgia, but my heart was warmed by this handsome, loving man. He was recovering from the loss of his left hand in an accident a month earlier.

A couple of weeks after we met, I became anxious about being away from home. I had ordered all sorts of fruit trees, shrubs and flowers from various catalogs. They'd be arriving in the mail any day, and I knew they wouldn't be safe just sitting outside. I had to get them planted!

"I've got to get out of this hospital and back home to put in my garden," I told Joe. "I've got so much to do!"

"I'll help," he offered immediately. Neither of us stopped to think that Joe no longer had his left hand.

Two weeks later, I was discharged from the hospital. Sure enough, I was greeted by box after box of plants. Joe called that evening to say hello. I told him what had been waiting for me.

The next morning, Joe called again. He had spoken with his doctor and been granted a day pass away from the hospital.

"If you still want help with the garden, I'll be glad to come over," Joe said.

"I'd love some help," I answered with relief. "It'll be a big job!"

Saturday morning I was in the yard getting organized when Joe arrived with a big smile on his face. I showed him where the shovel was, and I grabbed an armful of fruit trees.

When I got to the section of property where the trees were to be planted, my eager helper was all ready to get to work. All of a sudden, I stopped and focused on Joe's left arm. It was at that moment that it struck me what a challenge this was going to be for Joe.

"Don't worry," said Joe, as if reading my mind. "I had my therapist bandage my arm extra well so I won't get dirt on it. Now, where do you want these trees planted?"

After I showed him the layout, Joe wrapped his left arm around the shovel handle, grabbed the handle end with his right hand and started digging.

By sunset, Joe and I were planting the last shrub. Both of us were exhausted and hungry. We cleaned up and headed out to a nice restaurant.

Over dinner, we talked and laughed and had a wonderful time. Then Joe got really quiet. "I didn't think I could do it," he said softly.

I looked at him, puzzled.

Joe raised his left arm. "I didn't think I could do it," he said, as a beautiful smile spread across his face. "The end of my arm is really throbbing now, but I feel great! In fact, I've never felt better in my life!"

There is truth in the saying that "gardening is the best medicine." After that day, Joe often came to work in the garden with me. The exercise strengthened his arm, and he was out of the hospital much sooner than the doctors expected. Not only that, Joe fell in love with gardening. He was hooked for life. And best of all, we fell in love with each other. We were married six months later.

Today, Joe's even more passionate about gardening than I am. Sometimes I catch him pulling weeds in public flower beds! Our marriage, too, grows stronger every day.

I often think about how much we might have missed if we hadn't both been in the hospital and I hadn't been so eager to get my plants in the ground. Joe and I met by accident — or by accidents. But life's funny, isn't it? Those accidents brought us the best blessings of our lives.

~Joanne Bryan
Chicken Soup for the Gardener's Soul

47
Chicken Soup for the Soul

First Penny

I'd rather have roses on my table than diamonds on my neck.
~Emma Goldman

My husband and I had birthdays six days apart. We always celebrated on a day in between by giving ourselves a joint present. One year we decided to buy a rosebush. So, on a cold, blustery January day, we set off eagerly for the nursery to make our selection. After much thought, we chose a gorgeous, velvety, deep burgundy rose named Mr. Lincoln. With tall, straight stems, it's as stately as our sixteenth president. It was sure to do well in our Northern California climate. And since my husband's name was Abe, we thought it a good match.

We followed the planting directions and by early July, the Mr. Lincoln bush was loaded with lush burgundy blooms. I cut bouquets for most of July and well into August.

Years earlier, my husband and I had started a tradition. We loved to take early morning walks together. On our walks, the first one to spot a penny could keep the coin for the day's good luck. At the end of the day, the "First Penny" was deposited in a small crystal dish. When there were enough pennies in the dish, we'd go out for an ice cream treat for two.

Years passed, happy years when the roses bloomed and the copper coffer grew.

Then, it was over. On a July second, when Mr. Lincoln was in full bloom, my own Abe died. There would be no more walks, no more talks and no more First Penny contests. I went to the garden that day, cut a bountiful bouquet of the roses and tearfully closed a chapter of my life.

Or so I thought.

A decade passed and on another July second, I set out on my solitary walk. As I passed our rose garden, I thrilled to the bounty of blossoms on the Mr. Lincoln bush. My walk took me to a nearby park, and, as I came up behind the bandstand, there on the path, shining in the morning sunlight, was a bright copper penny! When I got home, I took the long-unused crystal dish from the cupboard and put my First Penny in it.

Each morning in July after that day, I took a walk and found a First Penny—sometimes shiny bright and sometimes tarnished—but always there. I began to look for it eagerly. I sensed that a countdown was underway, though I didn't know to what. One penny, two pennies, three pennies—more. At the end of July, thirty copper coins were in the crystal dish.

August first brought me the shining realization that the pennies were counting the days till our wedding anniversary on the eighteenth. If I found one every day between the anniversary of Abe's passing on July second and our wedding anniversary on August eighteenth, I would have forty-eight pennies.

Suddenly, I had a thought. Could it be? I counted out the years. Yes, it was true: This would be our forty-eighth wedding anniversary!

I'm not a superstitious person, but I got hooked. The small ritual became a consuming passion. Eighteen days until our anniversary! I scarcely slept at night waiting for the dawn and First Penny. I found the penny on the path in the park, in front of the convenience store, in the parking lot at the mall, and in front of the grocery store. Not a day was missed.

August eighteenth arrived. There were forty-seven pennies in the crystal dish. Would there be that last forty-eighth coin?

On the afternoon of our anniversary, I drove to the supermarket to pick up some groceries. On the way back to my car, I looked down and there it was: First Penny, shimmering brightly in the late-morning sun!

But there was more. When I returned to my car, there, on the hood, lay a single, long-stemmed Mr. Lincoln rose!

I picked it up reverently and pressed it to my lips, allowing the tears to flow unashamedly. How could this be? How had he done this? As I stared at the lovely flower in amazement, a young man closed the trunk of the neighboring car and walked up to me. "Oh," he said. "Sorry! That's for my wife. It's our anniversary."

"That's quite all right," I said, smiling at him through my tears. "Thank you. Thank you so very much." I handed him the rose, and he smiled at me.

"You must be thinking of someone special," he said gently.

"Yes," I replied, "and he's thinking of me."

~Bernice Bywater
Chicken Soup for the Gardener's Soul

48

Perennial

In the depth of winter I finally learned that there was in me
an invincible summer.

~Albert Camus, Lyrical and Critical Essays

The garden in front of my grandparents' red brick house is where the jonquils, tulips, crocuses and irises bloomed. Other bulbs remained beneath, still hidden in the darkness of the moist soil. As the days grew longer and stretched into summer, the deep pink star-gazers and trumpet-shaped lilies of pure white would also spring forth from the loamy earth and leaf debris.

In the springtime, a dear old friend who had known my grandparents for decades longer than I had even been alive came over to help with removing the storm windows. The air was warm, and any threats of wintry weather seemed to have passed.

After the task had been completed, he and my grandmother walked around to the front of the house where my mother and three aunts had spent their childhoods.

There, in the plot beside the front porch, a colorful congregation of flowers waved merrily in the breeze, a statue of St. Francis presiding over the petals.

My grandmother stopped to admire the flowerbed.

"I've been noticing these past few weeks," she said, pausing in contemplation, "and it just seems to me that the flowers are even more beautiful than usual, there just seem to be more colors."

The friend chuckled quietly. "Well," he said in response, "that probably has something to do with the extra bulbs Joe planted in secret last fall."

Joe was my grandfather, and although it was my grandmother who took most of the pride in the beautiful blossoms in front of their house each year, it was he who was the primary tender of the garden.

The friend shook his head, "Leave it to Joe to not tell you something like that." He continued, "I suppose the flowers speak louder than any words could anyway. And he was never one to make a big fuss over things, nor did he like it when other people would — especially when the fuss was being made over him."

"Well for heaven's sakes," said my grandmother. "But when could he have done it? We were together so much of the time."

"I reckon all those times he went to working on projects in the garage, he wasn't necessarily in the garage the whole time. And you did go to your ladies' meetings at church."

They both stood looking at the flowers.

"And he wanted it to be a surprise for you this spring." The man blinked several times in quick succession and cleared his throat, looking around the yard. "Is there anything else I can do for you today, Mary?"

She shook her head gently. "No, you've been such a big help already. Thank you so much."

"Well," he said brusquely, clearing his throat, "then I must be going now."

He rolled down his window in his car before pulling out of the driveway. "Mary, you be sure and let me know if there's anything you need."

She smiled and waved.

The car disappeared down the street, and my grandmother went to the porch swing. She sat down in a sunbeam, a small solitary figure with gray curls, swaying slowly back and forth. She gazed at the flowers, bathed in the warmth of the sunshine and thoughts of her romantic husband.

As long as she had known him, he was forever giving her

thoughtful gifts. They were a duo who had weathered a childhood in the Depression, and later had channeled much of their energy and financial resources into raising four children. Frivolous objects were a foreign concept to them, and the gifts he had given were never flamboyant or expensive. The few pieces of jewelry he had presented to her had been hard-earned after months and months of scrupulous saving.

She treasured the jewelry, but it was perhaps the other gifts that meant even more to her. The purchase prices had been smaller, but she recognized the thought that went into them, which made them so precious.

Throughout their courtship he had given her books that they would read sitting together on park benches. While he was overseas during the war, my grandfather wrote her letters almost daily, and sent photographs and small trinkets when he could. In 1944, he returned safely, and they began their lives together. Although he returned from Europe and they could see one another every day, he still sometimes wrote her love letters.

Even during the busy parenting years of crying babies, potty-training, skinned knees, school plays and proms, he still made time to be romantic, giving small gifts. The gifts and notes continued to appear, through the course of fifty-six years of marriage.

She turned her blue eyes again to the garden, breathing the sweet fragrances. A tear ran down her cheek, and the flowers became a blurred watercolor as her eyes welled with more tears.

He always found a special way to remind her and let her know how much he loved her.

Even now, three months after the cancer had so abruptly taken him, an angel gardener blew her kisses, carried on the scents and colors of the flower petals.

~Tinker E. Jacobs
Chicken Soup for the Grandparent's Soul

49

Butter Beans and Bulldogs

I shared so much with my husband, but not his passion for his vegetable garden. When we moved into the neighborhood in Lilburn, Georgia, back in the seventies, most everyone had a small garden. Jerry said that we should plant one, too.

"No, thanks," I declared. "I'm not a garden person." Undaunted, he went out and bought seed and an old, used tiller and began to till a corner of our backyard. He was so optimistic, he even bought a small freezer for storing the bounty. I threw a couple of loaves of store-bought bread into the shiny new freezer—all I ever intended to contribute. Smiling, Jerry raved on about how great it would be to have homegrown vegetables year-round.

"Who's going to pick them and put them in the freezer?" I asked, arms folded stubbornly.

"You might learn to enjoy it one day," he said.

I knew better.

Jerry spent countless hours in his garden. One night, when he had to work late, he came home and tended his tomato and bean plants by moonlight, whistling "Blueberry Hill." I watched from an upstairs window, convinced he was wasting his time and energy.

His garden was the talk of the neighborhood. Everyone came to marvel and sample. The green bean stalks were so tall, I had to look straight up in the sky to see the tops. The tomatoes were deep red, perfectly round and juicy.

Everything grew well in Jerry's garden, but the butter beans were his favorite. Homegrown butter beans—some people call them limas—and the University of Georgia Bulldogs football team were two of the most exciting things in his life. I cared about football and the Georgia Bulldogs about as much as I cared about that darn garden.

The years passed, and Jerry went on picking butter beans without me. Often our children helped him shell them and together they placed package after package in the freezer with all the fanfare of people putting the Hope Diamond in a vault.

Then Jerry became sick rather suddenly. He'd always been incredibly healthy and assured me he was all right. Nothing unusual turned up on the tests at the hospital. But I couldn't shake the feeling that we were dealing with a biggie. On the fifth CAT scan something showed up. Exploratory surgery revealed inoperable cancer had spread throughout his brain.

Jerry and I had been together for twenty-five years, and I had no idea how I was going to live without him. I was so afraid I hardly ate or slept, barely talked, couldn't even cry. I just stared at my husband, willing him to hang on, begging God to let life make sense again.

The doctors wouldn't permit Jerry to work or drive. After a while, he couldn't have anyway. Jerry went on like always, laughing, whistling "Blueberry Hill," rooting wildly for the Bulldogs, playing with our collie, signing our twin sons up for Little League and, of course, tending his garden. He'd never been a worrier. I don't think he even knew how to worry. Never mind—I could do it for both of us.

One day we came home from one of his hospital stays and plopped down on the sofa. "What do you want to do?" I asked, staring straight ahead, thinking, This can't really be happening. "I think the Bulldogs are playing," I said. "If you want, I'll watch the game with you."

I turned to glance at Jerry. He gave me his big, easy smile. "I'm going to pick butter beans," he said, as if this were just another early-autumn Saturday.

I looked at him. Really looked at him. He wasn't afraid. He didn't ask, "Why me?" He wasn't faking it. He wasn't even being brave for me. He was just very simply excited about his butter beans.

He stood up to go outside, and I stood, too. "I'll go with you," I said, still terrified of what my future held without him.

"You don't like to pick butter beans!" he exclaimed. Then he burst out laughing like he always did when he was really happy, his arms resting on my shoulders.

"I changed my mind." I'd never wanted to do anything so much in my whole life as pick butter beans with my husband.

Out in his tall, green garden we went to work under the broiling Georgia sun. Creepy things crawled over my feet. I'm sure I saw at least one snake. I got so hot I saw spots, and my back, arms and legs ached. I sweated. But every time my gaze met Jerry's, he smiled enormously. Once he winked at me. Finally, he announced that we were through in the garden, and we carried our reward inside.

Sitting at the kitchen table, Jerry and I began shelling the huge mound of butter beans. I could do this every day for the rest of my life and be happy and content, I suddenly realized, as my eyes lingered on my husband's large, square, freckled hands easing the beans out of their shells.

Jerry left this life the following summer. We still had some of those butter beans in the freezer.

The memory of that hot, early fall day we picked them together has stayed with me, one of the highest points of our long marriage. It helped give me the strength to go on, to see that the life God had given me made sense after all.

Now I love gardens. I have a small plaque that says, "Life began in a garden." For me, courage began in a garden, the courage to face life without my partner. It was a tiny seed at first. But like everything in Jerry's garden, eventually it grew and thrived.

~Marion Bond West
Chicken Soup for the Gardener's Soul

50

Say It with... a Rhododendron

Flowers are love's truest language.
~Park Benjamin

I read somewhere that starting a new job is one of life's most stressful events. So when my husband began behaving in a less-than-charming manner after he'd moved to a new workplace, I tried to remember that the source of his tension was probably elsewhere. I tried to hunker down and weather the unpleasantness until it ran its course.

I failed.

Eventually, one night at bedtime, he asked me if I was angry. We began to hash it out.

"Tell me, would you behave toward the people at work the way you've been acting toward me lately?" I asked.

"It's funny you say that," he answered. "Lately I've been thinking that they're a lot easier to deal with than you are."

"Maybe that's because your biggest criticism at work is only 'I think this paragraph needs revision' instead of 'I'm completely disappointed in everything about you.'" My voice broke. We continued trading accusations the way tired people at night should never do. Finally we went to bed, saddened and exhausted, with nothing resolved.

The next morning, we both acted carefully cordial. Our argument had succeeded in airing our tensions — only to have them hover oppressively all around us. It was a relief when the afternoon came and I got a chance to be alone; my husband was driving our daughter to a birthday party. It was far enough away that he was planning to wait there until it was over.

I gloomed around by myself for the next few hours. If being angry was bad, this uneasy peace was even worse. I dreaded his return and the resumption of our polite détente. Finally came the sound of the car in the driveway. Then my daughter stuck her head in the door and announced gleefully, "Daddy's got something for you!"

It is a historical element of our relationship, harking back to our courtship days: My husband will bring me flowers after his most dire offenses, even if he's not clear just what his offenses were. Yes, maybe it's a little trite, the typical way a male seeks forgiveness, but there it is. In times of romantic uncertainty, he is a man with a bouquet.

But this time he didn't bring just flowers. No, he struggled through the doorway with a large, balled-and-burlapped rhododendron, in full bloom. I couldn't help feeling a growing sense of amusement.

"I went with a shrub," he said with twinkling eyes. "I thought repeated flowering might be wise in the long run, considering how difficult I can be to live with." Then he added, "I hope you know I love you."

The hug that followed was warm and healing. I felt his embrace and, more important, felt the ease between us return.

The next day, we gave the rhododendron a careful planting out in the garden, tucking it into peat moss and compost. It has thrived, and when in bloom inspires many a knowing smile between my husband and myself. It is our special rhododendron, a fitting symbol of the romance between a gardener and her mate. Both the flowers and our love grow more beautiful as each year passes.

Did I say that flowers are trite? Well, maybe it's my turn to be wrong.

~Martine Caselli
Chicken Soup for the Gardener's Soul

51

Unspoken Love

You give but little when you give of your possessions.
It is when you give of yourself that you truly give.
~Kahlil Gibran, The Prophet

When it comes to flowery speech or emotional expression, my husband, Dave, is a man of few words. That was one of the first things I learned about him when we married thirty-one years ago.

One of the next things I discovered is that Dave has little use for rosebushes. He had no second thoughts about yanking out mature plants to widen the driveway when we purchased our home. To him, roses represent hours of pruning and spraying, mulching and fertilizing. As far as he's concerned, a lawn mower and hedge trimmers are all you need for the perfect garden.

On the other hand, I treasure my roses. I consider every minute of their care well worth the beautiful, fragrant results.

One winter, I spent several evenings drooling over rose catalogs and planning a small garden. In the spring, I ordered several English varieties of self-rooted plants. I removed an area of sod, worked and reworked the ground, and planted the foot-long starts. During the heat of summer, I watered them daily. In my mind, I saw the fruits of my labor: masses of color and fragrance perfuming the air just outside my kitchen window.

But as it sometimes does, life spun us around and redirected our attention. In the fall, I began to have pain in my lower abdomen. At first I passed it off as nothing serious. But instead of getting better, the pain intensified. I went to see my doctor. He ordered tests; when the results came back, he asked to see me in his office right away. He also requested that Dave come with me.

Our worst fears became reality: colon cancer. I'd need surgery immediately. After a short recovery period, I'd undergo a six-month course of chemotherapy.

We cried... and prayed... and cried some more. We had one week to inform our family and friends. Then, trusting God and my doctors, I entered the hospital.

One month later, as I lay on the sofa still recuperating from surgery, Dave and I watched the TV weather forecast. It promised bitter cold temperatures and possible snow.

"Oh," I moaned to myself, "I never did get the roses mulched."

Dave just sat and watched the end of the forecast. Then, always the practical, on-top-of-things handyman, he said, "I'd better go winterize the outside faucets." He bundled up and headed toward the garage.

Fifteen minutes later, I hobbled to the kitchen for a glass of water. What I saw from the window brought tears to my eyes. There was Dave, bending over the roses, carefully heaping mulch around every plant.

I smiled and watched as my quiet husband "said" I love you. You know, sometimes words aren't needed at all.

~Emily King
Chicken Soup for the Gardener's Soul

We Didn't Give Up on Us

The way I see it, if you want the rainbow,
you gotta put up with the rain.
~Dolly Parton

52

Desires of Your Heart

*I*t was late at night in front of my house. The floodlights were on, and worship music was playing. I sat in the dirt beside four flats of flowers waiting to be planted. My tears rolled down my cheeks as I thought back over the past twenty-five years. I had married this man when I was eighteen years old and now he wanted a divorce. He had just moved his belongings out that day, and I was determined to make myself happy by planting my flowers. When I was a child, my aunt had always told me that if you have lots of flowers outside your home it meant you had a happy home. For the first time in my forty-four years I was totally alone. The children were grown and on their own, and now I was, too.

In my early twenties, I realized I needed to be dependent on the Lord instead of my husband. Through the following years of his workaholism and unfaithfulness, I had struggled to make this wonderful provider happy. I doubled my efforts in being the best I could be, and prayed daily for God's guidance and wisdom for our family. I knew the only one I could change was myself, and I prayed daily for my husband to have God's salvation. In Psalms 37:4 it says, "Delight yourself in the Lord and He will give you the desires of your heart." My desires were to have a family and a husband who loved and adored me. It did not seem to be working out that way, but I hung on to that promise.

Times looked bleak as my husband and I, by the grace of God, managed to get through some very difficult years. We lived through our son's battles with attention deficit hyperactivity disorder (ADHD) and drug addiction, our daughter's depression and our own inner battles with each other.

Now, I was sitting in the dirt crying as I remembered. I knew I would be all right by myself because I was not really alone. I had built a relationship with God and He did love me.

It was a difficult time, but as I started looking forward to what God had planned for me, it became very exciting—and a relief—to have only myself to consider. I still prayed for my husband each day, but soon realized he had to find his own way. The divorce was in place and the time clock was ticking. I joined a Christian singles group and attended a divorce recovery workshop. I had gone on with my life and had just signed up for college when I got the call.

It was my husband. He was on his way over to tell me something. There he stood on the front porch with tears in his eyes, announcing his acceptance of the Lord. He no longer wanted a divorce and wanted to work on our marriage. It had been six months since he had left, and to be truthful, I was in doubt whether I even wanted to be married. Life was good, fun and exciting, and I was more content than I ever remembered being. Did I want to go back to the distrust and deception I had endured for so many years?

My answer to him was, "I need time." I separated myself from the activities I was involved with and took time to be alone and pray. The psalm had said the Lord would give me the desires of my heart. I had prayed for my husband for twenty-five years to come to know the Lord and now he said he had. I did not trust my husband, but I did trust God. If I chose not to work to save this marriage, I would be doubting God's power and grace.

My husband and I set up personal boundaries and had a lot of Christian counseling. We continued to live alone. As the months went by, God did the work of mending a very broken relationship. As I learned to know my husband and trust him, we fell in love, and Christ became the center of our marriage. We renewed our wedding vows in our church on our twenty-sixth wedding anniversary, with many friends and family in attendance. It was the happiest day of my life. Our beautiful daughter sang, "Let's Begin Again," and our drug-free son walked me down the aisle to meet a completely transformed man. All of my childhood dreams had come true, and I did receive the desires of my heart.

~Susan Lugli
Chicken Soup for the Christian Woman's Soul

53

House to Home

Snowflakes are one of nature's most fragile things,
but just look at what they can do when they stick together.
~Fay Seevers

"Mike, you need to leave work right now. I can see your house on the news and it's on fire." My friend's voice on the other line was filled with concern.

This cannot be happening to us. This is not happening to us, I thought. I was getting married in four days and the reception would take place in the backyard of our home.

I had met Lorena three years earlier and immediately developed a wonderful friendship. I soon knew my best friend was going to be my wife. A couple of years passed and after purchasing a home together, the conversation about getting married came up in passing.

"We should just do it," I impulsively suggested. Luckily for me, she agreed. With money tight, we planned a simple courthouse ceremony and a nice reception at our house. Little did we know our life plan would be turned upside down.

The wildfire started on a nearby hillside. Although we heard different updates, the final outcome was not good. "Your house got hit pretty bad," a friend informed me. I headed home from work as fast as I could.

My fiancée and I drove up at the same time and we couldn't believe our eyes. Why are all these people here? And the news media?

I thought. The house doesn't look that bad. The tall trees in the front yard hid our view.

The short walk past the people and media was the longest of my life. Despite the chaos surrounding me, my world fell silent. There, barely standing, was our only possession—our future. The one thing we owned as a couple, the one thing that held our belongings and sheltered our lives. Totally destroyed.

We hesitantly approached what was now walls and mortar and looked in the window to our bedroom. The entire roof had collapsed on our bed; embers and charcoal engulfed every surface; water-drenched belongings still dripped. Lorena's eyes filled with tears. Why did this happen? I thought. We have no money and no house. I was numb.

Bewildered, Lorena and I rummaged through the house. Suddenly, all I could think about was the wedding. Would Lorena still want to marry me? What if she wanted to postpone it or maybe even call it off? It dawned on me that, with time, the fire would be a mere memory. But if we didn't get married, it would affect the rest of our lives. We'd lost our home; I didn't want to lose Lorena, too.

A reporter began interviewing me. I told him about our upcoming nuptials and admitted my apprehension about Lorena's unwillingness to go through with it.

Little did I know the same reporter approached my fiancée and told her I had mentioned we were getting married on Friday. Moved, she looked at the grinning reporter, smiled and started crying in relief. In the midst of our crumbling world, we each thought the same thing—we didn't want to postpone our marriage.

As the day's mayhem settled, we were left alone to search our soaked, burned, broken belongings, looking for anything salvageable—including our wedding rings. By 3:00 A.M., hungry and heartbroken and with no rings in sight, we clung to a few salvaged photographs as if they were gold.

The days to follow were surreal.

We were bombarded by an outpouring of donations, support and kind wishes. Neighbors and strangers alike brought gifts, money, food and knickknacks. A local television station organized an on-air donation fund.

Having always worked hard for what we had, it was difficult to accept money and gifts from strangers. But with everything gone, Lorena and I knew we had to set aside our pride and let others help. The simple act of a pizza delivery woman giving us a blanket from her car filled our hearts.

And then the irony hit. In spite of our losses, we realized how lucky we were. Our newfound perspective left us thankful for community support and grateful to be alive and together.

The wedding was scheduled for Friday. Although the media asked to attend, we wanted this special moment alone. My mom and the priest were the only people present. Having no idea of the week's events, the priest commented that we seemed happy. After explaining why we were so emotional, he cried along with us.

We were happy. Happy for a new beginning and happy to move forward without looking back.

The day before the wedding, I received a call from the owner of a local café. George offered to host our reception at his restaurant after the wedding. Although it seemed a bit much, we accepted his offer to invite our closest friends and family for a small get-together.

Once again, I was shocked and overwhelmed to see the crowd that awaited us. Outside the restaurant we found reporters, news anchors, firefighters, Chamber of Commerce representatives—well-wishers wanting to congratulate us.

As reporters approached me, I thought, the real heroes were the firefighters. The real heroes were the community. I encouraged them to interview those who stepped up to the plate during a disastrous and wrenching time—the people who put their hearts first to help out a couple of strangers.

Inside the restaurant, we were overwhelmed with love and cheers from friends and family. We discovered generous donations: a keyboardist, a wedding cake, a honeymoon train trip to Arizona and a limousine ride to a night's stay at a local Hyatt.

Just when we thought it couldn't get any better, a stranger who noticed our party approached us. "Will you please accept this for your wife?" she asked. "It belonged to my grandmother." The sweet woman slid a beautiful ring on Lorena's finger and the three of us tearfully embraced.

Now we see our tragedy as a blessing in disguise. God intervened during a difficult time and gave us a fresh start. Not only are we more stable financially, but we've been blessed with a closer, stronger relationship.

Next, we plan to rebuild our house. After all, how could we leave a place filled with people who loved and supported us? More than ever, we look forward to the day that our house is our home again.

~Mike Zeballos
Chicken Soup for the Bride's Soul

My Vow

I knew I needed God, and I needed Him now. Ashamed and broken, I got down on my knees and begged Him. "Help me, Lord," I cried. "Forgive me, please forgive me, for my extramarital affair. For risking everything I loved. For pushing You out of my life."

Slowly, a peace I'd never known washed over me, proving what we all have been promised—God forgave me.

But could Allen forgive me? Could I ever forgive myself?

I knew if I trusted God, my marriage would be saved. That evening, armed with a new sense of hope, I asked my husband if we would try to work out our marriage or would we separate. With conviction he said, "I made a commitment to this marriage. I'm not going anywhere. If you want to leave, go ahead, but I'm not giving up."

I was stunned that he would want to stay, but told him I was willing to work it out as well. Then God's grace was shown through Allen when he said to me, "You are a great person. You stand up for your beliefs, and there could be no better mother for our children than you. I guess I didn't think you had any moral flaws. You made a mistake, and I forgive you."

The tears I thought I'd used up raced down my cheeks. My heart began to open up, and I wrapped my arms around my husband. I told him I would work hard to earn back his trust.

Changes began. We both agreed we needed God to be a part of our family, so we found a church and attended weekly. With the help of my newly found faith, I adjusted my attitude and began focusing on my family and all the blessings in my life. I made sure Allen knew where I was at all times and when he could expect me home. I went out of my way to prove he could trust me. His attitude changed as well. He didn't put in such long hours at work, and I could see he was really trying to get past this.

Even with all the positive changes, our relationship was still strained. The wound was still new and very deep. Life felt like a roller coaster. Everything would seem to be going along smoothly, and at any given time Allen would think about what I had done and all of the anger and hurt would surface. If the kids weren't around, he would go into a verbal rampage for a few minutes, or else he would just ignore me. I also got tired of giving a detailed itinerary every time I left the house, but knew it needed to be done. The guilt continued to weigh on my heart as I tried to maintain a positive attitude.

After a few months of emotional highs and lows, I questioned whether or not I could deal with it anymore. I wanted Allen to just forget what had happened so we could move on. It was then God showed us how to stay on the correct path. There were brochures at church giving information about an upcoming Marriage Encounter weekend. I brought it home and showed it to Allen. We decided we needed to do all we could to make our marriage work, so we signed up for the weekend.

On Friday we drove into the beautiful Rocky Mountains to a small retreat center. With our hopes high and our hearts still aching, we entered the weekend eager to heal. The days included a few large group meetings where the volunteer couples modeled good communication skills and then gave us a topic to take to our rooms to discuss. Over the course of the weekend, Allen and I rehashed recent events and talked about the kids, money, forgiveness and our future. There were a lot of tears, hugs, smiles and closeness.

On Sunday afternoon, following a short, uplifting church service, all the couples were asked to stand in a circle and face their spouses. Allen and I did as we were told. We looked at each other and smiled, unsure of what was next. The minister announced, "Today you are going to relive a special moment in your lives. You are going to renew your wedding vows." My heart skipped a beat. I wanted to do this, but was Allen ready? The men went first. My insides were shaking. Allen took my hands, lovingly smiled and with tear-filled eyes, he vowed he would "take me to be his lawful wedded wife, in sickness and in health... till death do us part." My heart opened up, and I accepted him completely. Tears welled in my eyes. It was now my turn. I swallowed the lump in my throat and looked at this man who I had put through so much pain. It was hard to believe he still loved me, but I knew at that moment that he did. I gripped his hands tighter and vowed with all my heart to love him for the rest of my life, in good times and bad.

We sealed the vows with a kiss, and I knew at that moment our life together would last. We left behind the crumpled pieces of a troubled marriage and rebuilt a stronger foundation—this time, with God in the center.

~Lyn MacKenzie
Chicken Soup for the Christian Soul 2

Meet Me at the Bridge

Hope is the feeling you have that the feeling you have isn't permanent.
~Jean Kerr

In the early years of our relationship, I found it harder and harder to walk away from a visit.... I thought a "forever" loomed in front of us before we could live our lives together. The loneliness that engulfed me as I left each visit seemed to stretch so far out that it seemed impossible to tolerate!

My husband has an incredible sense of humor. He finds the positive where only negatives seem to exist. Together, we found a way to "deal with it," not to constantly talk about next year, or three years from now. We learned to just "make it" from one visit to another... and visits became known to each of us as "the bridge!" In our correspondence, in our conversation, we refer to "making it" from one "bridge" to another. Honestly, the image of a bridge was in my mind because of a book that I and millions of others read, and then millions more flocked to see when it was made into a movie — *The Bridges of Madison County*. A "bridge" symbolized for us a special place to meet, a secret only we were sharing.

And what about that bridge? How have two hours spent at a wide table where holding hands is honestly uncomfortable (sitting in the midst of other visitors and under the watchful eyes of employees) become so special? First of all, we acknowledge that span of time is ours, and we talk. I honestly doubt that many married couples in the free world spend two whole hours at a time in their week really communicating! Elijah knows that I am sentimental, a "romantic" by nature. He kisses the palms of my hand; he takes all the blue M&Ms out of the package for me because that is my favorite color, and he unceasingly expresses gratitude. Gratitude is an attitude; I believe that! Elijah says thanks for every snack, for every mile I travel to see him — and his "thank yous" are sincere. I have learned through the years how special it can be to be genuinely appreciated! In the midst of a crowd, my wonderful husband is willing to blow me a kiss each week before he goes through a door and is out of my sight once again. It truly is the "little things" that count in life!

I truly do my best not to think about next month or next year, just the next bridge. I can recall how convinced I was that my husband would be paroled, but I don't get to vote. Setbacks have taught me to stop looking ahead and to appreciate what very little time we do have together.

Recently we tried something new that worked for us. I bought a paperback copy of *The Green Mile* for my husband, knowing that the movie would soon be released. He suggested that I buy a copy for me, too. We each read the book during the week and discussed it at our visits, and when I saw the movie, I was viewing for two. My "movie review" at our Sunday bridge was very real for my husband because we had just finished reading the book together.

Perhaps it sounds unrealistic to you, but when Elijah does come home, I want the bridge in our lives to continue. Every Sunday I want us to spend two whole uninterrupted hours talking to each other; I never want that level of communication to diminish in our marriage. I also believe that if we keep the bridge in our schedule, it will serve as a special reminder of where we came from: two people who met with glass separating them, who waited years for the first touch and the first kiss, who learned to appreciate every moment together.... For as long as we live one of us will look at the clock on Sunday afternoon and say, "Meet me at the bridge!"

~Nancy Muhammad
Chicken Soup for the Prisoner's Soul

To Begin Again

The restaurant was crowded, and I waited at the bar until my wife's and my table was called. A fire roared nearby and a real tree stood simply in the corner, covered in small white lights and nothing else. I ordered my wife a glass of wine and sipped at my draft beer while she lingered in the bathroom.

No doubt she was drying her eyes and reapplying a third coat of mascara, I thought bitterly as I remembered the heated words and nasty barbs we had exchanged on the first leg of our trip from North Carolina to Florida.

We were going home to get a divorce. There was nothing pleasant about it. Neither of us was even trying anymore.

We had pulled over at the first nice restaurant we saw. Of course, we had passed a hundred others that either hadn't lived up to her expectations or my price range. We blamed each other the more our hunger grew.

I grunted when the hostess told us that the wait was over an hour. My wife sighed and disappeared into the ladies' room.

As I chewed on stale peanuts and ordered another beer, I watched the happy couples at the bar, basking in the firelight and looking forward to the new year that they had no doubt roared in together romantically.

My wife and I had spent the first day of the new year storming around the house, dividing the CD collection and credit card bills. We had been married for four years, so there was a lot to go over.

I watched a young couple kiss. An older couple held hands. I recalled a happier time, not too long ago, when my wife and I would have been right there with them. Lingering over cocktails at the bar on purpose instead of just rushing in to get a table, eat and get it over with.

I thought of the past year and its few ups and many downs. It had started with a job transfer, and things had gone downhill from there. My wife said goodbye to her fourth-grade students, and we packed up the car and moved ten hours away. We had no friends, no family, and our first month's phone bill was enormous.

She found a job quickly and advanced easily, while I soon realized my new job was a big disappointment. She missed her family and her students, I missed my old job, and nothing worked out right. The move cost more than we expected, we rented an expensive apartment we really didn't need, and there was nothing to do in our new town but eat and watch TV. And fight....

Resentment grew with each passing month. But instead of talking to each other and sharing our problems as we had in the past, we turned to grumbling and grousing, fussing and fighting.

How could I tell her I felt unfulfilled and defeated at my new job? The job that had caused her to uproot her whole life and follow her husband to a small town in the mountains of North Carolina?

How could she tell me she hated going into work every morning and felt unfulfilled without being in a classroom?

In the end, neither of us told the other anything. When we spoke at all, it was to yell or accuse or snipe or bark.

My wife appeared at the bar, looking beautiful despite her puffy, cried-out eyes. I felt guilty at her tears, and each drop was like a knife in my heart. There was a time in our life when the thought of making her cry had brought tears to my own eyes. But now each drop was like some stupid point on an invisible scoreboard.

I watched her cross the room and felt a lurch inside my stomach as I thought of my life without her.

"How do I look?" she asked instinctively, and I had to laugh. It was a question she asked constantly, all through the day and night. An inside joke we'd shared for years, soon to be shared no more.

She thought I was laughing at her makeup, and she quickly downed her wine with a sour expression on her face that had nothing to do with the vintage.

Our last name was finally called, and we rushed through soup and rolls. Silver clinked on fancy plates and we chewed in silence. There was so much I wanted to say to her, but after all that we had decided, what was the point?

Telling her I still loved her would only make our decision that much more difficult.

After ordering dinner I excused myself to go to the men's room, stopping on the way to place a reassuring hand on her shoulder. Not surprisingly, her body clenched at my touch.

While inside the men's room I heard the door burst open behind me and then the sound of water running, but my flushing couldn't cover the sound of sobbing as I emerged from the stall.

A middle-aged man in a collared shirt and Dockers stood blubbering in front of the sink. He snuffled and snorted when he saw me, and I reached for paper towels and handed them to him in an unceremonious lump. He used them all and still the tears flowed. His face looked ruddy and flushed, and his washed-out eyes beseeched me to understand as he explained himself through his sobs.

"I'm sorry," he choked. "It's just... the tree and the lights. I thought I was ready. I thought I could do all this. But then I heard the Christmas music and I just... it's the new year already. Why do they have to keep playing them? I just couldn't do it. I'm sorry. I tried."

"Tried to do what?" I asked gently, hoping I wasn't prying. His pain seemed so intense, it was all I could do not to join him myself.

"Be... normal," he explained, blowing his nose shortly after. "My wife. You see... she died six weeks ago and I—"

"Six weeks!" I shouted, fear clutching my young heart. "I couldn't get out of bed if my wife had passed away six weeks ago." Despite the current state of affairs of my marriage, I suddenly realized this statement was all too true.

He nodded, as if I had any idea what kind of pain he was experiencing.

"I know," he nodded again. "I know. But... I managed to make it through Thanksgiving by drinking my way through a tropical cruise. I even managed to eat and sleep my way through Christmas. And... I thought I should be well by now.

"But Christmas was always her favorite. I never stopped to listen to all of those silly Christmas songs until this very night. My appetizer came, my drinks, my salad. It all just sat there while I listened to the words. Over and over. Then I just started bawling. I'm sorry, you must think me a fool."

Just then the men's room door burst open again, nearly knocking me to the ground. Two young men of college age rushed to surround the crying man. They wore expensive sweaters and grave expressions and called him "Dad."

They asked if he was all right and turned their backs to me as they cleaned their father up in private.

The small room grew crowded, and I left them to their task. I wanted to ask the man how long he and his wife had been married, but by the age of his grown sons I assumed it was well beyond twenty years.

I watched my wife's young face aglow in the candlelight, her fine hands curved around the stem of her wine glass. My legs felt leaden as I joined her at her seat, taking the chair beside her and pulling her into my arms just as the tears came.

"What's wrong?" she whispered into my hair as I clung to her chest. Her tone held no scorn, only bare and naked concern that her husband should feel pain.

After so many hateful words, so many petty barbs, I was still her husband.

"I'm sorry," I said, looking into her eyes.

Her tears spoke her truest fears, and in seconds we were tripping all over each other's apologies. Relief overflowed our hearts as we spoke.

"I'll find a job back home," I sputtered. "I'll work two jobs, whatever it takes. I miss our family, I—"

"We'll both find jobs," she joined. "You'll see. We'll be fine. We'll start all over. Last year was horrible. This year will be fresh and..."

When our apologies and plans were spent, she held me close and whispered two words in my ear: "What happened?"

But how could I explain that in one quick bathroom visit I had lost her, and then found her, all at the same time?

~Rusty Fischer
Chicken Soup for the Romantic Soul

57

The Game

Let your love be stronger than your hate or anger.
Learn the wisdom of compromise, for it is better to bend a little than to break.
~H.G. Wells

"Do you still love me?" I asked.

"I don't know." Ralph looked away.

It was a game we played again and again throughout our thirty years of married life. But today, something in his voice alarmed me. His eyes were not laughing when he said, "I don't know." This was not the way we played the game.

He was supposed to say, "Oh, I don't know" in a mocking way and then ask, "Do you still love me?"

And I would answer, with a deliberately provocative move toward him, "Mmm, let me see," then shrug regretfully and say, "I guess I don't."

Then, his brows arching mischievously he'd announce, "So what... I don't love you either. I guess I'll find another." And with head high and chest out he'd march away.

"Don't you dare find another!" I'd shake my fist and run after him. He'd turn with a start, and colliding he'd reclaim my lips in a most persuasive way and declare, "Mmm, I guess I was wrong. I guess I still love you after all."

That was the way we always played the game. But today Ralph remained uncomfortably still after uttering the words "I don't know."

Suddenly feeling as hollow as my voice sounded, I drew a deep breath, and forbidding myself to tremble, I repeated the question. "Do you still love me?" The words now seemed strange on my tongue.

And after an endless moment Ralph answered in a low, raspy voice. "I guess I don't."

A crow flashed black across the sky, its shadow skimming the earth. I was frozen into limbo where decisions and actions were impossible, where feelings were impossible. A defensive mechanism I supposed, a reflex taking over. Like a nothing I stumbled through nothingness. Pull yourself together and tell the kids, an inner voice roused my unconscious mind. What would they say?

I stood by the window with my back to John when he came into the room. "Your father and I are getting divorced."

I felt rather than saw Johnny's shocked movement. "Why?"

"Your father doesn't love me anymore, and I can't live without love. I mean I can't live with someone who... I mean...." Oh God, I mustn't cry. "Do you know what I mean?" I turned around.

There were lines of concern about John's eyes, masking his youth. He came toward me and put his arms around me. "I'm sorry, Mom. I'll always be here for you." His understanding and kind words barely registered on my numbed mind.

Peter masked his emotions with a deceptive calmness. He was a master at this. My defenses began to subside, puzzling over the feelings he was hiding.

Bobbie stiffened and didn't know what to say. I understood. She was very close to her dad. Yet her inability to show compassion threatened to shatter my last shreds of control.

Chris, our oldest, seemed not surprised. After all, divorce was the norm in today's life.

But it wasn't the norm for us. We were going to grow old together, Ralph and I. It was part of the game we always played, two old hopeless fools still in love.

Severely bent over and barely able to walk or talk, Ralph would call in a quavering voice, "Schatzi, where are you? Come here, I need a woman!" With my glasses at the tip of my nose I'd cast my eyes downward in a pretense of embarrassment and cackle, "You old devil you." Then with outstretched arms we'd shuffle towards each other in excited anticipation. But almost blind, we'd pass right by and take forever to come together, two old toothless clowns afflicted with tremors, and Ralph with a twitch. But in the end we'd always succeed. We'd lie side by side exhausted and spent, and deliriously happy we'd vow, "That's how it will be in the very end."

How long had it been since we pledged our love in this way? Lately, there was never time. Could it be that my involvement with Karen, my deceased sister's runaway child, took so much effort that I had neglected to realize Ralph's needs?

Or was Ralph merely going through male menopause?

I had waited to tell Karen last of the impending divorce. What would she say? I feared how it might affect her. Even though she was almost eighteen, she still needed a stable home.

"Huh? Don't worry! I'll stay with you." Perhaps it was the tone of unexpected casualness in her words, simple and plain, that dragged me out of my cocoon.

Karen, who for so long had been our confused, lost, tormented soul, in the hour of my greatest pain was the one who hauled me out of the depth of my despair. And I began to perceive a life without Ralph as possible.

Not long after, however, on a day in October when the valley was filled with unexpected thunder, Ralph came home early. "If you still want to see that counselor," he said, "I'll come along. Perhaps you were right. Perhaps we should give it another try."

Mystified by the unexpected, I asked, "What made you change your mind?"

And Ralph answered in a somber tone. "Yesterday, I went to look at an apartment." He paused and turned his back to me. "A very nice apartment, but all of a sudden it struck me," he turned to face me again, "you wouldn't be there when I would come home."

I gasped a sigh of relief, and while collecting the fragments of my heart I began to envision the possibility of, once again, playing the game.

~Christa Holder Ocker
Chicken Soup for the Unsinkable Soul

Chapter 8

Happily Ever After

Live, Love, Laugh!

We cannot really love anybody with whom we never laugh.
~Agnes Repplier

58

Happy Valentine's Day, Dear. Here's Your Mesh Body Stocking.

If love is blind, why is lingerie so popular?
~Author Unknown

Christmas is officially over. Today I dragged the tree with its fifteen remaining needles out to the curb, tied the Christmas lights into one great big ball like I found them, and dumped the odd remains of two ham-a-ramas and a jalapeño cheese log into the cat's dish, which caused him to immediately jump up onto the telephone stand and look up the address for the Humane Society's self-admittance wing.

But it's done. Kaput. Finé. The yuletide has ebbed. And not a moment too soon, because now it's time for... Valentine's Day.

Not to worry though, because this year I'm ready. Last February I was fooled by the pact my wife and I made that we weren't going to bother with Valentine's Day. What I thought she meant was that she didn't expect a gift. What she really meant was that only a chump would think it was okay not to get his wife—who was put on this earth for no greater reason than to serve her husband's every need, although said husband could count on serving certain needs himself until further notice—a gift.

And even though it was quite a bonding experience camping out in my backyard in February with my brother-in-law, who had wondered why everyone was buying flowers on Washington's birthday, I think I'd rather spend the rainy season inside this year.

So I grabbed the garbage bag full of Christmas cards and wrapping paper to drop off at the local landfill and headed off to the Hallmark store—that magical place full of those beautiful poetic musings that women love. I settled on a card with a romantic, soft-focus photograph of a young couple laughing and hugging in a wooded glen, taken no doubt just seconds before they realized they were standing waist deep in poison oak.

Then I headed across the mall to the lingerie store. The place was mobbed with guys all holding intimate apparel, trying to picture their wives in them. One guy was holding his selection upside down wondering, I suspect, why the thing had snaps at the neck. I was about to explain when a saleslady approached wearing a button that said "All Our Bras Are Half Off." She looked frazzled. Her hair was mussed. Her makeup was smeared, and she had bags under her eyes.

"Let me guess," she said. "Gift for the wife?"

Before I could compliment her on such a quick assessment of the situation, she moved me to one side and yelled over my shoulder. "Please don't mix the satin panties up with the silk ones."

Two guys, who were each holding a dozen pair of panties, smiled sheepishly, like they just got caught during a midnight raid at the female dorms.

"I hate Valentine's Day," she muttered. Then with a forced smile she asked, "So, what did you have in mind?"

"I dunno. Something sexy, I guess."

"Novel idea. What's her favorite color?"

"Uhh... brown?"

"Brown? Brown's her favorite color?"

"Green?"

"You don't know, do you?"

"Well, our cat is gray and white and she likes him a lot." I thought briefly about the cat and wondered if he'd still be there when I got home. Meanwhile, the saleslady moved me to one side again.

"Sir. Siiirrrr."

A large, bald man in a three-piece suit glanced up.

"It's Velcro," she said. "As you have no doubt observed, it will make that same sound over and over."

She shook her head, turned her attention back to me and was about to speak when a tall, thin guy approached us wearing a teddy over his T-shirt and boxer shorts.

"Whaddya think?" he asked.

I thought the red was a little too bright for his complexion and was about to say so when the saleslady jumped up onto a clearance counter and addressed the entire store.

"Okay. Here's what we are going to do. I want every one of you to take out the amount of money you want to spend and step up to the counter. I will hand you an item that costs that amount of money. Do not worry about the color or size. Your wives will be in here to exchange your gifts tomorrow. Now, who's first?"

We all hesitated. She held up her watch.

"The mall closes in fifteen minutes, gentlemen, and they are predicting a particularly cold February this year."

I thought I caught a whiff of damp tent. Then I quickly took out my wallet and got in line.

~Ernie Witham
Chicken Soup for the Romantic Soul

59

Dumbo

I was the nurse caring for the couple's newborn first child after his cesarean birth. Since the mother was asleep under general anesthesia, the pediatrician and I took our tiny charge directly to the newborn nursery, where we introduced the minutes-old baby to his daddy. While cuddling his son for the first time, he immediately noticed the baby's ears conspicuously standing out from his head. He expressed his concern that some kids might taunt his child, calling him names like "Dumbo" after the fictional elephant with unusually large ears. The pediatrician examined the baby and reassured the new dad that his son was healthy—the ears presented only a minor cosmetic problem, which could be easily corrected during early childhood.

The father was finally optimistic about his child, but was still worried about his wife's reaction to those large protruding ears.

"She doesn't take things as easily as I do," he worried.

By this time, the new mother was settled in the recovery room and ready to meet her new baby. I went along with the dad to lend some support in case this inexperienced mother became upset about her baby's large ears. The infant was swaddled in a receiving blanket with the head covered for the short trip through the chilly air-conditioned corridor. I placed the tiny bundle in his mother's arms and eased the blanket back so that she could gaze upon her child for the first time.

She took one look at her baby's face and looked to her husband and gasped, "Oh, Honey! Look! He has your ears!"

~Laura Vickery Hart
Chicken Soup for the Nurse's Soul

Ticketless Travel

You can discover more about a person in an hour of play than
in a year of conversation.
~-Plato

 y friend's brother, Cliff, is a very serious, dignified man, so his actions at an airport's check-in counter were totally unexpected.

It seems that he and his wife were placing their baggage on the conveyor when her purse accidentally fell onto the moving belt. She scrambled after it but it eluded her, so she climbed onto the belt to try to reach it.

Just as she was about to disappear through the doorway with the baggage, Cliff began to wave frantically, "No, no dear!" he shouted. "It's okay! This time we bought tickets."

~Jim Feldman
Chicken Soup for the Traveler's Soul

Level the Playing Field

Kindness is the greatest wisdom.
~Author Unknown

My husband, Terry, had performed the 6:00 A.M. and midnight wet-to-dry dressings on my abdomen and chest for several months. I battled post-operative gangrene following mastectomies and reconstruction surgery six months earlier. What was supposed to be an eight-day hospital stay and single surgery had turned into four surgeries, three months in the hospital, and then a nursing home because of aggressive infections and related complications. Now, visiting nurses came to our home twice each day while Terry was at work.

I knew living with me had not been a picnic. My pain and immobility kept me housebound and frustrated. I'm sure Terry wondered why he pulled so many strings to get me out of the nursing home early.

One night, we had an argument. It wasn't over anything significant, but it was the first since the surgeries. By bedtime, we had yet to make up. Terry still had the complicated dressing changes to complete. He had no medical training, but the nurses had taught him how to clean and dress the wounds that covered my front from hip to armpit.

Terry helped me roll onto my side. I sensed the tension in the air and still felt hurt from our disagreement. I didn't know how he felt, because he is quiet when upset. That night was no different.

I looked up at him and said, "This isn't fair. I feel too vulnerable here with nothing on while you take care of my wounds when you're still mad at me."

He walked away. A few minutes later he returned and stood in front of me, still silent with a half-smile on his face. He was stark naked.

"Terry, what are you doing?" I shrieked with laughter.

"Just leveling the playing field," he smirked—then tenderly changed my dressing.

~Linda S. Lee
Chicken Soup for the Caregiver's Soul

62

Drive and Determination

*Laughter is the sensation of feeling good all over
and showing it principally in one place.*
~Josh Billings

have to admit that I have never played golf. In fact, the only golf course that I have ever been on ended with me trying to hit the ball into a clown's mouth. That's why it is so strange that the game of golf had such an impact on my life.

I was nineteen years old and had just started dating a young man who I had met at work. We seemed to have chemistry together and both shared a love of competition. A lot of our time with each other was spent bowling or playing arcade games like pinball or Pac Man. Being a '70s kind of girl, I was determined to prove my capabilities and be an equal and worthy opponent. As it turned out, our skills were fairly evenly matched. We were both thoroughly enjoying our playful competitions.

One day, he came to my house dressed casually as always. Searching for something different to do he asked, "Have you ever been to a driving range?" I thought, My God! A driving range? What does he want to do now, race cars? He explained that he was talking about driving golf balls, not cars. Well, I had never tried it before, but surely it must be simple. After all, if I can hurl a fourteen-pound ball fifty feet down a lane and knock down ten sticklike pins at the far end, how difficult could it be to swing a club and hit a tiny ball perched right at my feet? I was confident that this little activity would not damage my athletic image, so off we went to the driving range.

We arrived at Bill's Golfland & Family Fun Park—a virtual megaplex of batting cages, arcades, go carts, mini-golf and, of course, our chosen destination, the driving range. After selecting our clubs, buying our balls and several embarrassing moments of scrambling to gather the bouncing balls that I spilled out of the top of the bucket, we were ready to start.

After brief instructions from my date, I then set out to prove my abilities. The first five or ten swings I took were either total misses or full-force collisions between my club and the rubber mat on the tee. I received more instruction from my teacher.

"Keep your eye on the ball."

"Bring the club back slowly."

Okay, there were a few more useless attempts and then... CONTACT! The ball took air and landed just shy of the fifty-yard marker, but it was a start! Over the next hour or so, it didn't get much better than that. Balls trickled off their mount and rolled into the grass in front of my station. Several fell off their tee, in a delayed reaction, caused by the wind from my swing passing its target. I admit it was pathetic, definitely not the piece of cake that I had imagined.

Each time that I turned to pick up a new ball from my bucket, I would catch sight of onlookers (a crowd was beginning to gather) wearing Titleist caps and Spalding sun visors. There were heads shaking and eyes rolling. Occasionally, I would hear a comment like, "Your feet are too far apart," or, "Bend your knees." I felt the pressure mounting. An audience formed behind me. To each side of me, a row of fellow golfers quested after swing perfection. In front of me, golf balls were flying through the air and landing at the 200-, 250- and even the 300-yard markers. At my feet the tiny white ball, which I thought would pose no challenge whatsoever, had grown fangs and horns. The sphere was sneering up at me, as if to say, "I showed you."

Snap out of it! I thought. You have a brain; IT does not. After all, the ball is just a lifeless piece of rubber that I command where to go. I felt a rush of determination come over me. I took a deep breath and repeated all of the directions to myself.

"Feet shoulder-width apart."

"Knees slightly bent."

"Bring the club back slowly."

"Keep your eye on the ball."

"Smooth and steady swing."

"Finish with your hands towards the target."

With an air of confidence, I approached the ball. I carefully acted out each mental step-by-step instruction. Before I knew it, I found myself following through with my swing with absolute perfection. My concentration was broken by the sound of whack. I raised my head to see the ball soaring through the air. I actually lost it in the sun's glare for a while, before it fell to earth somewhere around the 300-yard marker!

"Yes!" It was perfect! I jumped. I screamed. I rejoiced at my success.

I arrogantly turned to my date, "Did you see that? I knew I could do it!"

The laughter of my companion quickly dampened my celebration. He pointed to my tee, where my ball was still perched, tauntingly sticking its tongue out at me. The incredible 300-yard drive that I was claiming credit for actually belonged to the golfer on my left (who, by the way, was also laughing). The audience that had gathered began to chuckle, as did the range attendant. After taking several bows and curtsies, I quietly and humbly returned to my futile attempts at hitting a golf ball.

Needless to say, I never made it to the LPGA. The man who was my date that day became my husband and the father of my children. My determination, his patience and an ability to laugh at life, the very characteristics that we showed each other that day during the driving range episode, are qualities that have been the basis for a long, happy, strong and successful marriage. We occasionally return to the driving range with our two teenage sons. But now, when we go, it's not to prove anything or to compete with each other. It's strictly for the fun of it.

~Darlene Daniels Eisenhuth
Chicken Soup for the Golfer's Soul Second Round

63

Sleeping Through the Sermon

You can't deny laughter; when it comes,
it plops down in your favorite chair and stays as long as it wants.
~Stephen King, Hearts in Atlantis

I was the pastor of a small church in a rural community. Wilbur and his wife, Leah, attended every Sunday morning. Wilbur was a farmer, and whenever he came into the house from the field and sat down, he would fall asleep. It was such a habit that when he came into church and sat in the pew he would also soon fall asleep. I discovered that some of the members of the church were taking bets to see how long I could keep Wilbur awake on Sunday mornings.

Wilbur's wife was embarrassed by his behavior, especially when he began to snore. She tried everything to keep her sleepy spouse awake. She complained to him that she was getting calluses on her elbow from poking him in the ribs in a futile attempt to keep him alert. One day while shopping in the grocery store, she saw a small bottle of Limburger cheese. Leah bought it and dropped it in her purse.

The next Sunday morning I had just started the sermon when Wilbur began to nod. When I finished the first point in my three-point sermon, I could see I was losing him. As I started the third point, Wilbur began to snore. Quietly, Leah opened her purse, took out the bottle of Limburger cheese and held it under her husband's nose. It worked. Wilbur sat up straight and, in a voice that could be heard all over the church, said, "Leah, will you please keep your feet on your own side of the bed!"

~William Webber
Chicken Soup for the Christian Family Soul

Moving In with Frank

A hundred men may make an encampment,
but it takes a woman to make a home.
~Chinese Proverb

Although a bright and able man, my husband is almost completely helpless when faced with even the simplest domestic chore. One day, in exasperation, I pointed out to him that our friend, Beaa, had taught her husband, Frank, to cook, sew and do laundry, and that if anything ever happened to Beaa, Frank would be able to care for himself. Then I said, "What would you do if anything happened to me?"

After considering that possibility for a moment, my husband said happily, "I'd move in with Frank."

~LaVonne Kincaid
Chicken Soup for the Romantic Soul

My Love Is Like a Red, Red Marker

am, admittedly, a hopeless romantic. Not surprisingly, then, when my husband and I celebrated our anniversary recently, I bought him one dozen red permanent markers. These are, after all, the traditional gift for the man who spends many of his waking hours drawing shapes on the toes of his white tube socks.

Why does he do this? Because, he explains, for every white tube sock there is only one perfect partner. To preserve these sacred unions, my spouse assigns each pair its own symbol—a triangle, a square, a stick-figure wife throwing up her arms in despair.

For a man who on more than one occasion has mended his clothing with a staple gun, such conscientious sock matching seems strange. Just the same, I admit I find my husband's little eccentricities endearing and often make note of them in a growing file labeled "Mounting Evidence."

One recent entry reads: "Today husband is very happy. Seems the supermarket is having a buy-one/get-one-free rump-roast extravaganza. Spouse believes a freezer should always contain enough meat to host an intimate barbecue for all branches of the U.S. military."

I could understand hoarding power tools. Or fishing equipment. But discounted cuts of meat? My husband wasn't deprived of food as a child. He doesn't overbuy generally. And, to my knowledge, frozen hunks of beef do not increase in value over time.

His other fixations are no more easily understood. Take this recent notation:

"Today husband is mad at me. In what can only be described as a wild crime spree, I removed sixty-six cents from his change dish, in order to purchase two postage stamps."

To my husband, loose change is not actual, usable money, but some sort of endangered species he is determined to preserve. Every night he lovingly removes all coins from his pockets, and then gently places them in the dish. When the dish is full, he separates the change and stores it in large containers at an undisclosed location in our garage. As I understand it, the plan is to buy even larger containers at some point.

The Mounting Evidence file continues to grow with each tender entry. But yesterday, it closed with this startling observation: "Today husband claimed I'm sexy. Hmmm. Make sure to carefully match his socks, overstock the freezer and self-fund all future stamp purchases."

~Carrie St. Michel
Chicken Soup for the Bride's Soul

66

Last Outing

We love because it's the only true adventure.
~Nikki Giovanni

*I*looked out of my tent, and the snow was coming down so hard that I couldn't see a thing. It was blowing sideways and had already drifted up one side of my tent. It was cold, very cold. It must have been twenty or thirty degrees below zero. Why was I out there?

Snow in Michigan by the first of November is not unheard of, but this was a downright blizzard. I was sure this would be an all-time record. Thirty-two degrees and a foot of snow can be a beautiful, pleasant experience. This was not!

What is it about me that makes me do these things? Why do I take these chances? I love the outdoors, the sounds of the wild, the sunrises and sunsets, everything that you can only experience by getting outdoors and camping. I have all of the equipment to stay warm and dry in any weather, but this was ridiculous.

I was wishing that I had not ventured out that weekend, but there I was, and I was going to have to survive! The wind was making my tent snap and flap so hard and so loud that sleep was totally out of the question. My goosedown sleeping bag was supposed to be good to minus ten degrees, but I was already shivering quite a bit.

My last meal had been the night before, and it was going on 11 A.M. I hadn't eaten any breakfast, and I didn't have anything with me in the tent. My energy wouldn't last much longer.

My wife, Amy, was probably worried about me, too. She had warned me last night that it was going to be cold and windy. She is so loving that I know she would have joined me if I had asked her to. But I told her not to bother, that I just wanted to get this one last outing out of my system. She was probably snuggled up in front of the fireplace with a good book. I wished I were with her. I had carried a couple of my magazines along thinking I would read by flashlight, but I was too cold to enjoy reading about bass fishing.

With that thought, I knew I had to get out of there. My original plan was to try to wait out the blizzard, but I realized that wouldn't work. I was cold, and I was hungry. I would freeze or starve to death before this one was over. But how should I do it?

Should I try to take everything with me? I hated to abandon my equipment, but it would have taken too long to break down the tent, and the sleeping bag is too bulky if it isn't rolled up tight and stuffed in its bag. My hands were too cold to do that, and it's almost impossible to do with gloves on. I was sure my things would be all right here for a while. I would carry what I could and leave the rest behind.

I took another peek out the flap, and a blast of wind with tiny ice darts smacked me in the face. This wasn't going to be as easy as I thought. At thirty below your skin can freeze in a matter of minutes. Once that happens, well, I wasn't going to think about that.I was ready to make a run for it. I wasn't in great shape, and I couldn't run far, but I was afraid that if I walked I would freeze before I got there. I looked around inside the tent one last time to make sure I wasn't forgetting anything critical. It took a couple of seconds to get my glove around the tent zipper, but when I did, it jerked straight up to the ceiling, and I bolted out into the frozen landscape.

The snow was deep, but light. I kicked my way through the snow. How far would I have to run? Could I make it all the way? I was almost out of breath when I hit the back door of the house and burst through.

"Hi, honey, how did you sleep?" asked Amy. "I thought that bit of snow and wind we had last night might have woken you up sooner.

Are you going to bring the tent in from the backyard, or will you want to sleep out again?"

~James Hert
Chicken Soup for the Nature Lover's Soul

67

No Response

A good laugh and a long sleep are the best cures in the doctor's book.
~Irish Proverb

It was the third day my husband, Joe, had been in the intensive care unit following his fifth surgery for the removal of most of his remaining small intestine. The surgery took many more hours than expected. Joe was older and weaker, and he wasn't responding.

As I sat beside his bed, two nurses tried repeatedly to get him to cough, open his eyes, move a finger—anything to let them know he could hear them. He didn't respond. I sat praying to God to please help Joe respond—any sign that he might survive.

Finally, one of the nurses turned to me and suggested that perhaps if she knew something personal about our family, she could try to stimulate his response with that knowledge. She said, "Maybe you, as his daughter, could help us with such information." I smiled and said, "I'll be happy to give you personal information, and thank you for the compliment, but I'm his wife of forty-three years, not his daughter, and we're about the same age." The nurse looked at me and said, "The entire staff thought you were his daughter and had even commented how wonderful they thought it was that his daughter was with him all the time."

As they were expressing how I looked so young, a little cough came from my husband, and we all turned to stare at him. He didn't open his eyes, but loud and clear he said, "She dyes her hair!"

~Donna Parisi
Chicken Soup for the Caregiver's Soul

Chapter
9

Finding the Right Mate

It is the woman who chooses the man who will choose her
~Paul Géraldy

A Cure for Cold Feet

Winter finals were over, and the entire campus was ecstatic with relief. No more cramming, caffeine highs, tension headaches and cramped desks. We were free! We left campus en masse in the unusually crisp Seattle night, light on our feet, letting our hair down and our shirttails out. We were all going to the local dance club, the only place in the area that could accommodate a few hundred post-finals students who were ready to let loose. We squeezed ourselves into tight jeans and miniskirts, exposed some legs and bellies, and virtually wriggled with excitement. The music was loud and provocative, the figures on the dance floor sensuous, wild. The electricity was heart-stopping.

I looked pretty heart-stopping myself, poured into a barebacked white satin pantsuit with three-inch heels and a rose in my hair. Unfortunately, it wasn't my date's heart that was stopping. It was mine. More specifically, it was being bored to death. My date was Dumbe, a native of Cameroon, West Africa. Granted, it was our first date, so I hadn't really known anything about him, but I had thought we would at least enjoy the rhythm on the dance floor.

Multicolored strobe lights flashed over the table in our booth, and we had to yell to make conversation over the DJ's voice. I was bobbing and swaying to the music, frantic to get out on the dance floor—and Dumbe was telling me about his plans for the next few days: going to the bookstore to get a head start on his reading for next semester. I began to think maybe this wasn't going to work.

"It's important to get the majority of your science classes out of the way before you go on to the university," Dumbe yelled over the thumping on the dance floor.

It's important for me to get out of here, I thought. By now it was midnight, and even the shy kids who didn't know how to dance had finally jumped out on the dance floor. Dumbe and I were still talking about college credits.

"Let's go," I called out. Dumbe looked surprised.

"Are you sure you want to leave?"

Apparently, the look on my face was answer enough. This was definitely not working.

Dumbe politely drew open the door to the dance club and let me out. To our surprise, a three-inch blanket of snow had fallen, and our ears buzzed from the sudden change from the noise of the club as we stepped out into a soft, quiet wonderland.

It was beautiful. It was cold. And I was wearing three-inch heels with thin stockings.

The winter weather had caught the city by surprise; no buses or cabs were running. Dumbe didn't have a car, so with an exasperated sigh, I pointed the way home and we started our slippery trek through the streets. Dumbe shoved his hands deep into his pockets to keep them warm. I, in my bare-backed suit and flimsy heels, looked like the snow queen within fifteen minutes. I stumbled, and Dumbe reached to catch me.

"This, too, is not working," I said, laughing at the fiasco.

Dumbe looked up and saw a tiny restaurant that was still open. A rush of warmth blew at us when we opened the door. The customers were huddled close together, talking in hushed tones that matched the weather outside.

Dumbe ordered two hot chocolates, and we sat down. Ah, now we can talk a little more about scholarly habits, I thought morosely. I looked ridiculous in my outfit, and I was still frozen solid. Dumbe, however, didn't start any conversation this time. He watched me swallow a few, steamy sips, and then asked me to take off my heels.

I did, puzzled. He pulled his chair up close to mine, lifted my blue feet into his lap, and gently began to rub them between his hands, easing away the numbness and ache of the cold. I watched him, speechless.

"There, that should feel better," he said. He looked into my eyes and didn't say a word about classes or books. "You look beautiful," he said.

I smiled, and flushed a little, pulling away.

"Wait a minute," Dumbe said. He threw some napkins on the floor, then gently set my feet down on them. He slipped off his own boots, and took off his thick, warm socks. They were still dry.

He slipped the socks onto my own feet, then stood up and draped his sports jacket over my shoulders. The look he gave me when he smiled thawed me from the inside out.

"Come on," he said, turning to leave. "Hop up on my back. I'll give you a ride, and you can keep those pretty feet of yours dry."

I was so stunned I did what he said, and we stumbled our way up the four or five hills back to my dorm. By the time we got there, we were both laughing, talking freely about ourselves. I had completely forgotten about the dance. All I could think about was how gentle Dumbe was, yet strong, how quiet he was, yet full of dreams.

Before Dumbe left me in the lobby of my building, I reached down to return his socks.

"No," Dumbe said. "I'd feel a lot warmer knowing they were still on your feet."

He gave me a hug, waved goodbye, and moved slowly down the street. I stood there in his socks, virtually pulsating warmth, watching him till he was out of sight.

It's a routine we've kept for eighteen years now, Dumbe and I. That first night was four college degrees ago for the two of us, but no matter where my husband, Dumbe, is going, I follow him to the door, hug him, and stand there in his socks, watching him move down the street till he's out of sight. It warms me down to my toes.

~Pamela Elessa
Chicken Soup for the Single's Soul

Love and War

People always want to know who won.

When I tell them my husband and I met when we were opposing attorneys on a case, that's always their first question.

"Who won?"

"You decide," I say. Then I tell them the rest.

I was an aggressive young associate, newly hired by my law firm and anxious to prove myself. John was a seasoned pro who worked for another law firm in the same building. When I found out he was opposing counsel, I was nervous. I'd seen his name on countless appellate decisions and knew he was far more adept at this type of case than I was. I decided that what I lacked in skill and experience, I would make up for with hard work and bravado.

I devised a campaign of daily badgering: discovery requests, legal motions, correspondence, phone calls. If I wasn't satisfied with how quickly he responded, I walked down the hall and pestered him in person. I was relentless—a terrier yipping at his heels. My client and my boss loved it.

But somewhere along the way I started to like him. Maybe it was the way he overlooked my obvious lack of sophistication and treated me like a serious adversary. Maybe it was our verbal sparring that often left me walking away with a stupid grin, as though we'd been flirting instead of arguing. Whatever the reason, after a few months on the case, I decided my adversary was a decent guy. If we'd met under difference circumstances, I might want to see where the flirting could go. But since we were opposing counsel, ethics prevented us from becoming personally involved. Romance was out of the question.

One Friday afternoon, John left his office without giving me a set of documents I needed to review over the weekend. I tracked him down at home and demanded he turn over the materials to me that day.

"All right," he said, "I'll have them at my house tonight."

Skeptical, but not wanting to back down, I said, "Fine. I'll be there at 7:00."

That night changed everything.

Some people claim an instant familiarity with a place or a stranger, convinced they must have been there or known each other before. Walking into John's house, what I felt was not déjà vu, but more a sense of how things could be. I felt instantly at home, as I never have any place before or since.

The house was small, with wood floors and walls decorated with a strange combination of quilts and antlers. The furniture looked lived-in without being shabby. The place was modest, warm and comfortable—not at all like some of the palatial showcases I'd seen other lawyers strut through.

Seeing him in that environment, I felt more comfortable around John, too. Even though it was his house, it felt like neutral ground. I didn't have to act so tough anymore. I sank onto his couch and felt myself relax.

"So what's your story?" I asked, and he gave me a brief sketch of his life.

My answer to the same question was much briefer: "Work. That's all I do."

"I used to be like you," John said. "Trust me—it can't last. You need other things." He told me he was happiest when he was backpacking or sailing, running the power tools in his workshop, or simply puttering in his vegetable garden on the weekends. What a curious idea. I had always thought weekends were for more work.

I wished I were there under other circumstances. I wanted to talk longer. I wanted to know him better. But eventually duty called. I stood and held out my hand for the papers.

"I don't have them yet. Let's take a ride."

He drove me in his nine-year-old Honda station wagon (more bonus points—a modest car) to a house a few miles away.

"Come on," John coaxed. I followed him to the door.

John's client answered. It's hard to say who was more shocked, the client or me.

"You know Elizabeth," John said. His client raised an eyebrow, but politely shook my hand. Then he handed John the papers I'd wanted. John handed them to me.

Years later John confessed that what he'd really wanted to say when his client opened the door was, "Look! I have captured their queen!"

And it was true, he had.

My way had always been to rush into a relationship then see it flame out a month or so later. That couldn't happen this time. Being on opposite sides of a case forced me to get to know him slowly. I had the chance to see his character in action—his integrity, loyalty, honesty. By the time our romance began, I was already sold.

We had two choices: Wait until the case was over to pursue a relationship, or plunge ahead. If we weren't going to wait, one of us would have to withdraw from the case.

The next day I told my boss. He promptly fired me.

John's client still swears he paid John to date me, just to get me off the case. He says they both knew I was trouble.

Another lawyer took over for me and eventually the case settled. By then John and I had already been married three years. Good thing we didn't wait.

John and I have been married ten years now. We still live in the house where I felt so at home that night. There are still quilts and ant-lers on the wall, and we've only just now replaced the couch where I sat one Friday evening and wished I could know this man better. I still badger my husband at times, and he digs in his heels when I'm wrong. Ours is a marriage of negotiations and compromise, of flirting when we seem to be arguing. A worthy opponent, it turns out, makes a wonderful spouse.

So who won?

No doubt about it: I did.

~Elizabeth Rand
Chicken Soup for the Working Woman's Soul

New Year's Eve Dilemma

Don't refuse to go on an occasional wild goose chase —
that's what wild geese are for.
~Author Unknown

*N*ew Year's Eve was only a week away, and I didn't have even the prospect of a date for that important beginning to the New Year. Was the rest of the year going to be like this? Sitting in front of the television with my mother and younger brother watching other people enjoy themselves?

Six months ago, I had moved from the lush southeast coast to this desolate part of west Texas, in order to live with my mom while I recuperated from a serious motorcycle accident. Now that I was able to work again, I planned to hightail it back to God's country as soon as I was able to save enough money.

In the meantime, here I was, a twenty-one-year-old with a possible New Year's Eve at home looming in front of me. "Don't just sit there," an inner voice prompted me. "Do something." Usually, the thought of a blind date would have made me shudder, but I was determined not to spend the night in front of the TV.

I picked up the phone and called Penny, someone I'd met here who seemed to know a lot of people in town. Penny said she'd give the matter some thought and get back to me if anyone came to mind.

Two days later, she called back. A former coworker, who didn't know she was recently engaged, had asked her out for New Year's Eve. When she explained that she was no longer available, he asked if she had a friend to whom she could introduce him. "He's divorced with custody of his two kids, pretty clean-cut, and doesn't do drugs," she told me. Nervously, I accepted—then spent the next week regretting my impulsiveness. Several times, I almost picked up the phone to cancel.

But I made it through the week, and, finally, the night arrived. Now I couldn't decide how to dress. Would he expect casual or a dress and heels? About thirty minutes before he was due to arrive, I called Penny in a panic. What should I wear? Penny said she didn't think he was the "formal type." What did that mean, not the formal type? Now I was really confused. I finally settled on what I considered to be a happy medium, slacks and a sweater.

The doorbell rang. Should I answer the door myself, or ask my younger brother Jerry to get it? I sighed as I walked to the door, mentally composing various excuses that would allow me to exit the evening gracefully should it prove disastrous. Fixing a smile on my face, I opened the door.

I stopped short and stared as I took in the Stetson hat, western shirt, long blue-jeans-clad legs, and pointed-toe boots. A cowboy! My date was a cowboy! Then my gaze swept back up to his face, and I found myself looking into the greenest eyes I had ever seen, eyes full of laughter at the expression on my face.

I stuttered "hello" and politely held out my hand. Jerry struggled to contain his laughter, while I struggled to regain my composure. We chatted briefly, and suddenly I didn't care where we went or what we did.

Over dinner, we never seemed to run out of things to talk about. And I found my eyes kept coming back to those green eyes and that smiling mouth. After dinner, he took me to an action movie. I forgot to warn him how actively I participate in action adventures. He laughed as I screamed, hid my eyes and cowered in my seat, and lifted my feet off the floor when insects or rodents appeared on the screen. I think the really big adventure for him was watching me react to the show.

When the movie was over, he said he had to get home. I wondered if this was a brush-off. I also wondered if he would kiss me goodnight on this first date. He had been such a perfect gentleman the entire evening, he'd probably just shake my hand, and maybe I'd never see him again. I realized how much I wanted that goodnight kiss. Would he think I was too forward if I kissed him first? Would it drive him away, or bring him back? Once again, I was in an agony of indecision!

When we arrived at my house, he walked me to the door, came in for a moment, then turned to leave. What the heck? I thought to myself. Go for broke. I followed him out to his car and asked for that goodnight kiss. He obliged, and, lightheaded, I floated back to the house, hoping I would hear from him again.

I did. The next morning, early, he called. He liked me, too! Fifty-six days later, we became husband and wife. That was twenty-one years ago, and even after all these years together, his kisses still make me lightheaded.

Never underestimate the power of a blind date.

~Judith L. Robinson
Chicken Soup for the Single's Soul

Beautiful Music

If you're never scared or embarrassed or hurt,
it means you never take any chances.
~Julia Sorel (Rosalyn Drexler), See How She Runs, 1978

aulette, a divorced mother of two, began volunteering at a state prison in 1992 by helping organize a speaking group for the inmates. After a few months, she was asked by the prison chaplain if she would consider joining the prison choir—The Heavenly Voices. Loving to sing, or as she puts it, "making a joyful noise," she jumped at the chance to join the all-inmate, all-male choir. It wasn't long before Paulette became an integral part of the choir members' lives as well—writing letters for them, contacting family members on their behalf, or just listening when they needed to talk.

One of the inmates she grew close to was Reggie. In 1990, Reggie had received a twenty-year sentence for drug trafficking. Because of his incredible voice and ability to command respect, he soon became the director of the prison choir. The choir rehearsed every day, and the members had to be particularly dedicated in order to belong. In addition to concerts and programs, they sometimes put on plays or had special anniversary parties for some of the members. The choir became a family of sorts within the confines of the prison walls.

In 1997, Reggie had his sentence reduced and was ordered to attend a drug and alcohol treatment program that assisted inmates in their transition back to society. Reggie was instructed to find someone to be his "host" during the program. He wrote letters to three people he thought would accept the responsibility, but he only received one reply—from Paulette.

During their years in the choir together, Paulette had grown to respect Reggie and she didn't feel that she could refuse his request. After passing inspection by the state as an appropriate host, Paulette was cleared to assist Reggie in his journey back into society. At first, restricted by the few free hours he had a week, Paulette's responsibilities were merely to act as Reggie's taxi driver to choir rehearsals, as The Heavenly Voices also had an "outside" choir made up of several ex-inmates and their wives. Soon, however, Reggie had more and more free hours as the intensive transition counseling began to lessen. Paulette often included him in family events. She heard from more than one relative and friend that she and Reggie made a "perfect" couple.

Her first reaction was to laugh off these comments, but she soon found herself more and more anxiously awaiting Reggie's weekend visits. She told herself it was because he was such a dear friend, one whose company she cherished. It wasn't until the day that Reggie was to be released from the program that she realized the true extent of her feelings.

She and her teenage son arrived at the halfway house at 5:45 A.M. to pick up Reggie and his belongings and to take him to live in the basement apartment of her home. Instead, she was told that Reggie still had something on his record in his home state. Reggie was taken back to prison for possible extradition. Paulette, usually calm and in control, began to cry. She got in her car and raced home to begin a series of phone calls to find someone to help Reggie with this new legal entanglement. Ultimately, Reggie was delayed for only another week before being released into Paulette's custody. She realized then that she could no longer hide her feelings for him.

Although it had taken her more than five years, Paulette had finally realized that she had slowly but surely fallen in love with Reggie. If he hadn't known her feelings before, Reggie certainly knew when Paulette kissed him the day he was released. Paulette braced herself for the negative comments she was sure would come her way, but not one family member or friend said anything negative. It seemed Reggie had won the hearts of everyone in Paulette's life, including her son's and daughter's.

Reggie and Paulette were married on Valentine's Day 1999 and are still making beautiful music together with The Heavenly Voices. Some would argue that the chain of events that brought Reggie and Paulette together was just coincidence or fate, but Paulette firmly believes God planned it from the start. How else would Reggie have had a long prison sentence miraculously shortened?

Reggie is now serving a life sentence with the woman who is, above all else, his best friend.

~Kimberly Raymer
Chicken Soup for the Prisoner's Soul

Catch and Release

I'm a guy with a passion for the outdoors. I spend most of my free time fishing. I have waders, both hip and chest neoprenes for stream fishing, two small fishing boats, and two Honda trolling motors to go with them. Of course one can't fish during winter without the appropriate ice fishing gear—ice fishing tent, propane heater and lantern, ice auger, micro-light fishing poles, ice fishing tackle box to sit on, extreme Artic cold weather gear, mittens, the works.

About ten years ago, my next door neighbor invited me over for Christmas Eve dinner. He happened to mention that his single, twenty-eight-year-old niece might be there. At the appointed time I arrived at his home, was introduced to his niece and her family, and we had a pleasant chat and turkey dinner with all the trimmings.

This girl seemed very nice, and the following day I asked my neighbor for her phone number. I called her and asked if she would like to go out.

"I would love to," she replied to my offer of dinner and a movie.

Dinner was pleasant, and she was easy to talk with. She even asked what I liked to do. I replied that I was an avid outdoorsman. I suggested for our next date we visit my comfort zone. I invited her ice fishing.

The following Saturday arrived, and I picked her up in my old '75 Dodge Ram Charger, four-wheel drive with a pop-up camper.

When we arrived at the frozen reservoir, I broke out the snow shoes and strapped them on both of us, filled the sled with all the gear, and off we went trudging through four feet of snow for probably a third of a mile.

We found an abandoned hole, so I didn't even have to drill a new one with the auger. I set up the tent, lit the lantern, set out a folding chair for her and pulled out a fat, juicy night crawler to place on the hook. I suspected she had never fished before when she grimaced as I impaled the night crawler with all three barbs on my size-14 treble hook.

From this point on events happened very fast. I flipped open the wire bail on my reel to allow the night crawler to sink to the bottom. As soon as the bait hit the bottom, my little micro-light bent at a ninety degree angle right at the rod handle, straight down the hole. I had never before had a hit like this. The fish was pulling so hard that I was sure the six-pound test would not stand the strain. "Quick, adjust the drag for me!" I pleaded.

"What's a drag?" she replied.

"That little wheel at the back of my reel," I said. "Can you turn it counterclockwise, please?" She found it very quickly, and immediately the line peeled off the reel. I thought I had a nuclear submarine by the tail. About five minutes later, I was pulling a rainbow trout through an eight-inch-diameter ice hole with less than a quarter-inch clearance. I reached down and grabbed the fish by the bottom lip and assisted it out of the hole, opened my tackle box and obtained my needle-nose pliers to remove the hook.

Just then my date became hysterical. "Don't hurt 'em! Don't hurt 'em!" she pleaded.

I watched her eyes well up with tears. She started to sob, "Let's throw him back! He's gonna die! He's gonna die!" Her reaction surprised me. In my family, everyone would have been doing the "high-five" thing, sharpening up the fillet knife, heating up the skillet or preparing brine for the smoker. That trout was a minimum of six-and-a-half pounds. His shadow probably weighed a half-pound. I couldn't wait to show all my fishing buddies this lunker.

I looked at this attractive young girl and then down at the fish, and I did what any true fisherman would do. I kept the fish and let her off the hook.

~Vic Dollar
Chicken Soup for the Fisherman's Soul

The Moment It Happens

Having someone wonder where you are when you don't come home at night
is a very old human need.
~Margaret Mead

I know when it happened... the exact moment.

Houston Intercontinental Airport, 11:30 P.M.: My flight was three-and-a-half hours late. I sat in a phone station in the baggage area to check my business messages, and like a bolt of lightning, it hit me. If I fell over dead at that very moment, no one passing by to get a rental car, or to get their suitcases, or to greet loved ones would know who I was, where I was coming from or where I was going. No one would know I was missing for quite a while. It was an odd, lonely and very important moment in my life. I then decided to find someone significant who would miss me if I failed to arrive.

After making that decision, I had dinner with a longtime friend who listened to my complaints about trying to "find someone." I said there were no decent men "out there" to find. Without hesitation, or even looking up from her salad, she asked what I had done about my search that very day. When I said, "Nothing because it's been a busy day for me," she said, "Either do something about it every day, or shut up."

After that "put up or shut up" encounter, I decided okay, but how!? I talked to myself about where "they" (decent men) were. The old conventional ways that everyone talked about — bars, classes, meetings, friends, blind dates, etc. — seemed uncomfortable and not for me. After all, it seemed I was doing some of that anyway in my regular day-to-day life and "they" just weren't there. So, my inner voice said, "Try something new."

I picked up my newspaper and read one hundred personal ads of women searching for "them."

The free five-line ads all seemed to say the same things. And I wanted to be different.

I called the newspaper and discovered the ads were free at that typical size but if I wanted a bigger one, it would be costly.

I have always believed if you want something, go all out. So I did.

A friend and her mother helped me write the ad that would end up changing my life. After seventeen drafts, I wrote the ad. It was twenty-three lines, expensive and really described me. I also recorded a voice-mail message that every one of "them" would hear.

The ad ended with "I miss being called 'Honey'," and it spoke the truth.

In the next two weeks, I had 104 replies. The messages they left for me told of delightful-sounding, accomplished men, in my area and in my age group, who were also tired of the tried and not-so-true methods of meeting potential mates. They had also grown weary of bars, groups, socials and the like. They were all intrigued with someone wanting to be called honey, and most of them, through nervous laughter, used that word somehow in their message. I made a long prioritized list on a legal pad. Three stood out. An FBI agent, a business owner and a firefighter. The firefighter turned out to be delightful on the phone, but reluctant to go any further. The FBI agent met me for lunch and was concerned about my motives in looking for him. I reminded him that he had answered my ad. I finished my lunch quickly and that name was crossed off the list.

In my recorded message, I had said the best movie I had ever seen was *The Day the Earth Stood Still* (still my favorite). The third man on my list, the business owner, left this reply: "Michael Rennie, Patricia Neal, Hugh Marlow, Sam Jaffe, Billy Gray, call me!" He had listed the major cast members of *The Day the Earth Stood Still*.

Because I was leaving town on a rush flight, time prevented me from answering his call immediately. Upon returning, I heard his second message. This time he listed all the cast plus the director, producer and key moviemakers. And he recited the key phrase in the movie ("Klaatu Barada Nikto") and said, "Call me." That was the phrase that Patricia Neal said to Gort, the robot, to get him to come to the aid of Michael Rennie, who was being destroyed by the frightened people on Earth.

Again fate stepped in and I couldn't get back to him immediately, so when I returned home this time, there was a message on the voice mail from his entire office staff chanting in unison, "Please answer this man—he is driving us nuts."

I learned later that upon hearing my voice message, this man had played it for his brother in California, who said, "If she ever answers you, you are going to marry her."

Finally we did talk, scheduled lunch and chose to see a movie. When he approached the restaurant (I was there first so I could see him), I knew I would marry him. His look, his swagger and his élan told me this was "him."

In the middle of lunch, he put down his fork and said, "I think we are going to be married." I smiled.

Because I come from a self-sufficient generation, I told him at lunch that I would like to buy the movie tickets. He smiled and pulled them out of his pocket, saying the Italian side of him wouldn't let me pay, and that he knew I was going to offer.

We dated for nine months, planned a wedding, had the ceremony under a huppa in a temple and took an Italian honeymoon.

Upon returning, he presented me with a gift. On the table at our home was a square of Lucite with our crushed wedding glass reconstructed. The inscription on the Lucite square was the date of our wedding and the words to Gort, "Klaatu Barada Nikto."

He said, "They were true in the movie, and they are true for me."

Loosely translated: "You saved my life."

~Carol A. Price-Lopata
Chicken Soup for the Single's Soul

74

Until Death...

May the sun shine, all day long,
everything go right, and nothing wrong.
May those you love bring love back to you,
and may all the wishes you wish come true!
~Irish Blessing

rian and I were in a serious relationship. But as a divorced mom, dating, for me, was more often than not a family affair. There seemed to be many more grade school basketball games, dance recitals and family movie nights than romantic dinners for two. When Brian and I finally planned a "real" date one weekend, we put a lot of thought into it.

Knowing my love of everything Irish, Brian suggested we attend a play called *Flanagan's Wake*. That sounded great to me, so Brian ordered tickets. Saturday arrived and, with kisses to my daughters and a thank you to the sitter, we were off to the show.

Flanagan's Wake was an interactive play with audience participation as part of the action. Everyone was given nametags. The men used their real names, followed by the name "Patrick." The women were all called "Mary," followed by our first names. We, or should I say "Brian Patrick" and "Mary Barbara," sat chatting as the actors entered the intimate venue from the back of the theater.

"Boo-hoo," sobbed the grieving widow of the poor, deceased Flanagan as she walked toward us. Stopping next to my aisle seat, she took my arm and sniffled through her thick brogue, "No one can coomfort like a girlfriend, Mary Barbara. Coom and sit wit me, will ya?"

Wouldn't you know, I thought, I'm the first one they pick on.

Nevertheless, I cooperated and followed the widow Fiona, the Irish priest and several other cast members to the small stage. As the play progressed, I tried to look consoling at the appropriate moments, but I felt so self-conscious I could barely think how to act appropriately. Sitting at Fiona's side as the "wake" proceeded, I wished I were back in the audience with Brian. Here we were, finally on a real date, sitting thirty feet from each other.

My thoughts were interrupted by the widow.

"Mary Barbara, haf ya ever looved someone like I looved Flanagan?"

Somehow I thought I should play along with the cast but, surely, no one had ever loved anyone the way Fiona had loved Flanagan.

"No," I said, shaking my head.

"Well," she continued, "doo ya haf a special soomeone to loove?"

Nervous beyond belief, I again shook my head. "No."

I could tell by her expression that I was not following her cues the way she wanted, but I felt too uncomfortable to reveal my feelings for Brian in front of the whole audience.

"Tell me, Mary Barbara, did ya coome here to mourn Flanagan ahl by yerself?"

"Yes," I answered, the lie slipping from my lips. A combination of shyness and stage fright kept me from telling the truth.

"Well, then," the priest jumped in. "Who's that over there? I saw ya wit him earlier. Is that your broother, then? Bring her broother oop here!"

They're picking on Brian, too, I laughed to myself. Now he would have to talk in front of the audience along with me.

An embarrassed-looking Brian walked forward and stood in front of the small stage on which I sat. Looking at him with a skeptical expression, the priest spoke again.

"Yer not her broother, are ya?"

"No." Brian shook his head.

"Well, then," said the priest. "Do ya have anything to say fer yerself?"

Brian turned to me with an ornery grin. Suddenly, I knew what was going to happen. I jumped to my feet just as he knelt on one knee. He gently tugged me back to my seat while I laughed and cried simultaneously.

"Barb," he held both my hands and my gaze. "I truly believe God has written your name on my heart. I love you with everything that's in me. So, I'm here to... ask you if you'll marry me."

"Of course I will," I whispered, tears in my eyes. "I love you, Brian."

We joyfully embraced and — amid the clapping, cheers and congratulations of the smiling audience — floated back to our seats. I can barely remember the rest of the play. I sat with my head and heart in the clouds, touched that my bashful Brian had orchestrated such a public proposal.

You know, I've always liked the Irish tradition of honoring a life well-lived with a joyous celebration. But, I don't believe anyone's ever felt more joy at a wake than I did!

~Barbara Loftus Boswell
Chicken Soup for the Bride's Soul

75

Six Red Roses

I still remember the day I first heard of my husband. It was Friday, June 14, 1985, but it would be a few days later before I actually saw what he looked like. Yet by September 6th that same year, we were engaged.

I'd been on my way out for lunch that fateful Friday when my supervisor called me. "Lori, there is a package for you at the front desk."

I turned to Janine, a friend and colleague. "Uh-oh. That doesn't sound good," I said.

We went down to the desk and saw my "package." It was a long narrow box, and since I'd never received flowers before, I didn't immediately recognize it as a florist's box. My brow scrunched in confusion, and I tore open the string. Inside were six exquisite red roses. The card was signed with an "X."

I looked to Janine. "Is this a joke?" I asked.

She shook her head. "Not that I know of."

Needless to say, we spent much of the remaining afternoon trying to figure out who had sent the flowers. Janine even called the florist for information. Although the lady was very helpful, she couldn't give us any names, since the transaction had been paid in cash. The only thing she could say was, "He seemed like a very nice young man." I rolled my eyes at that. It sounded like something my grandmother would say, and so far, her taste in men didn't exactly correspond with mine.

Later that afternoon, my supervisor joined our discussion. "You know," she said. "Someone was up here asking for your name the other day."

My eyes widened. "Me? What for?"

She smiled. "Well, now I'm wondering."

I continued to stare at her. I'm sure it was obvious this experience was totally new to me. "Well, who was he?" I asked.

"His name is Gerry. He works downstairs. I think his last name is Robidoux."

I had never heard of him. I looked at Janine. "Do you know who he is?"

She shook her head. "Rub-a-dub? No, I never heard of him."

"Great, I'm being stalked," I laughed.

Within minutes, several curious girls from our office went on a "tour." They returned with big smiles.

"So, how many horns does he have?" I asked.

They shook their heads. "He's cute!" they squealed, almost in unison.

I made a face. "Are you sure you were looking at the right guy?"

I still couldn't believe that someone even remotely male was sending flowers to me. The idea that he was cute, too, almost threw me into a tailspin. I was starting to think someone had made a huge mistake. Somehow, I must have walked in front of the girl he was asking my supervisor about at precisely the wrong moment, and she had given him my name by mistake.

When I brought the flowers home that night, my mother was there. "What on earth did you buy those for?" she asked as I arranged them in a vase. I shot her a look that said, "Thanks a lot, Mom." Clearly, this experience was new for all of us.

The following Friday, my supervisor approached my desk with a huge grin on her face. "Guess who has a package downstairs again?"

I raced downstairs and came back with another florist box. Inside were six more red roses, a bottle of Oscar de la Renta perfume and another card. It read, "Have a nice day." Again, the signature was a simple "X."

I looked up at the crowd assembled around my desk. I was stunned, and my reaction seemed mirrored in their eyes as well. "Well, this is kinda weird," I chuckled.

They laughed as I'd hoped they would, but I couldn't help wondering who was sending me these things. The other day, I'd walked right past the cute "Rub-a-dub" guy, and he looked right through me as if I weren't even there.

Right after that, I'd crossed him off my list of potentials. Now I could only wonder what kind of psychopath that left.

Later that night (yes, two dateless Fridays in a row if you're paying attention), I was telling the story to a girlfriend of mine. "It makes me feel a little creepy because I'm doubting that it could be this 'Rub-a-dub' guy. In the first place, he's too cute. In the second place, he had the perfect opportunity to talk to me the other day, and he totally ignored me. I just can't help picturing some stalker following me around now."

Well, as small worlds go, mine was no exception. My friend's boyfriend worked at the same place I did, and she promised to ask him if he knew this "Rub-a-dub" character. It turns out he did. He knew him, and he asked him.

The following week, I received a phone call.

"Umm... hello, may I speak to Lori, please?" the voice on the phone said.

I smiled. I knew right away. "This is Lori."

"Oh... well, um... you don't know me, but... well, you know those flowers you've been getting? Well... um... I sent them," he stuttered. I couldn't help grinning to myself. It's usually me who's so tongue-tied.

"Who is this?" I asked.

"Oh... my name is Gerry Robidoux," he said.

The cute "Rub-a-dub" guy? I couldn't believe it. I pointed to the phone, gesturing to my mom, who was leaning over me, trying to catch every word.

"It's Mr. X," I mouthed.

After a few minutes of stilted conversation, we agreed to meet at a local pizza parlor. I was still skeptical, but I needn't have worried. It was as if the fates wouldn't allow me to be disappointed now.

We met and talked for a few hours. The whole time I couldn't help thinking that I could really fall for this guy. He seemed so honest and sincere, and I could already tell how thoughtful and genuine he seemed. Of course, his big blue eyes weren't too hard to look at either.

Well, as I said, a couple of short months later, we were engaged. I know to others that it seemed awfully fast, but somehow we both knew it was right. We were anxious to begin our lives together, and we were confident in our love.

That alone prepared us for the commitment that so many couples seem terrified of.

As impulsive as it seemed at the time, it's a decision I've never regretted, not for one moment, and it's made me thankful I was blessed with such great instinct. I'm thankful every time he calls me just to say hello. I'm thankful whenever he runs me a hot bath after I've had a stressful day at work. And I'm especially thankful every night when he wraps his arms around me as we fall asleep.

I remember something my grandma said right after I received those first roses. She sighed and said, "Oh, it's so romantic. And it'll be a great story to tell your grandchildren some day."

At the time, I just rolled my eyes and told her she was jumping to conclusions. But after fourteen years of marriage, two children and countless roses, I realize she was right.

~Lori J. Robidoux
Chicken Soup for the Romantic Soul

76

A Perfect Match

O ne Sunday afternoon in the late fall, a few months into our relationship, my boyfriend and I went to the local animal shelter together to adopt two cats, one for each of us. The shelter was a dingy concrete building, unremarkable except for the large window flanking the entrance where the cutest of the shelter's residents—usually a litter of kittens or puppies—appeared daily. On the wall facing the street, a window at eye level showcased other strays, usually cats who, unafraid of heights, seemed to enjoy peering down at pedestrians.

The volunteer in the reception area, a shoebox-sized room crammed with a dented tan-and-black metal desk and a half-dozen mismatched folding chairs, explained the adoption process. Satisfied that we were serious candidates for adoption, she directed us to the door in the wall, half-hidden behind the cartons of donated pet food and bags of generic kitty litter, leading to the cat room.

At the end of the narrow hallway filled with the sounds of whining and barking, scratching and mewling, the cat room—a room no bigger than the reception area—glowed green under fluorescent lights. Cages lined the walls from floor to ceiling. On the left side, several families were clustered around the cages containing litters of kittens. Two volunteers in blue tunics were taking cats out of cages for people to hold.

My boyfriend and I separated. Bypassing the crowd around the kittens, I headed for the cages on the right side of the room. Index cards on the front of the cages listed the name and description of the occupants: Flossie (four years old, spayed female, family moved) was a luxuriant white cat with a squashed face and sapphire-blue eyes; Jojo (six months, male, owner allergic) was a stringy cat with black and orange splotches; Sam (two years old, male, stray) was a burly Maine Coon cat; Yin and Yang (one year old, male and female, too much work for owner) were a pair of mewling, undernourished Siamese. The last cage on the right at shoulder height appeared to be empty, although it had a card: Morris (one year old, male, stray).

I peered into the cage. The same blue-gray as the metal walls that surrounded him, Morris melted into the shadowy corner of the cage. Only the brilliant shield of white fur on his chest and the stripe of white across his nose reflected the dim light. His yellow eyes, flecked with brown and gold, glowed as though lit from within. He sat on his haunches, erect and motionless, like the stone statues of cats that guarded the pyramids of ancient Egypt.

"Hey, Morris," I whispered. "Hey, guy," I cooed, sticking my fingers in the cage and wiggling them. He blinked and inclined his head slightly, considering me.

A volunteer, a sallow woman in her mid-twenties with a stringy brown ponytail, appeared at my shoulder. She consulted her clipboard.

"Excuse me," she said, reaching across me to pull the card out of the holder. She checked the card against her paperwork, made a notation on her clipboard and fit the card back in the metal slot sideways, short end up. She turned to go.

I turned with her, withdrawing my fingers from Morris's cage.

"Excuse me," I said. "What does it mean when you turn the card like that?"

She looked around at the family of noisy children behind her. Turning back to me, she said, in a voice just above a whisper: "It means he's the next to go."

"He's being adopted? That's great!"

"Well, no," she mumbled, looking down at her clipboard again. "He's next to, you know, go."

I didn't know. I looked at her, but she wouldn't meet my eyes.

"He's been here ten days already," she said. "We can't keep him any longer."

"So, what happens to him?" I said, although I suddenly understood.

"If no one adopts him by the end of the day, he'll be put to sleep." She sighed. "He's an adult cat, and families want kittens. And he's not very friendly. He just sits in the corner."

A father with two children, standing in front of the kitten cage, called to her, and she excused herself. My eyes prickled and my throat felt tight as I watched her open the door to the cage, pluck two squirming kittens from the pile, and hand one to each of the shrieking children.

Across the room, my boyfriend was bent over, poking his fingers through the bars of a cage where two handsome ginger-and-white-striped cats vied with each other for his attention.

Something quick and light brushed my right ear, and I turned. Morris was sitting at the front of his cage, one white-tipped paw extended through the bars. I moved closer to the cage, and he reached out again, tapping my left ear with his paw.

"Excuse me," I called over my shoulder to the volunteer. "Can I hold him?" I asked as she came up beside me.

"Morris?" she asked. "Sure." She swung open the door and reached her hand in, but Morris had backed into his corner again.

"Let me try," I said as she backed away.

"Morris," I called softly. "Hey, Morris." He edged forward, and I lifted him out of the cage. He settled himself in my arms, his front paws on my chest. The tears that had been burning the back of my eyes threatened to overflow, and I bent my head low over him. He reached his bony, pointed face up to mine, and, with a purr that was almost a growl, licked my ear. My chest constricted. Tears ran down my cheeks.

I heard my name and turned. My boyfriend was still standing in front of the same cage. He had one of the orange cats in his arms.

"Hey, look at these guys," he said. "Snickers and Reeses. But we'll change their names. He'll be Calvin." He stroked the purring cat. "And he'll be Hobbes." He indicated the cat in the cage.

"No," I choked. "I want this one."

"What?" he said, staring at me. "C'mon, these guys are perfect. A matched pair."

"No!" I said, wiping my cheek on my shoulder. "They'll put Morris to sleep if I don't take him."

"Morris? Look, you can't rescue every cat in here. Besides, these two are so cute...." His voice trailed off as he smiled encouragingly.

"I'm not leaving him," I said. Morris reached up a paw and patted my face.

My boyfriend opened his mouth, thought better of whatever he was going to say, and closed it again. He sighed.

"Okay," he said. "Mine'll be Calvin. Yours can be Hobbes."

"Morris," I said. "His name is Morris."

My boyfriend shook his head, motioning for the volunteer.

"Calvin and Morris," he grunted. "Great."

Throughout the winter, Morris and Calvin played together often, but Morris never liked my boyfriend. Morris proved to be a good judge of character. By spring, my boyfriend was gone. Fifteen years later, Morris is still with me, as loving and lovable as the first day I met him.

~M.L. Charendoff
Chicken Soup for the Cat Lover's Soul

I'm So Grateful
to Have You in My Life

*A wise lover values not so much the gift of the lover
as the love of the giver.*
~Thomas à Kempis

A Different Kind of "Trashy Secret"

A soft answer turns away wrath, but a harsh word stirs up anger.
~Proverbs 15:1

It was one of those stupid fights a couple has after five years of mostly blissful marriage. I had just come home from another long day at work. Of course, as we were a modern married couple, my wife had only arrived home a couple of minutes before me, after HER long day at work.

"Hey, babe," I said cheerily, dropping my keys and wallet off on the wicker table in the foyer.

"Don't you 'hey, babe' me," she grunted over a load of laundry she'd just started.

Puzzled, I looked at her for a minute, just before the fireworks started, it turns out. She was still in her fashionable work outfit, tailored slacks, silk blouse, crested blazer. Her hair was pulled back and stray wisps from the long day spilled over her beautiful face. Even after five years, catching her in moments like this one still took my breath away. If she only knew how...

"Don't you stand there in front of me with that 'innocent dreamer' look of yours, either," she said, advancing on me with a handful of colorful plastic. "Would you mind explaining... these?" she finished with a flourish, opening her clenched fist to reveal several candy bar wrappers, no doubt left behind in the load of my khaki work pants she was slipping into the washing machine.

I smiled for a minute, hoping my still-boyish charm might soften her concern.

"That's it?" she asked instead, slamming the candy wrappers down next to my wallet and keys. "You're just going to stand there and smile while your arteries clog by the minute?"

The upscale publishing company I worked for had recently offered blood tests to all of its employees. When my results came in, my wife and I were both surprised to see my cholesterol levels so high. Since then, she'd been urging me to eat better.

Snickers and Baby Ruths were definitely not on her list.

"Fine," she spat, deserting her load of laundry and grabbing her purse and keys off the wicker table instead. "If you don't want to be around to enjoy our twilight years together, then I don't know why you ever married me in the first place."

Embarrassment at getting caught, frustration from a long day at work and the "mother hen" tones of her afternoon "scolding" suddenly combined to raise the hackles on my neck.

"Me either," I spat pettily, just before she slammed the door in my face.

Minutes later, of course, I felt the first twinge of post-flare-up guilt and quickly finished her load of laundry and began tidying up the house to make myself feel better.

Noticing a bulging trash bag in the middle of the kitchen floor, I caught my wife's not-so-subtle hint and headed out the front door for the quick trek to the apartment complex Dumpster.

On the way past the deserted tennis courts, a faulty seam in the dollar-store trash bag stretched to its limit and split right in two. Cursing myself for making such a cheap purchase, I began stuffing the scattered coffee grounds and banana peels back into the remaining half of the bag.

I stopped when I noticed the glaring labels of products we'd never bought before and that looked completely unfamiliar. Fat-free cheese slice wrappers hastily rewrapped around regular, oily slices of cheese. Low-fat sour cream containers still mostly full. Healthy Choice cereal boxes full of regular raisin bran and Apple Jacks. A coffee can claiming it contained "Half the caffeine of regular brands" still full of rich-smelling, regular coffee. "Lite" lunchmeat and dessert wrappers. Low-fat potato chip bags in which the chips had been replaced by regular, greasy Ruffles!

No wonder things had been tasting differently lately! She'd been switching healthy products out with my usual, fattening ones! But when did she find the time? In between our hectic schedules and long workdays, I could only imagine her getting up half an hour early each morning and stealthily replacing my usual chocolate chip cookies with dietetic ones by moonlight. The socks on her always-cold feet padding around the darkened kitchen floor while I slept two rooms away snoring peacefully, none the wiser.

Maybe she really did want me around for the rest of her life, after all.

Gathering up the devious garbage, I made two trips and dumped all of her "evidence." Then I washed my hands, grabbed my wallet and keys, and drove to the one place I knew I'd find her: the deserted movie theater near our apartment complex.

Once a week she called from her office and asked if I wanted to see a twilight movie with her after work. And once a week I declined, claiming some fictional last-minute meeting or looming deadline. The fact was I liked my movies at night, where crowds swelled, laughter roared, popcorn flowed and everyone had a good time.

Twilight shows were for little kids and old folks. Not to mention one lonely wife who was quietly begging her husband for a little weekday romance....

I parked next to her car in the empty parking lot and bought a ticket to the first chick-flick I saw. Out of habit, I headed straight for the concession stand.

Balancing a diet soda, licorice and a huge bag of popcorn, I found her in the third theater I tried, watching exactly the kind of blaring action-adventure movie she never let me rent in the video store!

Creeping up behind her, I sat down with a flourish. She looked startled to see me, but not just because I'd snuck up on her.

"What are you doing here?" she smiled, our fight quickly forgotten. "You never come to the movies with me after work."

"I missed you," I said honestly, not telling her about the garbage bag discovery. "I'm sorry I blew up at you.... I'm just..."

"We're both tired," she finished for me, reading my mind. "And you shouldn't be such a sneak and... I shouldn't be such a nag."

I held her face in my hands in that darkened theater and told her, "No... you should."

She smiled warmly until she saw the bag of popcorn resting gently on my armrest. "Honey," I explained, "I didn't get any butter on it. And look, it says these Twizzlers are 'low fat.'"

She looked surprised, if not exactly happy. "Well," she grunted, holding my hand as yet another car chase played out across the giant screen in front of us, "that's a start, I guess."

Not really, I said to myself, still amazed at how much effort she'd made to keep me healthy and how much she loved me. It was more like a new beginning.

~Rusty Fischer
Chicken Soup for the Romantic Soul

78

Love: A Novel Approach

You have to walk carefully in the beginning of love;
the running across fields into your lover's arms can only come later
when you're sure they won't laugh if you trip.
~Jonathan Carroll, "Outside the Dog Museum"

*I*t was reading romance novels that let me know—my relationship with David is fizzling rather than sizzling. David is sweet, sensitive and reliable, but he's also becoming way too rational for my taste. He folds his underwear before climbing into bed, sits in an easy chair instead of snuggled next to me on the sofa and is too busy doing yardwork to slip away for an afternoon tryst. I decide to be brave and find out how bad things really are.

"Darling," I say to David, as I hand him a dish of chopped onions for the stir-fry he is making, "do you ever have to suppress a sexually charged groan when you step close to me?"

"Huh?" he asks.

"Does the passion rise so fiercely that you have to groan to keep yourself from tearing off all my clothes and ravishing me?"

"No," he says and adds broccoli to the frying pan.

My worst fears are confirmed. In the romances, the handsome heroes frequently have to suppress passionate groans. And that's just from being in the same room with the long-legged, tousle-haired, full-bosomed heroine.

While David and I eat dinner, he tells me about his out-of-town client from Nebraska. I'm discouraged to note he does not suddenly shove away his half-eaten dinner and impetuously pull me toward him for a rousing embrace. In fact, he goes back for seconds.

"Do you ever longingly look at the hollows of my knees?" I ask, as we clear the dishes.

"No," he says. "But I did notice you seem to be biting your fingernails again." He smiles as if this observation should win him a sensitivity award.

"How come you never cry out my name in a hoarse, impassioned whisper?" I ask.

"You mean like this?" He lowers his voice and hisses "Deborah" like he is a spy about to be caught.

"Well, with more of a sense of sexual urgency," I coach.

He pants a couple times, flexes his jaw muscles and says my name like a steam engine with laryngitis.

In the books, the guys emit these throaty unrequited whispers all the time. What's wrong with David? Why is he causing me to miss out on love as it's truly supposed to be?

Maybe David needs a little more assistance in transforming himself into my romantic ideal. Accordingly, I make a list of gestures that will enhance and strengthen our relationship.

At dinner the next evening, I read David the list:

1. *Gaze longingly at me.*
2. *Crush me in your impassioned embrace.*
3. *Watch me hungrily when I enter a room.*
4. *Push back my tousled hair and smile into my eyes.*
5. *Groan with the impossible task of suppressing your surging sexual urges for even a second more.*

David frowns. "I thought we had a great sexual relationship," he says. "I thought you were happy."

"I am," I tell him, "but more romance will deepen our relationship."

He stares at me with a stricken look.

"What's wrong?" I say, as the silence stiffens.

He keeps looking, his mouth turned down, his eyes in pools of agony.

"David," I put my hand on his. "Darling, what's wrong?"

"Nothing," he says blithely, "I'm staring longingly at you." And he continues his mournful gaze. I feel as though a basset hound has developed a huge crush on me.

He follows me into the kitchen and lurks about as I clean up the dishes. Suddenly he seizes my arms, pulls me to him and envelops me in a huge bear hug. I can barely breathe.

"You're crushing me," I tell him, pulling loose.

"Exactly. Isn't that what you've been yearning for?"

I don't know whether to kiss him or kick him.

The next day, I worry that my romantic ideas are being misconstrued. Maybe I should start with something simpler, like a loving missive tucked under my pillow or slipped into my briefcase.

I intend to discuss the nature of such a missive at dinner, but David stops me by plunking down a pile of paperbacks on the table.

"I've been doing some reading," he says. "How come your nipples never strain against the gauzy fabric of your enticing summer frock? How come you never moan out my name and bite your full, fleshy lower lip in a beguiling profusion of confused sensuality? Why don't you shudder with ecstasy at my merest touch? What is it with you—don't you love me anymore?"

He reaches out to me. I do feel a little row of goose bumps when he touches my arm. Not quite enough for a full-blown shudder but plenty for a gentle little shiver.

I look at David and smile. I pick up one of the books and open it toward the end, wanting to get to the "good" part. David begins to read and I move closer, hanging on to him and his every word. Neither one of us can wait to see what will happen next.

~Deborah Shouse
Chicken Soup to Inspire a Woman's Soul

79

The Gift of Life

*f*ell in love with my husband, Mike, after our first date. I had invited him to a Sadie Hawkins dance. He wasn't my first choice, but I am so glad fate had it that he was my second! A friend had encouraged me to invite him, saying, "Mike's the type of guy you could be with for the rest of your life." What wisdom from a sixteen-year-old!

He had every quality a girl could want. Handsome, kind, respectful, loving and caring... basically the very best friend a girl could have! He was a big high school football player, and I felt like a princess when I was with him.

We dated into college, and with the Vietnam War facing us squarely in the face, we decided to get married. Yes, we were too young, but we would not back down on our decision, even without the support and blessings of our family. Love knows no obstacles.

On a short honeymoon trip to Corpus Christi, Texas, Mike developed serious stomach pains. Terrified, I called the hotel desk to be referred to a local physician. The doctor said he was passing a kidney stone, and we should return home immediately. I remember the long, four-hour drive home. The wind was horrendous, and in those days cars did not have power steering! I could not hold the car on the road, so Mike, suffering incredibly, took the wheel of the car and took us safely home. He was my hero.

This incident began a long journey of living with chronic kidney disease. Mike never made the trip to Vietnam as he was immediately given a medical discharge from the service. He finished college and started a career as a manufacturer's rep in the furniture business. We had two wonderful sons. I made a career of being a full-time wife and mother.

Over a period of twenty years there were many hospital stays, kidney biopsies and some very scary moments. But with Mike's character and positive attitude, he would always bounce back and return to being a normal father and husband. On the outside looking in, we seemed to be an average, happy family, but on the inside, I lived each day wondering when the black cloud over us would finally burst.

In 1987, his time was running out, and the only alternative was to be put on a dialysis machine and go on the list for a transplant. Before starting the treatments, I surprised him with a trip to the beach, where he played one of the best rounds of golf he had ever played. He was so weak and so gray in color, and it was his fortieth birthday. For the first time in our married lives, he told me he felt defeated. He had fought going on the machine for as long as he possibly could. My heart was broken, even though I was grateful that this machine would keep him alive.

He approached the dialysis just like everything else he did in life. He made a game of it and would never allow it to bring him down. He would leave the treatments weak as a cat, eat a meal and go right back to work. People were just amazed at him.

Meanwhile, the list of people ahead of him was long, and relatives were ruled out for the transplant. To this day, I still cannot explain where this strange feeling came from, but I remember vividly sitting in the doctor's office with Mike's sister. He was explaining to her why she could not be a donor, when a voice in my head said, "You will do it." It was so clear and so precise, and I have never before nor since heard a voice speak to me like that. I never doubted from that moment that I would be the donor, even though it sounded impossible at the time.

I kept thinking about it, and the answer came to me very easily. On the next visit with the doctor, I told him, "Look, Mike and I have the same blood type, is this correct? A cadaver kidney only has to match by blood type, correct? Okay, so if I got run over by a car today and killed, then my kidney would work for him, correct?" The doctor just looked at me as I pleaded my case. "So, let's let him have it while I'm alive to enjoy the rest of our lives together.... How about it?"

Sure sounded easy to me, but the answer was a flat no. A living, nonrelated donor could not donate a kidney. Saying no to me was like waving a red flag in front of a mad bull.

I spent hours researching and found that in the state of Wisconsin, husband-and-wife transplants had been done several times. So why not in Texas?

I gathered some support from a few physicians, and the case went before the hospital board. It took a while for them to reach a decision, and they even asked us to go through psychological testing. (I guess they wanted to make sure I wasn't crazy.) We both laughed driving home from the testing, because we could almost read each other's minds. He'd say, "I knew you would give that answer for that question," and I would reply, "Yeah, and I know which one you chose too!" Thank God we could laugh a little!

The Methodist Hospital board and staff in Dallas were finally convinced and ready to go. I never dreamed the delay might come from my own husband! The more he thought about it, the more he could not stand the idea of me going into surgery for him. After all this, he said he didn't think he could go through with it. In a quiet and very emotional moment, I just asked him the simple question, "I have watched you fight and be there for our family for the last nineteen years. We have been through all this together. Now what if it were me on that machine, and you knew you could do something to make me well? What would YOU do?" The surgery was scheduled.

Fourteen years ago, Mike and I made Texas history as the first husband/wife (living, nonrelated) transplant. I received phone calls from people all over the country wanting to do the same thing. Now it is not uncommon for nonrelated donors to be allowed to give "the gift of life."

Making history has never impressed me that much, but having

a healthy husband for the last fourteen years, and looking at many more to come, is far more important.

~Margo Molthan
Chicken Soup for the Romantic Soul

80

The Last Quarter

In the coldest February, as in every other month in every other year,
the best thing to hold on to in this world is each other.
~Linda Ellerbee, Move On: Adventures in the Real World

When I decided my girlfriend Maria was the woman I wanted to marry, I told her I wanted to date her exclusively. A good friend of ours suggested we start "courting."

Since neither Maria nor I knew the difference between courting and dating, our ever-helpful friend quickly pointed out they were similar, but with significant differences. "Appropriate physical boundaries" needed to be respected; and a dedicated commitment would enable us to grow individually and as a couple.

Finally, according to my friend, courtship meant every time Maria and I saw each other, I was to give her a quarter. Yes, that's right—a quarter. Is this some mysterious, ancient ritual, I wondered? "Never mind," said my friend. "Just do it."

So I took the "quarter" challenge, and decided to make a game of it. It became second nature to check my pockets for the appropriate pieces of silver. A dime wouldn't do. I hid quarters under her plate in a restaurant or left them with notes on her steering wheel, or gently slipped them into her hand as we walked to the movies.

I loved to see the excitement and joy in her face every time I gave her a quarter. She saved each one and collected them in a green corduroy drawstring bag. When we were apart, Maria would hold the bag and think of all the fun we shared.

Finally, the right time came for me to ask the Big Question. Almost finished with our premarital classes at the church, I'd never been more positive about a decision in my life. But doubt crept into my mind—did Maria feel the same way?

More than anything, I wanted the proposal to be special and to incorporate our "quarter theme." Carefully, I formulated my plan.

First, I chose a nice restaurant across from the performing arts center and bought tickets to a jazz show I knew she wanted to see. Then, I put words onto paper about how much Maria meant to me:

The Last Quarter
In the first quarter a comfort level was formed,
In the second quarter a friendship was spawned,
In the third quarter silver tokens of affection did abound,
And in this final quarter—my true love I have found.

This is the last "quarter" I will give you to celebrate our "court-ing" stage. For today I ask you to be my wife, and in exchange for the silver tokens that daily show my love, I humbly ask you to accept a silver ring, and thus daily share my life. I love you, Maria.

Ward

I framed the poem and letter and placed a quarter inside, too. I arranged with the manager of the restaurant to have the frame placed on a secluded table with the menus set directly over it. My plan? When Maria lifted the menus she would find the poem and, at that point, I would drop to my knees and propose.

On the way to the restaurant, I felt confident. At least until Maria grabbed hold of my hand in the car.

"Your hand is clammy. Are you nervous about something?"

I made some lame joke in response while thinking, "This woman knows me pretty well." I took that as another sign I'd made a good decision.

About five minutes after we sat down, Maria lifted her menu and saw the framed poem beneath it. She picked it up and exclaimed, "Hey, they've got a quarter theme, too!"

I didn't say a word. Maria was still reading. A look of confusion crossed her face. I guessed she reached my name at the bottom. That was my cue.

I knelt down beside her and asked her those four little words: "Will you marry me?"

Well, would she? There was a tantalizing moment before everything sank in. Finally, Maria said the one word I most wanted to hear.

"Yes."

The waiter brought the champagne on cue. As we laughed and held each other, I handed Maria my cell phone, programmed with her mother's number, so she could tell her mom the good news.

Within a short while, Maria and I married. All the quarters I gave her remained in the same bag, sitting next to the framed poem.

Our marriage was wonderfully happy, but I found I missed our quaint little custom. So I planned another surprise. Over a year later, we moved into our new home and had a special dinner on Valentine's Day. When Maria opened a box of chocolates she found—wrapped in tissue in place of a chocolate—a quarter.

She looked at me, mystified. "Why am I getting a quarter?"

"I miss 'quarting' you." I rolled the quarter up her arm. "I want to quart you and court you for the rest of my life!"

Since then, I've been giving Maria a quarter every day. Sometimes I put them in the most unexpected places.

Maria puts all the "new" quarters in a ceramic jar on her night-stand. She stores them in quart-size mason jars in her hope chest and promises to keep them forever. I've no idea how many are in her collection, but I do know that many quarters make infinite riches—of love.

~Ward Nickless
Chicken Soup for the Bride's Soul

81

Head to Toe

Do I love you because you're beautiful,
Or are you beautiful because I love you?
~Richard Rodgers and Oscar Hammerstein II, Cinderella

Now that I'm four kids past twenty-five, my body shows some signs of wear and tear. So when we vacationed at a Washington coastal resort I was — I'll admit it — jealous of the flat-stomached, stretch-mark-free bachelorettes frolicking in the pool.

When the kids pulled out their swimsuits, I looked pleadingly at my husband, Andy. "Please take them in," I said. "I just can't go out in a swimsuit in front of all those twenty-somethings." He gave me a puzzled look, but took the children swimming while I watched the baby nearby.

That night Andy came in with a mysterious bag, from which he withdrew a bottle of fuchsia nail polish!

"I'm going to paint your toenails," he announced.

"You're going to what?"

"Paint your toenails," he said, taking off my socks.

This is silly, I thought. I don't even paint my toenails.

But my husband was insistent.

"Why are you doing this?" I asked.

"Because," he answered, brushing on the first coat, "I want you to know you're beautiful from head to toe."

I looked at the guy who's been with me through fifteen years of bills and babies. He had not only protected me from embarrassment, but adorned me. I thought of those twenty-somethings with the flat stomachs and I didn't feel jealous anymore. Instead I felt grateful.

~Katherine G. Bond
Chicken Soup for the Romantic Soul

Twenty-Six Years – An Unfolding Romance

"**N**ow, who is it that's getting married?" my husband whispered to me as we settled into our pew after being led down the church aisle by a solemn-faced young usher.

We'd had this discussion at least three times. Once when I discovered the calligraphied envelope buried under a pile of discarded grocery flyers after he'd reached the mailbox first. Another when he knocked the invitation off its magnet on the refrigerator door—where I had mounted it in plain view. And a few days earlier when I reminded him we couldn't go to the opening of an action flick because we were going to the wedding of a teaching colleague of mine.

Despite all this, I wasn't concerned he'd forgotten the names embossed on the invitation. After twenty-six years of marriage, I've learned that the mere mention of the word "wedding" seems to trigger a memory lapse in my husband.

So, as we took our seats, I calmly whispered back, "The computer teacher and the Bible teacher's son."

"Sounds like the title of one of those romance novels you read on the treadmill at the gym," he muttered and settled down, probably to count the number of women sitting by themselves who had left their lucky husbands behind.

The ringing chords of the organ accompanied a lilting soprano and filled the flower-scented air. It reminded me of my own wedding day and the joy-tinged nervousness that made my stomach dance with butterflies as I stood hidden from guests, awaiting my cue. I wondered if the bride was calming her own fluttering emotions.

I knew the groom was. He was a quiet man who didn't seek the limelight and for whom, according to his mother, the anticipation of standing to face four hundred guests was daunting.

When, tuxedoed and handsome, he led his entourage to take their places at the altar steps, I looked for signs of distress. Fidgety hands. Sweating brow. Restless feet. Instead, I saw the sweet smile of a happy man as he anticipated the sweeping entry of the woman he loved. And I didn't need the strains of the "Trumpet Voluntary" to know the bride was poised to enter. The groom's face reflected her presence.

As we rose in honor, I felt a twinge of envy. It had been a long time since my husband had looked at me with that kind of glow. Maybe twenty-six years of marriage does that, I thought. Maybe the day we said our vows, the day he looked at me in my bridal white and his eyes said, "I love you and you are beautiful" was the climax of our own romantic saga, the best it was ever going to get. And maybe our confidence in the first blush of love became a memory buried under years of hard work to keep our marriage going.

The last strains of music faded and the bride's glowing face, shadowed by layers of pearl-encrusted tulle, turned from her father to her groom. That's when a little tear threatened to slip down my cheek. In the candlelit softness, they did look like a perfect couple from one of those romantic novels I liked to sneak into the gym.

A tiny part of me mourned the loss of my storybook-romance illusions as the groom reached for his bride's hand. I wanted to be them again—partners facing a clean slate, oblivious to all but their love. I wanted to steal a piece of the mystical magic of new love and rediscover its feelings of hope, promise and possibilities—the same fresh feelings my husband and I shared on our own wedding day.

Suddenly, as if he knew my thoughts, my husband turned to me and whispered, "I like the way you look in that red dress, Kris." His eyes filled with a warmth that still melts my heart, and his thumb stroked my palm like it did twenty-six years ago when we stood in a rose-perfumed garden and he said, "I do."

Inching into the shelter of his encircling arm, I remembered the long-ago wedding promises we made and have honored over many good and some not-so-good years. I thought of our mutual respect, of the love that drew us together, of the sure foundation of trust and commitment we continued to build on.

All too soon, the groom kissed his bride and, beaming, they walked hand-in-hand down a petal-strewn aisle... into a star-studded night.

As the bride left to face her future, I wished her happiness. But I no longer wanted to be her. I was glad I was right where I was. With the man I love. Hand-in-hand, we followed the newlyweds into the luminous night—and a beckoning future of romance.

~Kris Hamm Ross
Chicken Soup for the Bride's Soul

83

The Wrong Person

Rick's face shone with wonderful news. "Robin, the Lord wants us to continue with our honeymoon for a long time!"

In utter joy, I hugged him.

"He called me to the mission field." His eyes filled with purpose. "India is in my heart." My arms fell to my side. What about me? I thought we would pastor a small country church in the States—near a mall. Had he heard God's call correctly?

Soon I received my call—from his mother. "Robin, when God called Rick to the mission field, he called you too."

She began making plans to return our wedding gifts "since you will not need them anymore."

I gritted my teeth. I would inform Rick when his parents were not around. I was not going to India. "Lord, you have the wrong person," I said.

I was not going when I had my shots and my passport picture taken.

As we lent our car to my best friend, I still was not going.

While we bought our new luggage, I was not going.

As I resigned my teaching position, I asked for a new application.

As we sold all our earthly possessions at a yard sale, I was not going.

I felt happy at our going-away party, for I was staying.

Sitting on the overseas flight to India, I planned on turning around the moment the plane set down in Iran to catch our connecting flight. The only thing I had to do was inform Rick of my decision. I was not going to be a missionary. I wanted my house inside the safe perimeters of a white picket fence with clothes in dresser drawers and clean sheets on the bed. The Lord simply had the wrong person.

But when I looked into the wonderful blue eyes I fell in love with, I couldn't bear the thought of leaving him. Rick and God were a package deal. Just where did I fit in? Was I limiting God from working in my life? Did my attitude scream out, "This far and no further, God?" How did that translate in my marriage?

Changing planes in Iran, we learned the Shah was fleeing the country to save his own life. I wanted to flee with him to save mine. The Iranians were in revolt. I understood the feeling. While Americans were at the airport trying to get out, we were at the airport trying to get in, like salmon swimming upstream.

I decided to break my news to Rick during our two-hour layover. My speech was prepared. My courage gathered, I was at last ready. Rick would soon learn I was returning to the States and my dog. While standing in line, handing my boarding pass to the flight attendant, I opened my mouth to tell him I was not getting on the plane. Just then the announcement came: The airport was now closed due to the revolution. Rick looked rather startled, so I decided to postpone my own startling news for a less stressful moment.

As we drove up to the Commodore Hotel in Tehran, I couldn't help but notice all the large tanks with cannons pointing toward it. My refuge was the bull's eye.

Okay, I would tell him a little later. I still had time. Perhaps after he had his morning devotions; scriptures always perked him up.

The next day was Sunday. Rick directed, "Get ready for church."

"Church? We are in a Muslim country." I shook my head at him.

"I am sure there is a Christian church somewhere. Let's go find one."

"There are people out on the streets shooting Americans!"

"Don't make excuses, Robin. Just get ready."

After looking through the phone book, we found a Christian church, and it was only twelve city blocks away. No cabs were available, so we walked.

Shortly after arriving, I decided I would pass Rick a note during church saying I was not going to India. Only first I had to use the restroom. Slowly, I circled down the cement steps and found the room at the end of a long, dark hall in the basement. I locked the creaking door behind me. Ready to rejoin my husband and the lively congregation on the floor above, I tried to unlock the door. It would not budge. I twisted it. I pulled it again and again and again.

"Help!" I cried hysterically into my hands. I surveyed the small room, searching for a window to make my escape. There was none. Three-foot walls of stone surrounded me. I envisioned a revolution taking place on the street above my head while I remained locked in the water closet below. How long would it take for Rick to notice I had been gone too long? He might get sidetracked praying for someone infirmed and forget about his reluctant wife.

As I pulled and pushed the bathroom door I muttered, "God, if Rick's plan is the center of Your will, why am I so miserable?" Was I fighting against Him as hard as I was against the lock on the door? At that moment, I surrendered totally to Him. I quit pounding and pushing and rattling and struggling. His will was now my will, no matter where it took me — to America, to India or to Niagara Falls.

God had called Rick during a church service; He called me in the restroom under the street.

I pressed the lock one more time and it flew open. "Lord, as easily as this lock opened, please allow me to do Your will. Help us leave this country for India."

Arriving back at the hotel as giggly honeymooners, Rick and I heard the airport had miraculously opened for only two hours. Our jet awaited us on the tarmac. It was heading east, toward the rising sun. Amazingly, my courage and prayers began to take root.

Stepping out into India, sights, sounds and smells I had never imagined enveloped me; some delightful, some frightening, but all wonderful.

In the mission field, I learned the true meaning of being a child of God and the wife of a committed Christian man. Missionaries and marriage both require teamwork. God and Rick and I were a team.

I had been the right person all along.

~Robin Lee Shope
Chicken Soup for the Christian Soul 2

84

The Porsche Factor

Remember, we all stumble, every one of us.
That's why it's a comfort to go hand in hand.
~Emily Kimbrough

I held my ring under the light and watched it sparkle. Newly-married life was as bright as my new diamond... except for one nagging shadow of doubt. The Porsche factor, I called it secretly. Yes, my new husband actually owned one of those sleek, red cars that belonged in a James Bond movie.

The Porsche was a constant reminder of the different worlds we came from. His family belonged to a country club, donated generously to charities and took exotic vacations. My family struggled to make ends meet. We shopped at thrift stores, cut coupons and took public transportation.

Rich people seem to care so much about stuff, I thought. After the honeymoon was really over, would my husband love me more than his stuff? If only there was some way to be sure.

On his first morning back to work, he handed me his keys. "I'll take the bus," he said. "You drive the car."

I fingered the worn leather key ring. "Are you sure?" I asked. I'd never driven the Porsche, although he'd been offering it ever since my ancient car died a month before the wedding.

"Sure," he said, "but... be careful."

I felt a twinge of irritation even though I knew he couldn't keep himself from adding the warning. I said a prayer as I started the engine. After all, this was no ordinary car.

My father-in-law had driven it home for the first time almost fifteen years ago. Under his care, the car gleamed like a jewel and purred like a well-fed tiger. The boy who grew up to be my husband spent hours beside his dad, handing over a needed tool, studying the correct way to wax and learning the well-crafted intricacies of a Porsche engine. Sometimes he'd even sneak out to the garage in the middle of the night and climb carefully into the driver's seat. Without actually touching anything, he'd pretend he was driving fast along the curves of an empty road.

One day, his dad took him aside. "Son, if you save the money by the time you turn sixteen, your mother and I will sell you this car."

The amount he named was far less than what the Porsche was worth, but it was a big amount for a boy to earn and save. My husband found a job cleaning the garage in an apartment complex, emptying garbage cans, sweeping and mopping. He worked after school and on weekends and saved every penny he earned. On his sixteenth birthday, he proudly handed his dad a check and took the Porsche out for a drive.

There was a mystical male bond between my husband, his dad and that car. Even now, when we drove the shiny Porsche into the driveway of my in-laws' house, his dad came out to check on it.

"Good job, son. The car looks great."

With all that history in mind, I drove slowly at first, like I was handling a piece of heirloom china. I pulled to a stop at the first hint of a yellow light and clung to the right lane on the freeway. As the car picked up speed, my confidence grew. I rolled down the window, turned up the radio and nosed into the fast lane.

After doing some shopping, I couldn't wait to drive home. I walked eagerly to where I'd parked the car in the crowded lot—and stopped. The Porsche had moved a good three feet forward in the parking space.

Somebody must have hit it from behind.

I stood for a moment, trying to gather my courage to inspect the damage. The back end wasn't bad; the bumper seemed to have absorbed most of the shock. But when I saw the crumpled fender and the dent on the hood, my heart sank. A sign that read "ten-minute parking only" leaned over it like a warrior gloating over a fallen enemy.

Oh no! I thought. I'd left the gearshift in "neutral" instead of "park," and the car had lurched forward when it had been hit.

I drove home slowly, fighting my tears. For the first time since our wedding, I didn't want to see my husband. He found me hiding under the covers.

"What's wrong, honey? Are you sick?"

"The car," I said, my voice muffled. "Something bad happened. I left it in neutral and somebody crashed into it while it was parked and they didn't leave a note."

I waited while he went down to the parking garage to inspect the damage. When he returned, the sadness in his eyes made me hide my face in the pillow.

"It's okay, honey," he said. "Don't worry about it."

But we both knew that this was no ordinary car. To make things worse, we were scheduled to drive that very night to his parents' house.

"Do you want me to tell them you're not feeling well?" he asked.

"No," I answered grimly. For better or worse I'd promised just a couple of weeks earlier. And this was definitely the worst day so far.

As we drove to my in-laws' house, I felt a rush of hatred for the Porsche. Why was this material object such a treasure, anyway? It was a pile of metal welded together with some wiring inside, destined for rust and decay.

When we pulled into the driveway, I shrank in my seat. My in-laws were coming out of the front door, both of them beaming as usual.

My father-in-law began walking around the Porsche with an appraising glance. When he reached the front of the car, I caught my breath.

"Oh no!" he shouted. "What happened?"

Feeling like a criminal about to be sentenced, I waited for my husband's answer.

"We had a little accident," he said.

As the two of them began to discuss repairs, I wondered if I'd heard wrong. Had he really said, "we"? I was responsible for the first damage ever done to this family treasure. Surely he'd explain to his dad that there was no we about it at all. Before I could speak up, my mother-in-law pulled me into the house.

"I'm going to tell them the truth," I told him, when the two of us had a moment alone later. "It's not right for you to take the blame."

"Who cares who did it?" he answered. "It's just a car."

I felt like shouting for joy, but I hugged him instead. I was still determined to tell his parents the truth, but that didn't matter now. The secret shadow of my last doubt was gone. Without the Porsche factor, our life together sparkled even more brilliantly than the diamond on my finger.

~Mitali Perkins
Chicken Soup for the Bride Soul

Military Marriages

All the survivors of the war had reached their homes and so put the
perils of battle and the sea behind them.
~Homer, The Odyssey, line 1

85

The Commissary Roadblock

Thoughtfulness is a habit—
a way of life well worth cultivating and practicing.
~Brough Botalico

It was just another harried Wednesday afternoon trip to the commissary. My husband was off teaching young men to fly. My daughters went about their daily activities knowing I would return to them at the appointed time, bearing, among other things, their favorite fruit snacks, frozen pizza and all the little extras that never had to be written down on a grocery list. My grocery list, by the way, was in my sixteen-month-old daughter's mouth, and I was lamenting the fact that the next four aisles of needed items would have to come from memory.

I was turning into the hygiene/baby aisle while extracting the last of my list from my daughter's mouth when I nearly ran over an old man. He clearly had no appreciation for the fact that I had forty-five minutes left to finish the grocery shopping, pick up my four-year-old from tumbling class and get to school, where my twelve-year-old and her carpool mates would be waiting.

The man was standing in front of the soap selection, staring blankly as if he'd never had to choose a bar of soap in his life. I was ready to bark an order at him when I realized there was a tear on his face. Instantly, this grocery-aisle roadblock transformed into a human.

"Can I help you find something?" I asked. He hesitated, and then told me he was looking for soap.

"Any one in particular?" I continued.

"Well, I'm trying to find my wife's brand of soap." I was about to lend him my cell phone so he could call her when he said, "She died a year ago, and I just want to smell her again."

Chills ran down my spine. I don't think the twenty-two-thousand pound mother of all bombs could have had the same impact. As tears welled up in my eyes, my half-eaten grocery list didn't seem so important. Neither did fruit snacks or frozen pizza. I spent the remainder of my time in the commissary that day listening to a man tell the story of how important his wife was to him—and how she took care of their children while he fought for our country.

My life was forever changed that day.

Sometimes the monotony of laundry, housecleaning, grocery shopping and taxi driving leaves military wives feeling empty—the kind of emptiness that is rarely fulfilled when our husbands don't want to or can't talk about work. We need to be reminded, at times, of the important role we fill for our family and for our country. Every time my husband comes home too late or leaves before the crack of dawn, I try to remember the sense of importance I felt in the commissary.

Even a retired, decorated World War II pilot who served in missions to protect Americans needed the protection of the woman who served him at home.

~Paige Anderson Swiney
Chicken Soup for the Military Wife's Soul

86

Destination: Military Wife

When I was in college, my roommate found an address in a magazine where you could send your name and receive the names and addresses of single soldiers who were looking for pen pals. Amy sent in her name, and it wasn't long before her mailbox was crammed with letters from soldiers all over the world. She did her best to reply to each letter she received. One of the soldiers, J.D., was from Rhode Island, just a few miles from where we went to school. He was coming home on leave and wanted to meet her. Amy was nervous, but they hit it off. So well, in fact, that after that weekend, she stopped corresponding with all the other soldiers and focused only on writing to J.D.

A few months after they met, J.D. was deployed to Saudi Arabia in support of Desert Storm. They continued being pen pals for the nine months he was gone. Through their many letters, Amy and J.D. bonded, and their relationship bloomed and deepened.

The summer J.D. returned home from the Gulf War, Amy and I took a road trip to Fort Bragg, North Carolina, to see him. I was not interested in meeting a soldier, though Amy and J.D. had other plans: they had arranged to set me up with his roommate. Knowing I would protest, they kept it a secret from me until the day before we arrived. That's when J.D.'s roommate had to return home for a death in the family, completely foiling their secret plan. J.D. wanted to find someone else to fill in at the last minute. He told Amy about another squad leader in his platoon, Mitch. Mitch was from Tennessee and wore cowboy boots and liked to sing country music.

Amy leaked this information to me on our way to Fort Bragg. I was understandably upset. First of all, I was embarrassed that they felt they had to fix me up on a blind date. I realized they were doing it so I wouldn't be the third wheel, but it still offended me. Second of all, I am 100 percent Yankee, born in Boston, and I had lived in New England my entire life up until that point. The thought of a "redneck" from Tennessee was not only unappealing, but honestly, quite horrifying. How would I ever relate to a guy who wore cowboy boots and listened to country music? Irritated with my friend despite her good intentions, I told her they could tell Mitch from Tennessee that I weighed five hundred pounds and had unsightly facial hair. They got the point and stopped their scheming.

Amy nevertheless continued to tease me about "Mitch from Tennessee" for the rest of the drive, and it became a joke to us. When we arrived in Fayetteville, my intentions were to collapse in the hotel room for the remainder of the weekend, only leaving to use the pool. When J.D. showed up at the room twenty minutes after we arrived, they talked me into taking a ride to Fort Bragg for a "quick tour." The last thing I wanted to do was go for a ride, but Amy's eyes pleaded with me to go.

We saw the sign that welcomed us to Fort Bragg, and our surroundings were immediately transformed. I had never been on an army post before. There were soldiers everywhere. It was intimidating, exciting and interesting. When J.D. pulled into a parking lot and motioned for us to follow him into a building, I glared at Amy. I was haggard and harried from our long journey. "I'm not going anywhere," was what I tried to say. But I knew Amy needed my moral support.

The building we followed J.D. into was the barracks where he lived. As we got close to the door, a guy in army PTs ran past us. When he saw me, he stopped. He was cute and polite and had blood dripping down his forehead from what I later found out was a racquetball accident. He reached his hand out to welcome me to Fort Bragg. "Hi, I'm Mitch," is what he said.

I looked at Amy, and we couldn't contain our laughter. I suddenly wished I had taken a moment to freshen up before we left the hotel room, put on lipstick or at least comb my hair. I knew how bad I looked. Mitch left us to go upstairs, but, a few moments later, he was back, freshly showered and dressed, and following us to J.D.'s truck.

"So where do you want to go eat?" he asked.

I wish I could say we hit it off that night. But, in truth, we did not. I thought he was very attractive and had a great sense of humor. But Mitch was six years older than I, and I found him to be arrogant and overly assertive. Still, we had a fun evening.

When I returned to Rhode Island, I could not stop thinking about him. We started writing, and, after a few more visits to Fort Bragg, our relationship flourished. I graduated from college in May 1993, and I married Mitch from Tennessee in June. We even beat Amy and J.D. to the altar. They said their vows in September of the same year.

As I write this, Mitch and I have been happily married for ten years. I know it wasn't luck that led me on that fateful trip to Fort Bragg twelve years ago. It was destiny. We have two beautiful daughters, and Mitch is now a captain with a promising military career ahead of him. He is deployed to the Middle East once again, but this time as a husband and father, rather than a single soldier.

Over the years, I have met many military wives with stories like mine. Nowhere will you find a more diverse group of people than on an army post. We have created a true melting pot in our neighborhoods. I have neighbors from across the globe—from places like Honduras, Korea, Africa, Germany, Vietnam and Croatia. I know wives who met their husbands in bus stations, in airports, in the town squares of foreign countries. There are language barriers, but no barriers stand between our love for our husbands, or the unique friendships we have formed with one another. In the past ten years, a new world has opened up to me. I have been shown that the only race is the human race. I have experienced suffering, and, as a result, I have seen the true strength of the human spirit and the power of support and friendship. There are thousands of military wives, and each one of us has a story to tell about how we got here.

The next time you meet a military wife, take a minute to ask her, "So how did you meet your husband?" It might renew your faith that God has a plan for us all.

~Bethany Watkins
Chicken Soup for the Military Wife's Soul

Picture the Waiting

*I*n my grandmother's home, there is a framed image of a young girl with long blond hair sitting on a high, rocky ledge overlooking the sea. The intense colors of the darkening, star-filled night sky mix with the deep blues of the calm ocean. She wears a white dress that glows in the light of the moon. Her tiny, sharp-featured face is sullen and sad, and her arms wind loosely around her legs. Her eyes gaze out longingly over the sea, but she cannot see what lies many miles away.

On September 18, 1917, my grandmother was sitting alone in her tiny one-room shack holding a newborn baby girl. The only things that adorned the walls of her home were a medicine chest that her grandfather had made for her and the picture of a young girl looking out toward places unseen.

Attached to the picture's corner was a letter. It read:

Dearest Lenny,

Woodrow called me to serve and you know I had to go. I'll send back my pay so that you and Grace will be taken care of. Pray for my comrades and me, and give Grace a big kiss. I'll be home soon.

With all my love,
Jim

Her Jim was a man who never wrote, and this note was a surprise to her. She folded it neatly several times and tucked it safely in her apron pocket.

She did what she had to do, but the nights were long as she walked and rocked her young, crying daughter. A tiny radio foretold the possibility of war, and, on October 23, 1917, her throat tightened and her heart pounded as the news reported that "the first American Doughboys were stepping onto foreign soil."

Grandma knew Grandpa was one of them.

Within two months, Grandma received Grandpa's first check and was able to pay up the bills. An enclosed letter said that her husband had made arrangements for his checks to be delivered directly to her the first of each month. That comforted her because she knew as long as the checks came, Grandpa was okay.

As the months wore on, Grandma was grateful that the army hadn't visited her door. Neighbors and friends were already dealing with the loss of husbands, brothers, uncles and children. Her own sister received an official letter that stated her husband was missing in action.

Grace started walking at six months. Grandma packaged a picture of their beautiful daughter stepping lightly across the floor with a long family letter. Sealing it with a kiss, she wrote, "Miss you much," on the envelope and mailed it off. After several weeks, the letter and picture were returned with the handwritten message, "Unable to locate soldier," scrawled across its front.

Grandma tucked the letter in her apron pocket and slumped into the big, overstuffed blue chair that faced the picture. Her tears flowed as she stared into the picture and placed herself into the body of the girl. She felt her hollow heart skipping beats as the Atlantic slammed her soul.

Taking a deep breath, Grandma prayed for all the men who were lost and scared this night. With a strong "Amen," a calm came over her. She realized that the young woman in the picture was also waiting for her love to come home. Suddenly, she didn't feel so alone. She had someone to wait with.

When the months had rolled into the second year of America's involvement in World War I, Grandma had settled into a quiet routine. Grace was walking and talking, the house was immaculate, and life went on. Grandpa's checks were arriving each month and she told no one about the returned letter.

On the eleventh hour of the eleventh day of the eleventh month of 1918, a cease-fire went into effect for all combatants. The war was over, but before the official armistice was declared, nine million people had died on the battlefield, and the world was forever changed.

On April 6, 1919, Aunt Martha handed Grandma a letter that she had received by accident. It was official army issue, stamps, seals and all. She carried it inside and sat heavily in the chair. She called Grace to her lap and cradled her close as she opened the envelope with trembling, cold hands. As she pulled the letter out of the envelope it fell to the floor. Two words jumped out at her: coming and home. Retrieving the letter, she smoothed it out and started reading. Jim's unit would be coming home on April 7, 1919, at 9:00 A.M. That was tomorrow!

The next morning, she dressed Grace and herself in their finest attire, and they arrived at the dock at 8:30 A.M. The ship was already there, and she placed herself at the end of the gangplank. A serviceman came over and asked her whom she was there to see. She told him but then asked, "Why?"

"We have special messages for some of the wives. Let me see if you're one of them." With that, he walked away.

Soon cheers were heard from the ship and men of all ages were running down the plank toward waiting arms. As the last of the men were embraced, Grandma found herself manless. Swallowing hard, she squeezed Grace's hand tightly and scanned the ship. Suddenly, the serviceman appeared at the top of the gangplank with a handful of envelopes and a high-ranking officer. As they descended the plank, Grandma stepped back and caressed Grace's hair. She closed her eyes and started to pray.

"Mrs. Adams?"

"Yes," a weak voice sprung up from behind the crowd.

"We are sorry to inform you that Robert J. Adams was killed while in the service of his country...."

Grandma's heart fell almost as far as the just-widowed wife's did.

"Mrs. Becker?"

Another note was passed on.

By the tenth passing, Grandma turned and started the long walk home.

"Mrs. Creed?"

Grandma's heart stopped.

"Don't you want to go home with your husband?" the voice said.

She turned slowly to greet the face that asked the question. Grandma fell to her knees and sobbed into Grace's dress as Grandpa knelt beside her and hugged his family for the first time in almost a year and a half.

After they tucked Grace into bed, Grandpa found Grandma sitting in the big blue chair staring at the picture. For the first time, it looked to her as if her friend in the painting was smiling.

~Candace Carteen
Chicken Soup for the Military Wife's Soul

88

Hidden Treasures

Grow old with me! The best is yet to be.
~Robert Browning

Ike was closed-lipped about our Valentine's weekend getaway. I was to be ready to leave from the Air Force base where we both worked by 6:00 P.M. He gave no other clues.

A few hours after our departure, we arrived at the beautiful cabin he had rented near a Northern Georgia mountain town. Valentine's Day morning, we had breakfast, exchanged gifts and cards, and then headed into Helen for some sightseeing.

After a full day, Ike informed me he had brought some work he needed to do. Knowing him to be a workaholic, I was neither surprised nor disappointed. He went to the bedroom while I curled up on the couch to watch a Doris Day movie.

Sometime later and half asleep, I felt Ike gently shaking my shoulder to rouse me.

"I forgot to give you a few presents," he said, sitting down next to me. I sat up, groggy but curious.

Ike handed me several small boxes and told a story about each present as I opened them one by one.

I unwrapped delicate pearls from Hawaii and listened as he painted a picture of turquoise water and white sand paradise. Next was a pair of exotic gold earrings from Saudi Arabia and I listened as he described the stark deserts of the Middle East. I opened box after box of jewelry and enjoyed Ike's descriptions of the distant places where he'd found them.

Then he pulled out several sheets of paper—the "work" he had been doing. A list of everything he liked about me. A beautiful love letter. A letter that reduced me to a blubbery, weepy mess.

"Michelle, each one of these gifts I've given you were purchased on different occasions, in many different locations during my ten years in the Air Force." Ike paused. "They were all purchased with my future wife in mind."

As I tried to process it all, he slipped down on one knee, took my hands in his and asked me to marry him. I drew him into a passionate embrace with my equally passionate answer.

Today, a beautiful jewelry armoire cradles those wonderful, worldly gifts. But my most cherished treasure is the man who so lovingly thought and planned and shopped for his future wife. My jewel of a husband.

~Michelle Isenhour
Chicken Soup for the Bride's Soul

89

Only Joking

It is the ability to take a joke, not make one, that
proves you have a sense of humor.
~Max Eastman

I was a military wife stationed in California in the mid-1980s. My helicopter pilot husband was gone much of the time. He handled the separations in his way, and I handled them in mine.

During this time, he was often in Panama for three to four months at a time. He was able to call me at home once a week, for five minutes. I was often not at home when he phoned and would keep his messages on the answering machine tape to listen to over and over again until he returned.

Once, just before he was due to return, he phoned, and during the conversation said he had bought something for me. The very next night he was able to surprise me with another phone call. He had only a minute to talk, saying he had been celebrating the night before and didn't remember what we'd talked about. I reminded him that he said he'd bought me lace table linens and a gold bracelet. He hung up before I could tell him that I was only joking and that he hadn't told me what he'd bought for me at all.

When he got home three days later and was emptying his duffel bag, there they were: the hand-embroidered lace tablecloth and napkins, and a lovely gold bracelet—all of which he had quickly gone out and bought for me after that second phone call.

I finally told him the truth about that second phone call, but only after I'd put the linens on the table and the bracelet on my wrist. We had a good laugh, and he never again used his five-minute phone call to telephone me after he'd been "celebrating."

~Vicki A. Vadala-Cummings
Chicken Soup for the Military Wife's Soul

90

Navy Pilot's Wife

*You can kiss your family and friends goodbye and put miles between you, but
at the same time you carry them with you in your heart, your mind, your
stomach, because you do not just live in a world but a world lives in you.*

~Frederick Buechner

When you are a navy pilot's wife, every phone call makes
you stiffen, and every knock at the door brings a lump
to your throat and a knot to your stomach. The dangers of combat are obvious, but even routine flights have inherent
dangers. Flying is a perilous business, and families of pilots face that
on a day-to-day basis.

It was a difficult six months when my husband was deployed as
a helicopter pilot in the Persian Gulf region. We had two daughters,
and I was pregnant with our third. Dennis and I e-mailed each other
as much as we could, trying to support each other from opposite
sides of the world. I faced the challenges of being a temporarily single
parent back home, and he faced the challenges of long, hot flights
over the Persian Gulf.

We talked about everything except the dangers he faced. He
didn't bring it up because he didn't want to worry me. I didn't
bring it up because I didn't want to burden him with my worries.
But the dangers were real, and we both knew it. I knew he was a
good pilot, but that didn't stop the nightmares I had of him flying
in slow motion, the sand whirling around, the smell of burning
fuel and the sound of clicking rotors as his helicopter plummeted

to the ground. I never told him about the nightmares, but every time I had them, I awoke shaking and sweaty, with the taste of sand in my mouth.

During spring vacation from school, the girls and I took a trip to South Carolina with my parents. For the first time during Dennis's deployment, I relaxed and let go of the constant worry. He would be home in another month, and all was well. Truthfully, I was relieved to be out of our house, where I had to wonder if every knock on the door might be that of a Navy chaplain.

We were walking in from a bike ride when I heard my cell phone ringing. I ran to answer it but could only hear a lot of noise on the other end. "Hello?" I said, then yelled, "HELLO?"

Then, on the other end of the line, I heard, "Sarah? It's me. I'm okay. I need you to know that it wasn't me and that everyone got out okay. I'll call you as soon as I can..." and then the phone went dead.

What was he talking about? I had no idea, but I felt my throat tighten and a sandy taste filled my mouth.

"What's wrong, Mom?" my daughter asked.

"I'm not sure, honey," I said, and I walked to the TV and turned it to CNN. The scroll line at the bottom of the screen said: "NAVY HELICOPTER CRASHES."

I got a chill and started to shake. He was okay. I took a deep breath and patted my pregnant belly. "Daddy is okay."

I didn't find out the whole story until later. My husband had been the pilot of one of two helicopters set to fly in formation. He took off first, and, when he turned to spot the other helicopter, he saw it on the ground in flames. Everyone had gotten out of the aircraft, but he didn't know that at the time. He landed nearby and found out that his squadron mates were okay. When he saw a news crew pull up, his first thought was how scared I would be if I saw video of the crashed helicopter on TV. He remembered he had his cell phone in his flight suit pocket, and, just moments after the accident, he called me. Amidst all the chaos, despite how close he and his fellow pilots had come to disaster, he was thinking about protecting me. His selflessness touched me and brought us even closer together.

I haven't dreamed about helicopter crashes since.

~Sarah Monagle
Chicken Soup for the Military Wife's Soul

Chapter

12

Holding Memories
Close to Your Heart

*Throughout our years together, we had built up a history and a close-
ness so subtle we didn't even know it was there.*
~Erma Bombeck

91

Seven White, Four Red, Two Blue

believe every object in our lives holds a memory. The most prized object in my life, and the one that holds the most memories, is a rusty tin box. I need only look at the beat-up old tin box, resting obscurely on my bookshelf next to a picture of my five-year-old daughter, to unleash a flood of memories and emotions. Some happy—some sad—all mine.

The first true love of my life, and the one that still causes the most pain, was a Japanese girl named Hitomi. In Japanese her name meant Pure Beauty, but you didn't need to speak the language to understand that. You just had to look at her. I was twenty-six and she was twenty-one when we first met at a nightclub in Okinawa, Japan. I swear she came straight out of a fairy tale. She had long, straight, silky black hair that flowed to her perfectly shaped waist and high-lighted her hundred-and-five-pound frame. Her skin was soft and tanned and seemed to glow in the sunlight; but what I remember most were her eyes. Her eyes seemed to pass right through me and touch the very depth of my soul. I was in love.

We started dating shortly after that first meeting. Hitomi was a very sentimental person. Every day held special importance to her. I would soon understand why.

One day, after we had been going out for about a month, she showed up at my apartment and handed me something. "Present," she said. I opened the carefully wrapped handkerchiefs she had used as gift wrap. What I saw surprised me—a beat-up, old, rusted, lime green, tin cigar box. The lid had the remains of a picture on the outside. Through the rust and chipped paint I could only make out what appeared to be a finger and an ear. The rest of the box looked just as bad—like it had been dragged behind a car after a wedding sixty years ago.

"Thanks," I told her. "If we're exchanging junk, let me get something out of my garbage for you."

She didn't understand my attempt at humor. "Open," she said, picking up the box and handing it to me. Paint and rust fell from it as I gripped the box in my hands. I was reluctant to open it, fearing it might still contain the remains of the world's first fruitcake. "Open," she said again, this time smacking me on the side of my head and pushing the box into my chest. I opened the box and was amazed. The inside was finished in gold leaf, polished and shined like a mirror.

In the box was a single, white, origami paper swan. "Every month we are together I will make you a white swan to put in our box," she said. "After one year, we will string the swans together to hang on the praying tree in front of Nishihama Temple. This will be our way of thanking God for our time together. I will make you a blue swan to put in the box to show our one year of love together. And if we ever have an argument or fight, I will make us a red swan, so when we see it in our box we will remember what we did wrong and learn from it as a couple." We placed two strings of white swans on the tree at the temple while we were together. And in time, a few red ones appeared in our box as well.

It was during the middle of our third year together that Hitomi began to get sick. She had told me she had health problems in the past, but they were nothing for me to worry about. That was the only lie Hitomi ever told me. I found out through her best friend that she had leukemia and was in the final stages of that sickening disease. Her parents admitted her to the hospital, and after several weeks of pleading, they finally let me see her. I sat next to her bed and softly kissed her lips. When she saw me she smiled.

"Hello, honey," she whispered. Then she pointed to the night-stand next to her bed. "Please open for me." I opened the nightstand and saw within it a single, white paper swan. "I want to take to your house but too sick. I'm sorry. Now you please put in our box, okay?"

I nodded and kissed her forehead—tears flowing down my cheeks. I didn't notice how frail she had become. Or that her skin, once tanned and glowing, was now pale and gray. I also didn't notice that the long, silky hair she meticulously combed every day was gone, due to heavy doses of chemotherapy. I didn't see any of that. To me she was as beautiful as the first day we met, maybe even more so. It was then that I realized I wasn't looking at her—I was looking inside her. I saw the beauty in her that could never be changed. I saw what was important. I now understood the meaning of that tin box she gave me. It was her way of preparing me for what she knew would inevitably become of her—her way of teaching me that pure beauty is on the inside. And that no matter how broken or old the outside may appear, what's important—what's real—is that which is held inside.

Hitomi died two days later. Her family didn't allow me at her funeral. I was a foreigner. That was fine. I knew she was with me, and she always would be—every time I opened that old tin box.

I once read, "No one knows what any object means except he or she who owns it." When I look at that tin box I think how true that is. Since her death, people have asked me about the relationship I had with Hitomi. My answer is as perplexing to them as it is simple to me: "Seven white, four red and two blue."

~Robert P. Curry
Chicken Soup for the Grieving Soul

92

A Romantic Hammer

The miracle is this—the more we share, the more we have.
~Leonard Nimoy

During the story that follows, you will gain insight into an especially romantic evening amidst a very difficult financial time in my life. My husband, our two children and I lived on a very tight, shoestring budget for a number of years. We were in the ministry and our little church could barely afford to pay us as their pastor and family. But out of lack come great things from the heart, things that make memories, things that mold character, things that make strong marriages, things that will never be forgotten. And from this, I tell my story....

As I walked into the room that had earlier been off limits to me, I could see that careful preparation had taken place to assure that our wedding anniversary celebration would be a wonderful surprise. Most of the day had been spent carefully following my husband's instructions to spend the afternoon outdoors, which in itself made me suspicious. For several months, I had become totally absorbed with juggling our financial situation—so much so that the word "surprise" wasn't even in my vocabulary. I certainly was not prepared for what I was about to receive. My husband knew that we didn't have the extra finances for an evening out, so instead he and our two children worked together to create the most romantic anniversary evening right in our very own home.

Standing directly in front of our dining room entrance was my husband, who said with a smile, "The evening awaits you, my lady." My face blushed like a new bride anticipating what was to happen next. My eyes were immediately drawn to the table, which was beautifully covered with a fine linen cloth and my best china dishes. Napkins were neatly folded by each plate, but above one of the plates were several packages wrapped in brown paper. A single source of light came from the center of the table, where a rather large candle was burning. Balloons of varied shapes and sizes danced along the ceiling as if in accompaniment to the beat of the soft music playing in the background. My daughter emerged from the kitchen proudly carrying the cake she had just baked for the celebration while my son stood tall with a strong posture as he wore a white linen towel draped carefully over his arm, taking on the position of maître d' for the evening. My husband was dutifully orchestrating all the last-minute details before he pulled out the chair for me as guest of honor at the head of the table. It was obvious that each member knew his or her assigned duties and had rehearsed them several times for this occasion.

Only a queen could feel this regal, I thought. Glancing at my husband throughout the evening, I could sense romantic overtones to his smile and the way in which he addressed me to the children. This was life at its finest, and I was savoring every moment of it when my son said, "Come on, Mom, it's time to open your presents!" I could see in their eyes that this was the moment, the unveiling if you will, the frosting on the evening. So I proceeded to unwrap the first gift. It was from my daughter. She had given me a book of coupons on which were written different chores that she would do for me as I had need of them. The second gift was from my son. It was his treasured silver dollar.

Then there was the last gift. It was from my husband. Anticipation loomed across their faces like you would see seconds before a touch-down. At this point, I felt like part of the winning team, and that this box contained a special something just for me. And as I removed the last piece of wrapping paper and opened the tightly closed box, there was a still silence, and then, there it was!

"A hammer?" As they were cheering, I was gasping as I tried to hide my bewildered expression. Was this a joke? Had I missed something? Not knowing what else to do, I gave my husband a quick kiss, hoping this diversion would eliminate any detection of ungratefulness on my part. Gathering my composure, I said to my husband, "How did you know that I wanted my own hammer?" All the time, my son was saying, "Gee, Mom, this is great!"

Sometimes, we cover our disappointments with gratitude, especially when our spouse has that special sparkle in his eyes that speaks loudly of the pride he feels after having purchased the perfect gift. How could I be anything but happy for all they had done for me? But the romance was fading fast! How could I be ungrateful when in all reality we had very little money for anything extra? Yet I had secretly hoped for a bottle of perfume or a renewal of my favorite magazine subscription. Had I forgotten to convey that to my husband over the course of the week before our anniversary? A hammer? What was he thinking? Next it'll be a tool belt or staple gun. Doesn't he know that a woman savors the romantic things, especially on her wedding anniversary? And here I was at forty, already feeling my esteem fading with the discovery of new facial wrinkles, graying hair and a thicker waist. I tried to keep in mind that it was the thought that counts, but every time I envisioned that hammer, my heart sank even deeper. How could our thinking be so far apart? My resolve would be to simply misplace the hammer, perhaps in a box under my bed, and never let on about my disappointment.

But there is a moral to the story.... My husband was much more discerning than I ever gave him credit for being. I have always been a decorating bug, always changing and rearranging the furnishings in our home. Since then, I have realized that his hammer was a gift that spoke volumes to me of the confidence my husband had placed in me and my abilities to transform the interior of our simple little home into a place of beauty. The hammer was like receiving his stamp of approval. Today I can see the purpose in the gift in a far greater way than I did the day I received it. And I am impressed with the fact that my husband knew me better than I knew myself.

As I look back on that situation, I can laugh and even tell you the story. I've also learned an important lesson about prejudging a gift. What I would have chosen for myself at the time would not have benefited me half as much as this gift has. And you know what else? Every time I have used this handy tool throughout the years, I have thought of my husband and the romantic anniversary evening he so lovingly planned for me. It generates a continuous romantic feeling each and every time. So it really was a romantic hammer after all.

~Catherine Walker
Chicken Soup for the Romantic Soul

93

Romeo Sets the Stage

*A*s a flight attendant for a major airline, I've had many memorable moments attending to passengers' special needs. Most of the memories bring a smile to my lips. Some make me grin from ear to ear.

My all-time favorite occurred a few years ago on a Friday night flight to Denver. A passenger asked the flight attendants if we could do him a favor. The young man's girlfriend was meeting him at the airport in Denver, and he was planning to propose. He had brought with him ninety-nine long-stemmed red roses and one long-stemmed white rose. Nestled between the petals of the single white rose was an engagement ring. Our Romeo wanted ninety-nine passengers to deplane before him, each handing his girlfriend a red rose. He would come out last, carrying the white rose with the ring, and propose to her.

We made an announcement explaining the gentleman's plan and asked for volunteers. Immediately, hands waved and people called out. Everyone wanted to be a part of the romantic event! The lucky ninety-nine were thrilled to be entrusted with a rose. Throughout the flight, the young man went through the cabin showing the engagement ring and receiving congratulations. Many passengers shared stories of their own engagement, wedding or honeymoon, and waves of laughter rang through the cabin. The warm wishes and feelings of joy were overwhelming.

When we arrived in Denver, the passengers deplaned in a buzz of excitement, and the crew followed our Romeo out of the jetbridge. There, under a mountain of roses, we found Juliet—and a planeful of passengers patiently waiting to spy on this special moment. Romeo took the roses from his sweetheart's arms, laid them on a chair, dropped to one knee and professed his love. Then he handed her his single white rose. Through her tears, she said "Yes!" and the audience broke into cheers. Cameras flashed and best wishes were given.

Truly, all the world loves a lover!

~Jill LaBoy
Chicken Soup for the Gardener's Soul

94

The Tale of the Goose

He felt now that he was not simply close to her,
but that he did not know where he ended and she began.
~Leo Tolstoy

More than a decade ago, my wife Barbara and I bought a wonderful five-acre property on a small mountain. We feel incredibly lucky to live where we do. Every day we marvel at the beauty of our land, and we like sharing it with the fish, ducks and deer, as well as the hordes of birds that grace it year-round.

The geese are a different story entirely. I must confess that for the most part I have never liked geese. They tend to travel in large flocks, make an awful din, are unpleasantly aggressive, and above all, they make a terrible mess. When they come in waves each spring and fall, it's a war of attrition. I want them to go; they are determined to stay. They settle at the edge of the pond and I run at them, flapping my arms and shouting.

The idea is to make them so edgy and uncomfortable they will decide to leave. For years I won; each gaggle would stay a few hours, or at most a day or two. Then they would decide it just was too unfriendly a place and off they would go.

Six years ago they came again, but something was different. Two of the geese, clearly a pair, stayed away from the others, both on land and in the water. It was as if they were saying, "We're different. Don't include us with our brethren." When the others finally left, honking in anger, the pair left with them, but I knew something was up. I was sure they would be back. Two days later, they came back, quietly, in the evening, alighting in the pond.

They watched with concern as I walked to its edge. I knew they were waiting to see what I would do. As I looked at them, trying to figure what approach to take, Barbara joined me. "They are a pair. You know they mate for life. They won't bother us. Let them stay."

And so I did.

The ducks continued to come for their regular feedings. At first, the geese watched from a distance as the ducks ate. A few days later, I could see them watching from the far side of the pond and then, suddenly, with a huge flourish of honking, they charged over to join the ducks.

For six years they held sway on the pond. Each year the female nested, but only once did that result in goslings. When they were gone for any period, you could hear them coming from miles away; it sounded like an entire gaggle. And when they landed in the pond with great fanfare, they would talk to each other, honking loudly for a few minutes before settling down.

They were clearly devoted to each other, and gradually we found ourselves becoming quite attached to them. They had decided this was their pond: Ducks were okay, but not other geese.

At first they left it up to me to get rid of the other geese. Finally, after one particularly difficult time persuading some unwanted geese to leave, I turned to Mr. Goose whom we had named George and said, "Some help you are. It's your pond; you get them to leave."

Now I know geese do not understand English, and I knew it was pure coincidence, but after that George and Mrs. George took a very active role in flying at the intruders. Most of the time they succeeded, but when they couldn't make the invaders fly off, I would help out.

Our geese, like most geese, were very smart. Often they would join the intruders, and when I rushed them, they would squawk loudly and fly off. Invariably the whole gaggle would follow. Then the next morning or later that night, George and Mrs. George would return, boisterous as ever.

Almost always when we arrived home, as our car passed a small bridge at the bottom of the pond, the two of them would start a huge din, necks out straight, honking at the top of their voices.

"Our watch-geese," said Barbara. And so they were.

After any event on the pond that aroused their attention, they would face each other and talk. Their conversations were a marvel to watch. They communicated more in a given day than most human couples do in a week.

Their devotion was extraordinary. They were paired for life, together twenty-four hours a day, never far apart either in the confines of the pond or on the adjacent rolling lawns. It was easy to tell they enjoyed each other's company.

Gradually, they began to trust us. At first, they would stand on the edge as I fed the ducks, waiting impatiently until I went off a distance, then they would rush in, pushing the ducks aside to grab their share. It took several years before they led the run (or more properly, the waddle) for the food. George always came first, hissing if he felt I was too close.

They spent the day in the pond or at its edge. Sometimes George would stand on one leg, his neck and head buried in his wing, but at our approach, even fifty or a hundred yards away, he would stretch his neck and keep one eye riveted on us, suspiciously watching our every move.

As he became more trusting, George would stay with his head buried, but I could still see that eye fixed on me. It took a year before he would completely ignore me, letting me come within ten feet of them as I removed algae or leaves from the pond.

Then one day as I threw the corn, he came running up ahead of the ducks, stopping seven or eight feet away and talking softly without any hissing. And when I threw the corn on the ground, George eagerly pecked at it, eating and talking at the same time. I marveled at this feat—I couldn't figure out how he could eat and talk all at once.

And so it went. They became our friends; we were captivated by their devotion. We never spoke about it, but I think we both wondered if it could be that their bond to each other was greater than ours, even though we had been married for decades.

In early April they made a nest, but it was in a different site. Every other time it had been on the far side of the pond, behind a willow tree. This time it was close to us, in a wooded, protected area at the edge of the pond. I could see Mrs. George sitting on that nest—awake, watching, protecting. Perhaps they thought that a change of scenery, of nesting site, would change their luck and produce a gaggle of goslings.

At the same time George's personality changed dramatically; he would not permit the deer on the front lawn. He would honk loudly and angrily, then charge, running or flying just above the ground, wings fully spread, making an enormous din.

His behavior was clearly purposeful. He wanted a full pail of corn on the ground, and he saw to it that the marauding deer did not gobble it up. He tolerated the few ducks, but he knew they would not eat much of it. He wanted it there for the infrequent occasions when Mrs. George would leave the nest, eat and drink hurriedly, and then return to her maternal labors.

Sometimes when Barbara was gardening, he would come close to her and stand there until she got up and filled the pail with corn and threw it on the ground near the pond. Then Mrs. George would appear and feed while George, eating nothing, would stand guard.

And so it went for weeks. Then one day early in May, I arose as usual, dressed and ambled to the garage to get the pail of corn. George was in the pond, but unlike every other day he seemed uninterested in my activities. I walked to the area at the edge of the pond where I ordinarily threw the corn. He remained in the pond, still uninterested. I threw the corn on the ground as usual. Thirty minutes later when I left for work, eight deer were there, and George didn't chase them. That's strange, I thought.

The next day George was sitting at the edge of the pond, not far from the nest. Again I threw a pail of corn. Again he paid no attention. I had a very queasy feeling. Something was wrong. I tried to locate Mrs. George, but she wasn't visible; perhaps she was behind the tree.

On the morning of the third day, George was sitting in the same place. I threw the corn down. Still no response. I looked at him. Something was very wrong. I walked to within a few feet of him and asked, "What's wrong, old man?"

With that he turned to me, and as I looked at him, I gasped, for in that eye there was an unmistakable look of terrible despair, of sadness, of overwhelming sorrow. And in that moment of communication between goose and man, I blurted out, "I'm so sorry."

Then, shaken by that look, I walked around to the nest. It was empty, but undisturbed. There were no eggs, no sign of a struggle.

I was to learn later that a coyote had killed Mrs. George in the middle of the night. Not knowing that his beloved partner was dead and puzzled by the benign appearance around the nest, I walked back to where George had been sitting, but he had left.

Later, after we knew the full story, Barbara said, "Maybe he has not gone forever. Maybe he'll be back. Sometimes they find new partners."

She was giving voice to that wellspring of inner hope that helps us all deal with tragic events. But we knew it was not to be. George, heartbroken, was not coming back.

That look of overwhelming sorrow in his eye has haunted me ever since.

Of course, life goes on. The flocks of geese returned almost immediately. There was no goose couple to tell them the pond was already taken and to drive them off. I still didn't want the pond over-run with geese, and, as in the past, I made it clear they were not welcome. They were tenacious, but so was I, and I harassed them until, protesting loudly, they flew off.

This went on for several weeks, and then I noticed that a pair stayed apart from the rest. One day after the larger gaggle had gone, they came back and stayed a few hours. They watched me closely, obviously testing whether I would let an isolated pair stay. When I left them undisturbed that first evening, they got the message. The next afternoon they were back, and the day after that. They haven't adopted the pond as their own just yet, but we think they will.

I hug my wife a lot more now. Whenever we walk, she has always been the one to take my hand. Now I seek her hand as often as she takes mine. She thinks it's my mellowing with age.

There is some truth in that, but for the most part it's George and his wife. Mostly, it is the tale of the goose.

~Donald Louria
Chicken Soup for the Nature Lover's Soul

95

A Forever Kind of Love

*For you see, each day I love you more
Today more than yesterday and less than tomorrow.*
~Rosemonde Gerard

One of our favorite patients had been in and out of our small, rural hospital several times, and all of us on med-surg had grown quite attached to her and her husband. In spite of terminal cancer and resulting pain, she never failed to give us a smile or a hug. Whenever her husband came to visit, she glowed. He was a nice man, very polite and as friendly as his wife. I had grown quite attached to them and was always glad to care for her.

I admired their expression of love. Daily, he brought her fresh flowers and a smile, then sat by her bed as they held hands and talked quietly. When the pain was too much and she cried or became confused, he hugged her gently in his arms and whispered until she rested. He spent every available moment at her bedside, giving her small sips of water and stroking her brow. Every night, before he left for home, he closed the door so they could spend time alone together. After he was gone, we'd find her sleeping peacefully with a smile on her lips.

On this night, however, things were different. As soon as I entered report, the day nurses informed us she had steadily taken a turn for the worse and wouldn't make it through the night. Although I was sad, I knew that this was for the best. At least my friend wouldn't be in pain any longer.

I left report and checked on her first. When I entered the room, she aroused and smiled weakly, but her breathing was labored and I could tell it wouldn't be long. Her husband sat beside her, smiling, too, and said, "My Love is finally going to get her reward."

Tears came to my eyes, so I asked if they needed anything and left quickly. I offered care and comfort throughout the evening, and at about midnight she passed away with her husband still holding her hand. I consoled him, and with tears running down his cheeks he said, "May I please be alone with her for awhile?" I hugged him and closed the door behind me.

I stood outside the room, blotting my tears and missing my friend and her smile. And I could feel the pain of her husband in my own heart. Suddenly from the room came the most beautiful male voice I have ever heard singing. It was almost haunting the way it floated through the halls. All of the other nurses stepped out into the hallways to listen as he sang "Beautiful Brown Eyes" at the top of his lungs.

When the tune faded, the door opened and he called to me. He looked me in the eyes then hugged me saying, "I sang that song to her every night from the first day we met. Normally I close the door and keep my voice down so as not to disturb the other patients. But I had to make sure she heard me tonight as she was on her way to heaven. She had to know that she will always be my forever love. Please apologize to anyone I bothered. I just don't know how I will make it without her, but I will continue to sing to her every night. Do you think she will hear me?"

I nodded my head "yes," unable to stop my tears. He hugged me again, kissed my cheek, and thanked me for being their nurse and friend. He thanked the other nurses, then turned and walked down the hall, his back hunched, whistling the song softly as he went.

As I watched him leave I prayed that I, too, would someday know that kind of forever love.

~Christy M. Martin
Chicken Soup for the Nurse's Soul

96

"Falling" in Love

During World War II, I was employed at a research lab in Oklahoma. Men were pretty scarce at that time, of course. One day after the end of the war, a friend called me to come to her lab to meet the new fellow who had come to work for the summer while attending college on the G.I. Bill. So I went down for a short talk and to meet the guy.

As I left I heard a loud crash behind me. When I went back to see what had happened, he was sprawled flat on the floor. He had been sitting at a desk by the door in a swivel chair and had leaned back too far to watch me walk down the hall. All during our fifty-two years of happily married life, including eleven moves with three children, I have loved telling people this story of how my husband fell for me. He hastens to assure them that he actually was only leaning over to pick up a pencil.

~Mary Mikkelsen
Chicken Soup for the Romantic Soul

The Last "I Love You"

I like not only to be loved, but to be told I am loved.
~George Eliot

Carol's husband was killed in an accident last year. Jim, only fifty-two years old, was driving home from work. The other driver was a teenager with a very high blood-alcohol level. Jim died instantly. The teenager was in the emergency room for less than two hours.

There were other ironic twists: It was Carol's fiftieth birthday, and Jim had two plane tickets to Hawaii in his pocket. He was going to surprise her. Instead, he was killed by a drunk driver.

"How have you survived this?" I finally asked Carol, a year later.

Her eyes welled up with tears. I thought I had said the wrong thing, but she gently took my hand and said, "It's all right; I want to tell you. The day I married Jim, I promised I would never let him leave the house in the morning without telling him I loved him. He made the same promise. It got to be a joke between us, and as babies came along, it got to be a hard promise to keep. I remember running down the driveway, saying 'I love you' through clenched teeth when I was mad, or driving to the office to put a note in his car. It was a funny challenge.

"We made a lot of memories trying to say 'I love you' before noon every day of our married life.

The Last "I Love You": Holding Memories Close to Your Heart   333

"The morning Jim died, he left a birthday card in the kitchen and slipped out to the car. I heard the engine starting. Oh, no, you don't, buster, I thought. I raced out and banged on the car window until he rolled it down.

"'Here on my fiftieth birthday, Mr. James E. Garret, I, Carol Garret, want to go on record as saying I love you!'

"That's how I've survived. Knowing that the last words I said to Jim were 'I love you.'"

~Debbi Smoot
A Second Chicken Soup for the Woman's Soul

98

The Camping Trip

Anywhere is paradise; it's up to you.
~Author Unknown

*I*t was raining sideways and thundering so loud that the house shook. Anne sat in the middle of the hardwood floor surrounded by sleeping bags, camping stove, groceries and a tent. She wondered if the tent would be able to float in the ocean-sized puddles that were forming on the leaf-covered ground.

In a few minutes Sam was supposed to arrive for their anniversary camping trip. They had hardly seen each other the last few weeks. They were both bogged down with graduate thesis and research projects. In addition to their schoolwork, Anne taught two classes a week and Sam worked full-time for his mentor. They knew the only way they could spend some time together was to go out of town, away from phones, computers and professors asking for last-minute favors. This trip was going to be their reunion as well as their one-year anniversary celebration.

"Just my luck," Anne said out loud. "We finally have plans and it has to rain on our camping trip. We're cursed!"

The front door opened and there was Sam, clad in soggy hiking boots and clothes so wet they looked like they were melting.

"Who's cursed?" he asked, plopping down on the splayed sleeping bags. "Certainly not us. Two wildly in-love newlyweds about to go on the world's most fabulous camping trip?"

Anne shook her head. "You don't really want to go camping in this weather?"

"You bet I do!"

Before Anne could answer, Sam stood up and walked around the room. First, he unplugged the phone, then the computer. He pulled down the shades and covered the television with the orange afghan they kept on the couch. Then he began setting up the tent in the middle of the living room floor. He brought the George Foreman grill in from the kitchen and set it up next to the tent and lit a fire in the rarely used fireplace.

"Now," he said smiling, "have you ever seen a more beautiful campsite?" He opened his arms wide and Anne rose and stood in his embrace, laughing as she surveyed their campsite.

"Never."

That night after they roasted hot dogs on the George Foreman grill and toasted marshmallows in the fireplace, they were tucked inside their sleeping bags. Sam circled his arms around Anne's waist.

"Sam," Anne said, "when we planned this night, I imagined that by now we would be watching the sunset behind House Mountain and sipping on some champagne, but, somehow, this makes it all the more special. We don't need a romantic sunset, or a fancy bottle of champagne or beautiful scenery—we just need each other, forever. Together we can make any situation work out right."

Anne and Sam just celebrated their ten-year wedding anniversary. To celebrate they did the usual; they went on a romantic camping trip—right in their own living room.

~Meghan Mazour
Chicken Soup for the Romantic Soul

99

Chicken Soup for the Soul

The Fisherman and His Femme Fatale

It's not where you go or what you do, it's who you take along with you.
~Anonymous

Saw her across the room, sparkling with sequins. She flipped her eyes up at me under a heavy fringe of false eyelashes and my knees turned to water. Patting her bouffant hairdo, she wiggled her way upstream, through the crowded party, toward me. She looked like an enchanting mermaid in that silvery dress, and as she neared I felt for the first time in my life like a piece of bait.

It was Halloween 1964. I was wearing hip waders and a fishing vest because my passion in life was fishing, and I indulged my passion every opportunity I got. As she neared, gazing at me hypnotically with her sea-green eyes, she told me she was born under the sign of the fish. I laughed, not knowing whether to believe her or not. One thing I knew, I was in trouble. She told me I was tall, dark and handsome. I told her she was bewitching. By the end of the evening she had me hooked, and by the end of the following summer, she had me landed in a small courtroom, slipping a gold ring on her dainty finger.

On our honeymoon I took her from the lights of the city to a remote valley nestled deep in the heart of grizzly bear country. For one week, we pitched our tent by an emerald flowing river and fished to our hearts' content. But wait. She liked to fish too, didn't she? I asked somewhat belatedly as we rumbled down the dirt road in a battered pickup truck. Her answer? She batted her magical eyes and just smiled.

Every day of our honeymoon, I fished. Every day, she also fished; precisely at noon, she donned a fishnet bikini, toss her gleaming black hair down her back and walk barefoot to the river. I, too, was in that river, chest deep, casting my line far downstream. She always managed to lure me to shore. Well, almost always. Sometimes a line would tighten, or a reel would spin crazily, a conquered fish leaping to the surface. At those times I'd see her shrug her shoulders and head back to the tent.

I took her canoeing and she managed to look impressed at the salmon I threw at her pretty painted toes, telling me I looked like a Greek god throwing tribute at her feet. One day we rounded the corner, heading back to camp and saw the savage evidence of a grizzly bear foray. Our belongings were strewn everywhere as if they had been chewed up and spit out. Upon investigation, I noted claw marks imbedded deeply in the lid of our food chest. Giant paw prints in the soil left no doubt whatsoever as to whom the predator had been. She broke down in tears and started to pack.

I prepared an airtight plea bargain that got me three extra days on the river. That evening she dabbed on her favorite perfume and I smiled as I hung my chest waders in the log cabin I rented for her.

The day of our departure arrived, and I didn't share her feelings of elation at going back to the city. As I closed the truck door, I tried not to appear morose. Looking longingly at the crashing waterfalls that tumbled over the majestic mountains, the deep secret forest and the shining river that I loved, I asked what she thought of the valley.

"Very beautiful," she replied absently, checking her makeup in the windshield mirror. I thought she was beautiful as I saw the eagerness on her face.

I made up my mind then and there, kissed her soundly and told her bluntly, "I'm glad, because this is where we're going to live."

A look of horror crossed her features as I realized my blunder.

That eager look of hers had been to high-tail it out of the wilderness, not live in the wilderness. Desperately, I began to play my line. I was a new stepfather to her five children—I had to think of the welfare of my new family, didn't I? In the valley there was no danger, except for bears, and I had a rifle. There were gardens, and game to hunt in the fall. I always hunted with a fishing rod in one hand and a rifle in the other, because I never knew when I might run into a stream. There would always be plenty to eat for the children. And—I told her dramatically, saving the pièce de résistance for last—I would build her a dream house.

That did it. She agreed. But somehow I suspected she knew the real reason for my wanting to move the family twelve hundred miles—for the fishing. I hadn't mentioned that little fact, but if she had asked, I would have confessed. I knew I had married a wise woman when she didn't ask.

Happy with her dream home—a beautiful custom-made log cabin—we moved the entire family to paradise. On our first Christmas, I bought her a fishing rod. Now she could fish with me! Our girls took me to task, and on her birthday I bought her perfume with the money from the sale of the rod. But, to her chagrin, I also bought her a canner to can the steady supply of coho and spring salmon I regularly brought in from my daily forays to the river.

She always wondered where I got the feathers to tie my flies. One day she pulled her hatbox from beneath the bed, lifted the lid and gazed into it, stupefied. Like naked chicks, embarrassed for lack of feathers, laid her hats. One by one she picked them up, not knowing whether to laugh or cry. A lone feather floated to the bottom. I had forgotten one. She picked it up and stuck it in my wallet beside my credit card. That year she had the best vacation ever.

Time passed. The children left home. She packed away her false eyelashes and got rid of the bouffant hairdo. I packed away my rifle, but there was no way I was going to get rid of my fishing rod. As much as my declining health allowed, I still fished.

On our thirty-fifth anniversary, outside a log cabin not far from where we had once pitched our honeymoon tent, I unwrapped a framed collage of photographs. Stormy rivers bleak with snow, rain swollen or hotly sun dappled, fishing through the years, casting, reeling, angling, in the glory of it all, I stood. Wiping a tear from the corner of my eye with an arthritic finger, I told my femme fatale that she was the best thing I had ever caught. Then I kissed her and together we walked into our log cabin and closed the door, forgetting my fishing rod outside.

~Graham Hall
Chicken Soup for the Fisherman's Soul

100

The Wedding Gift

More in a garden grows than what the gardener sows.
~Spanish Proverb

I had picked out the flowers in my wedding bouquet carefully, with thought for the meaning of each one. There was blue iris, my fiancé's favorite flower; white roses, symbolizing purity; and strands of green ivy, to represent faithfulness.

Midway through our wedding reception, I found myself breathless and happy, chatting with friends and juggling a full champagne glass and my flowers. Suddenly, I felt a hand on my shoulder. I turned to see a woman I had met only briefly, a friend of my new mother-in-law. In her hand, she held a tendril of ivy.

"This fell out of your bouquet when you were on the dance floor," she said. I thanked her and began to reach for it, when she added, "Do you mind if I keep it?"

I was startled at first. I hadn't even tossed my bouquet yet. And I barely knew this woman. What did she want with my ivy?

But then practicality kicked in. I was leaving on my honeymoon in the morning and certainly wouldn't take the bouquet along. I had no plans for preserving it. And I'd been given so much today.

"Go ahead. Keep it," I said with a smile, and congratulated myself for being gracious in the face of a rather odd request. Then the music started up, and I danced off in the crowd.

A few months later, the bell rang at our new home. I opened the door to find that same stranger on my porch. This time, I couldn't hide my surprise. I hadn't seen her since the wedding. What was this all about?

"I have a wedding gift for you," she said, and held out a small planter crowded with foliage. Suddenly, I knew. "It's the ivy you dropped at your wedding," she explained. "I took it home and made a cutting and planted it for you."

Years ago, at her own wedding, someone had done the same for her. "It's still growing, and I remember my wedding day every time I see it," she said. "Now, I try to plant some for other brides when I can."

I was speechless. All the quirky thoughts I'd had, and what a beautiful gift I'd received!

My wedding ivy has thrived for many years, outliving any other effort I made at indoor gardening. As the giver predicted, a glance at the glossy green leaves brings back memories of white lace and wedding vows. I treasure the ivy's story and have shared it many times.

Now, nearly twenty years later, I'm the mother of three growing sons. Someday they'll be married, I know. And although I don't want to be an interfering in-law, surely the mother of the groom can suggest that the bride's bouquet contain a bit of ivy?

I know just the plant to cut it from.

~Carol Sturgulewski
Chicken Soup for the Gardener's Soul

Red Shoes with Gold Laces

Gilda was a dancer,
a ballroom dancer,
her billowing skirts,
held to a tight waist,
by a belt made of
a rainbow of tiny conch shells.
Gilda wore red shoes, with gold laces.
When invited to come play bridge,
even with the luring promises
of meringue coconut cream pie
at the end of the bidding wars,
Gilda would apologize, say her thanks,
and instead go dancing in her
red shoes with gold laces.
Some nights folks at the condo
convoyed to the bingo palaces,
They'd come home smelling from
cigarettes, their fingers tainted
with bingo markers, and sometimes money.
But Gilda preferred to go dancing,
in red shoes with gold laces.
That's where Gilda and Bill met.
His dancing uniform was a tie

with Nittany Lions on it.
His shoes were old U.S. Navy issue,
with leather soles that could slide,
and never step on the toes of a woman
in red shoes with gold laces.
They slow-danced, an easy, gliding song.
He felt her soft skin and looked into her eyes
but Bill kept his distance,
hummed Glenn Miller in her ear,
and smelled her cologne,
something as old
as his GI Bill college days.
What was that name? It drifted
through memories, White Shoulders,
and he dipped his new Gilda deep and low,
Gilda kept her sweet-smelling balance
Safe in red shoes with gold laces.
And could that Gilda jitterbug.
Her grin picked up the spinning mirrored ball.
Bill didn't throw her over his shoulder,
nor did she leap up to wrap her legs around his hips,
but for the first time out,
he had no doubt that this was a dancer,
Gilda of the red shoes with gold laces.
Bill knew she was here alone,
There was no wedding band on her pale hand,
so he asked in between sets, about where
love had two-stepped right by her,
Just as it had polka-ed all over him,
She answered, not with vanity,
and not with false modesty.
Her eyelids fluttered like a muted tombstone,
"That husband just didn't dance enough."
She made it clear that if the new ones don't,
"I simply fox trot out of here, and go home alone,

in my red shoes with gold laces."
A whole dance card later,
Back at her place, trim and neat,
Bill undid those gold laces for her,
Softly, to the rhythm of a Sinatra
tune that danced in his head.
Then Bill kissed those toes
that had twinkled under that soft red leather.
He could tell she liked her feet
Held in reverence like an icon.
Gilda Hoffman kissed Bill on his ear,
And whispered in it, breathlessly,
That he sure knew how to dance,
even if he had never owned
a pair of red shoes with gold laces.

~Dr. Sidney Simon
Chicken Soup for the Golden Soul

Share with Us

We would like to know how these stories affected you and which ones were your favorites. Please e-mail us and let us know.

We also would like to share your stories with future readers. You may be able to help another reader, and become a published author at the same time. Please send us your own stories and poems for our future books. Some of our past contributors have launched writing and speaking careers from the publication of their stories in our books!

Your stories have the best chance of being used if you submit them through our web site, at:

www.chickensoup.com

If you do not have access to the Internet, you may submit your stories by mail or by facsimile. Please do not send us any book manuscripts, unless through a literary agent, as these will be automatically discarded.

Chicken Soup for the Soul
P.O. Box 700
Cos Cob, CT 06807-0700
Fax 203-861-7194

Chicken Soup for the Soul: Woman to Woman

Women Sharing Their Stories of Hope, Humor, and Inspiration

Women have always been wonderful sources of inspiration and support for each other. They are willing to lay bare their souls and share their experiences, even with perfect strangers. This new volume includes the 101 best stories and poems in Chicken Soup's library for women of all ages, written by women just like them.

978-1-935096-04-7

Just for Women by Women!

The Wisdom of Dads

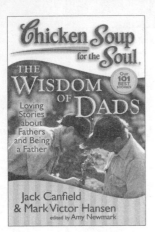

Children view their fathers with awe from the day they are born. Fathers are big and strong and seem to know everything, except for a few teenage years when fathers are perceived to know nothing! This book represents a new theme for Chicken Soup – 101 stories selected from 35 past books, all stories focusing on the wisdom of dads. Stories are written by sons and daughters about their fathers, and by fathers relating stories about their children.

Dads & Daughters

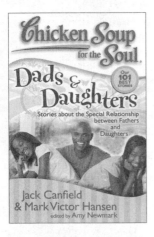

Whether she is ten years old or fifty – she will always be his little girl. And daughters take care of their dads too, whether it is a tea party for two at age five or loving care fifty years later. This wide-ranging exploration of the relationship between fathers and daughters provides an entirely new reading experience for Chicken Soup fans, with selections from forty past Chicken Soup books. Stories were written by fathers about their daughters and by daughters about their fathers, celebrating the special bond between fathers and daughters.

On Being a Parent

Parenting is the hardest and most rewarding job in the world. This upbeat and compelling new book includes the best selections on parenting from Chicken Soup's rich history, with 101 stories carefully selected to appeal to both mothers and fathers. This is a great book for couples to share, whether they are just embarking on their new adventure as parents or reflecting on their lifetime experience.

Check out our books on

Moms Know Best

"Mom will know where it is…what to say…how to fix it." This Chicken Soup book focuses on the pervasive wisdom of mothers everywhere, and includes the best 101 stories from Chicken Soup's library on our perceptive, understanding, and insightful mothers. These stories celebrate the special bond between mothers and children, our mothers' unerring wisdom about everything from the mundane to the life-changing, and the hard work that goes into being a mother every day.

Like Mother, Like Daughter

Fathers, brothers, and friends sometimes shake their head in wonder as girls "turn into their mothers." This new collection from Chicken Soup represents the best 101 stories from Chicken Soup's library on the special bond between mothers and daughters, and the magical, mysterious similarities between them. Mothers and daughters of all ages will laugh, cry, and find inspiration in these stories that remind them how much they appreciate each other.

Moms & Sons

There is a special bond between mothers and their sons and it never goes away. This new book contains the 101 best stories and poems from Chicken Soup's library honoring that lifelong relationship between mothers and their male offspring. These heartfelt and loving stories written by mothers, grandmothers, and sons, about each other, span generations and show how the mother-son bond transcends time.

Love & Family

Our
101
BEST
STORIES

More books for Women

Chicken Soup for the Woman's Soul
1-55874-415-0
A Second Chicken Soup for the Woman's Soul
1-55874-622-6
Chicken Soup for the Single's Soul
1-55874-706-0
Chicken Soup for the Couple's Soul
1-55874-646-3
Chicken Soup for the Romantic Soul
0-7573-0042-1
Chicken Soup for the Single Parent's Soul
0-7573-0241-6
Chicken Soup for the Bride's Soul
0-7573-0140-1

Books for Teens

Chicken Soup for the Soul: Preteens Talk
Inspiration and Support for Preteens from Kids Just Like Them
978-1-935096-00-9
Chicken Soup for the Soul: Teens Talk Growing Up
Stories about Growing Up, Meeting Challenges, and
Learning from Life 978-1-935096-01-6
Chicken Soup for the Soul: Teens Talk Tough Times
Stories about the Hardest Parts of Being a Teenager
978-1-935096-03-0
Chicken Soup for the Soul: Teens Talk Relationships
Stories about Family, Friends, and Love
978-1-935096-06-1
Chicken Soup for the Soul: Christian Teen Talk
Christian Teens Share Their Stories of Support, Inspiration and Growing Up
978-1-935096-12-2
Chicken Soup for the Soul: Christian Kids
Stories to Inspire, Amuse, and Warm the Hearts of Christian Kids and Their
Parents
978-1-935096-13-9

Books for Pet Lovers

Chicken Soup for the Soul: Loving Our Dogs
Heartwarming and Humorous Stories about our Companions
and Best Friends
978-1-935096-05-4

Chicken Soup for the Soul: Loving Our Cats
Heartwarming and Humorous Stories about our Feline Family Members
978-1-935096-08-5

More Favorites!

Chicken Soup for the Soul: Older & Wiser
Stories of Inspiration, Humor, and Wisdom about Life at a Certain Age
978-1-935096-17-7

Chicken Soup for the Soul: Tales of Golf and Sport
The Joy, Frustration, and Humor of Golf and Sport
978 1 935096-11-5

Chicken Soup for the Soul: Christmas Cheer
Stories about the Love, Inspiration, and Joy of Christmas
978-1-935096-15-3

Chicken Soup for the Soul: Stories of Faith
Inspirational Stories of Hope, Devotion, Faith and Miracles
978-1-935096-14-6

About the

Chicken Soup for the Soul®

Authors

Who Is
Jack Canfield?

J ack Canfield is the co-creator and editor of the *Chicken Soup for the Soul* series, which *Time* magazine has called "the publishing phenomenon of the decade." Jack is also the co-author of eight other bestselling books including *The Success Principles™: How to Get from Where You Are to Where You Want to Be, Dare to Win, The Aladdin Factor, You've Got to Read This Book,* and *The Power of Focus: How to Hit Your Business and Personal and Financial Targets with Absolute Certainty.*

Jack has recently developed a telephone coaching program and an online coaching program based on his most recent book *The Success Principles.* He also offers a seven-day *Breakthrough to Success* seminar every summer, which attracts 400 people from fifteen countries around the world.

Jack is the CEO of the Canfield Training Group in Santa Barbara, California, and founder of the Foundation for Self-Esteem in Culver City, California. He has conducted intensive personal and professional development seminars on the principles of success for over a million people in twenty-three countries. Jack is a dynamic keynote speaker and he has spoken to hundreds of thousands of others at more than 1,000 corporations, universities, professional conferences and conventions, and has been seen by millions more on national television shows such as *The Today Show, Fox and Friends, Inside Edition, Hard Copy, CNN's Talk Back Live, 20/20, Eye to Eye,* and the *NBC Nightly News* and the *CBS Evening News.*

Jack is the recipient of many awards and honors, including three honorary doctorates and a *Guinness World Records Certificate* for having seven books from the *Chicken Soup for the Soul* series appearing on the *New York Times* bestseller list on May 24, 1998.

To write to Jack or for inquiries about Jack as a speaker, his coaching programs, trainings or seminars, use the following contact information:

Jack Canfield
The Canfield Companies
P.O. Box 30880 • Santa Barbara, CA 93130
phone: 805-563-2935 • fax: 805-563-2945
E-mail: info@jackcanfield.com
www.jackcanfield.com

Who Is
Mark Victor Hansen?

Mark Victor Hansen is the co-founder of *Chicken Soup for the Soul*, along with Jack Canfield. He is also a sought-after keynote speaker, bestselling author, and marketing maven.

For more than thirty years, Mark has focused solely on helping people from all walks of life reshape their personal vision of what's possible. His powerful messages of possibility, opportunity, and action have created powerful change in thousands of organizations and millions of individuals worldwide.

Mark's credentials include a lifetime of entrepreneurial success. He is a prolific writer with many bestselling books, such as *The One Minute Millionaire*, *Cracking the Millionaire Code*, *How to Make the Rest of Your Life the Best of Your Life*, *The Power of Focus*, *The Aladdin Factor*, and *Dare to Win*, in addition to the *Chicken Soup for the Soul* series. Mark has had a profound influence in the field of human potential through his library of audios, videos, and articles in the areas of big thinking, sales achievement, wealth building, publishing success, and personal and professional development.

Mark is the founder of the *MEGA Seminar Series*. *MEGA Book Marketing University* and *Building Your MEGA Speaking Empire* are annual conferences where Mark coaches and teaches new and aspiring authors, speakers, and experts on building lucrative publishing and speaking careers. Other MEGA events include *MEGA Info-Marketing* and *My MEGA Life*.

He has appeared on *Oprah*, *CNN*, and *The Today Show*. He has been quoted in *Time*, *U.S. News & World Report*, *USA Today*, *New York Times*, and *Entrepreneur* and has had countless radio interviews, assuring our planet's people that "You can easily create the life you deserve."

As a philanthropist and humanitarian, Mark works tirelessly for organizations such as Habitat for Humanity, American Red Cross, March of Dimes, Childhelp USA, and many others. He is the recipient of numerous awards that honor his entrepreneurial spirit, philanthropic heart, and business acumen. He is a lifetime member of the Horatio Alger Association of Distinguished Americans, an organization that honored Mark with the prestigious Horatio Alger Award for his extraordinary life achievements.

Mark Victor Hansen is an enthusiastic crusader of what's possible and is driven to make the world a better place.

Mark Victor Hansen & Associates, Inc.
P.O. Box 7665 • Newport Beach, CA 92658
phone: 949-764-2640 • fax: 949-722-6912
www.markvictorhansen.com

360   About the Authors: *Who Is Mark Victor Hansen?*

Who Is
Amy Newmark?

A my Newmark was recently named publisher of Chicken Soup for the Soul, after a thirty-year career as a writer, speaker, financial analyst, and business executive in the worlds of finance and telecommunications.

Amy is a graduate of Harvard College, where she majored in Portuguese, minored in French, and traveled extensively. She is also the mother of two children in college and has two grown stepchildren.

After a long career writing books on telecommunications, voluminous financial reports, business plans, and corporate press releases, Chicken Soup for the Soul is a breath of fresh air for Amy. She has fallen in love with Chicken Soup for the Soul and its life-changing books, and found it a true pleasure to conceptualize, compile, and edit the "101 Best Stories" books for our readers.

The best way to contact Chicken Soup for the Soul is through our web site, at www.chickensoup.com. This will always get the fastest attention.

If you do not have access to the Internet, please contact us by mail or by facsimile.

Chicken Soup for the Soul
P.O. Box 700
Cos Cob, CT 06807-0700
Fax 203-861-7194

Acknowledgments

Thank You!

Our first thanks go to our loyal readers who have inspired the entire Chicken Soup team for the past fifteen years. Your appreciative letters and e-mails have reminded us why we work so hard on these books.

We owe huge thanks to all of our contributors as well. We know that you pour your hearts and souls into the stories and poems that you share with us, and ultimately with each other. We appreciate your willingness to open up your lives to other Chicken Soup readers.

We can only publish a small percentage of the stories that are submitted, but we read every single one and even the ones that do not appear in a book have an influence on us and on the final manuscripts.

As always, we would like to thank the entire staff of Chicken Soup for the Soul for their help on this project and the 101 Best series in general.

Among our California staff, we would especially like to single out the following people:

- D'ette Corona, who is the heart and soul of the Chicken Soup publishing operation, and who put together the first draft of this manuscript

- Barbara LoMonaco for invaluable assistance in obtaining the fabulous quotations that add depth and meaning to this book

- Patty Hansen for her extra special help with the permissions for these fabulous stories and for her amazing knowledge of the Chicken Soup library and Patti Clement for her help with permissions and other organizational matters.

In our Connecticut office, we would like to thank our able editorial assistants, Valerie Howlett and Madeline Clapps, for their assistance in setting up our new offices, editing, and helping us put together the best possible books.

We would also like to thank our master of design, Creative Director and book producer Brian Taylor at Pneuma Books, LLC, for his brilliant vision for our covers and interiors.

Finally, none of this would be possible without the business and creative leadership of our CEO, Bill Rouhana, and our president, Bob Jacobs.

www.chickensoup.com